Featuring North America's Most Popular Comic Strip

Laugh 'n' Learn

SPANISH

Lynn Johnston • Brenda Wegmann

¡ES UN PLACER APRENDER ESPAÑOL!

¡BAU!

McGraw·Hill

New York Chicago San Francisco Lisbon London Madrid Mexico City
Milan New Delhi San Juan Seoul Singapore Sydney Toronto

Library of Congress Cataloging-in-Publication Data

Johnston, Lynn Franks, 1947–
      Laugh 'n' learn Spanish : featuring North America's most popular comic strip
  For better or for worse / Lynn Johnston, Brenda Wegmann.
        p.   cm.
    ISBN 0-07-141519-X
    1. Spanish language—Textbooks for foreign speakers—English.
  I. Wegmann, Brenda, 1941–   II. Johnston, Lynn Franks, 1947– For better or for
worse. Spanish. Selections.   III. Title.

PC4129.E5 J64   2003
468.2'421—dc21
                                    2003052780

10 11   QDB/QDB 3 2 1

ISBN 0-07-141519-X

McGraw-Hill books are available at special quantity discounts to use as premiums and
sales promotions, or for use in corporate training programs. For more information, please
write to the Director of Special Sales, Professional Publishing, McGraw-Hill, Two Penn
Plaza, New York, NY 10121-2298. Or contact your local bookstore.

This book is printed on acid-free paper.

Contents

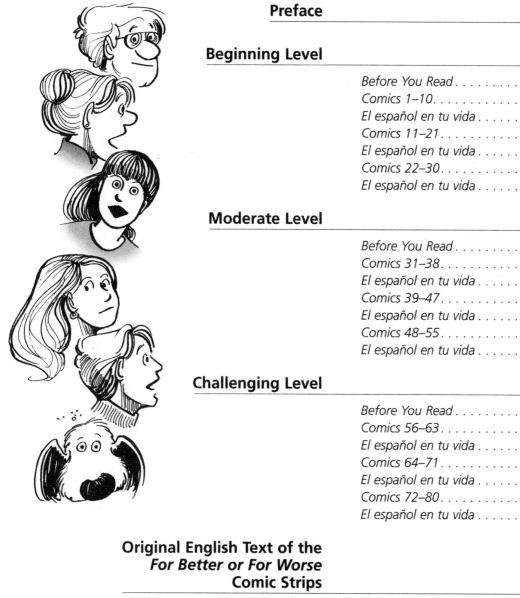

Preface

This book is for people who already know some Spanish and want to improve on what they know.

Learning Spanish can be fun! It is musical and dynamic and spoken around the world in many places of exceptional beauty. As English speakers, we have a great advantage because most of its sounds exist already in our own language. (It is much harder for Spanish speakers to learn English pronunciation because many sounds in English do *not* exist in Spanish.)

Our ideas about how to learn a foreign language have changed radically in the last fifty years, moving away from the grammar/translation approach to the communicative. But how exactly to accomplish this *communication* has not been easy to discover, and many courses remain "grammar-driven." This book is not grammar-driven; if anything, it is perhaps driven by smiles, interest, and the desire to find out what will happen next.

Reading is a good way to improve and retain your Spanish (once you have learned some), because in contrast to English and French, Spanish is quite phonetic. There is a close correspondence between the spoken and the written word. Most experts agree on this, but the difficulty is in finding reading matter that is easy enough to be understood by early learners and at the same time engaging enough to hold their interest.

This is the idea behind *Laugh 'n' Learn Spanish*. We have taken 80 selections from Lynn Johnston's popular comic strip *For Better or For Worse*, presented in Spanish as they have appeared over the years in Latin American newspapers. The most popular, most-read family comic in the U.S. and Canada, it presents the life of the Patterson family, their triumphs and misadventures, with a gentle irony that has won the hearts of readers all over the world.

Two Ways to Use This Book

There are two ways to use this book effectively:

1. **The Systematic Learning Method.** Read the book from beginning to end, including the pre-reading preparations called *Before You Read* that come before each of the three sections. Say the vocabulary out loud and read the *Working with Words and Patterns* part. Work out the comprehension exercises and the fill-ins that appear at the end of each group of comics in the review sections called *El español en tu vida*. Check the answers at the end of the book to see how much you have remembered. Take your time. Enjoy.

2. **Pick-and-Choose Browsing Method (The Lazy Way).** Flip through the beginning section until you find a comic you really like. Read it a few times and browse through the vocabulary, notes, and comprehension exercise. Skip to another part that catches your eye. Then stop and enjoy it. Although the comics are presented to some extent in a sequence of graduated difficulty, each comic is an independent lesson that can stand on its own and teach you something. Try your hand at the exercises and review sections. Check the answers at the back. Read on. Have fun.

Either one of these two approaches will work—as long as you actually do it!

Why It's Worth Your Time to Read This Book

There is no magic bullet, injection, or pill that you can take to learn Spanish. There is no secret method either, and no amount of money paid will guarantee you learn it. You simply have to stuff into your brain enough words, phrases, and structures to be able to communicate. You need repeated, attentive contact with Spanish, including review and reinforcement. You need to acquire many words, phrases, and patterns in order to comprehend and speak Spanish fluently.

Recent research using databases and recordings of authentic speech show that vocabulary is best acquired by studying chunks of language, commonly used phrases, and words in context. It is helpful if you can visualize or feel the context or interaction between you and a Spanish-speaking companion to retain the meaning in your memory bank. This makes sense, and it agrees with what experienced teachers have always tried to do.

This is why the *For Better or For Worse* comics in Spanish are so effective. They present humorous situations we identify with and use everyday speech we can imitate. Since the Patterson family is familiar to us, we don't suffer the misinterpretations that come from not understanding cultural cues.

Extra Steps for Acquiring Vocabulary

Here are a few suggestions to aid in your vocabulary acquisition.

- Use a highlighter to mark words and phrases especially relevant to your lifestyle and special interests. Then you can page through the book later and quickly reinforce them.
- Concentrate on images, and try to connect words and phrases to them. Add synonyms and alternate phrases in the margins. Practice using some of these when you get the chance to speak Spanish.
- Find drawings in the comics that you especially like, and label in Spanish as many of the items in them as you can find.
- Make lists and group words with associations (foods, opposites, insults, etc.). You need "hooks" to fasten words and phrases to in your memory.
- Highlight useful patterns and practice using them in different contexts (e.g., **tengo que** + **trabajar/salir/estudiar**).
- Review the grammar sections. Read them over from time to time. They will make more sense each time.

One final suggestion: go back and do it all again! Hey, it is just reading the comics, after all. Then read it again after some time has elapsed. Each time you will be reinforcing the words and phrases. Laugh and learn Spanish!

Presentando a los Patterson

Los Patterson son una familia canadiense que se enfrenta con los altibajos típicos de las familias de nuestros tiempos.

Eli (*Elly*) es la madre que cuida a todos.

Juan (*John*), el padre, es dentista.

Hay tres hijos. Miguel (*Michael*) es el mayor,

Isabel (*Elizabeth*) es la de en medio y

Abril (*April*) es la más pequeña.

El abuelo materno (el padre de Eli) se llama Jaime. Es viudo y también participa mucho en la vida familiar. Los Patterson tienen mascotas: el perro Edgar (*dog, Edgar*), la perra Dixie (*dog, Dixie*), y el conejo Sr. B. (*rabbit, Mr. B.*).

Beginning Level

Before You Read (Comics 1–30)

Do you want to improve your Spanish? Read through this section for a quick look at basic words, phrases, and patterns. Then read the beginning level of *For Better or For Worse* in Spanish, referring back to these pages when you want to recheck something, and do the practice exercises (called **El español en tu vida**) that occur after every 8–10 comic strips. Then you may be ready to move on to the moderate level. (Or, you may decide to read the beginning level through a second time. Repetition is the key to language learning.)

Remember to enjoy the lively adventures of the Pattersons in Spanish!

Learn the Links

Learn the following small words that appear often and link ideas.

ahora/luego	*now/then*
algo/nada	*something/nothing*
aquí, acá	*here/around here* or *over here*
bien	*well, fine, OK*
casi	*almost*
cuál	*which, what*
en	*at, in,* or *on* (en la universidad = *at* the university)
esto/eso	*this/that*
mucho/un poco	*a lot/a little*
no	*no* or *not*
o	*or* (it becomes **u** in front of words beginning with an **o** sound)

qué/que	(with accent mark) *what?*/(without accent mark) *that*
sí/si	(with accent mark) *yes*/(without accent mark) *if*
sólo	*only*
también	*also, too*
tan	*so*
todo	*everything, all*
y	*and* (it becomes **e** in front of a word beginning with an **i** sound)

Tener for Useful Descriptions

Many common expressions that use *to be* in English, use **tener** (*to have*) in Spanish. For example, you say *I'm 30 years old* in English, but you say **Tengo 30 años** (literally, *I have 30 years*) in Spanish. These expressions are used in everyday life and throughout this book. They are well worth learning.

tengo . . . años	*I am . . . years old*
tengo calor	*I am hot*
tengo frío	*I am cold*
tengo hambre	*I am hungry*
tengo miedo	*I am afraid*
tengo prisa	*I am in a hurry*
tengo razón	*I am right*
tengo sed	*I am thirsty*
tengo sueño	*I am sleepy*

Master the Magic of Cognates

Cognates are words similar in form and meaning in two different languages. Fortunately, Spanish has many cognates with English! Some are very obvious, like **gasolina**/*gasoline*. Others are more challenging. Here are some that appear in the Beginning Level, Comics 1–30. Can you find them in the box and match them to their English equivalents? (Answers are on page 216.)

HINT: Some cognates do not start with the same letter in English and Spanish. For example, many English words starting with *st-* or *sp-* have cognates in Spanish that start with **est-**, **ext-**, or **esp-** (*stadium*/**estadio**, *special*/**especial**). Also, some cognates are closer to less common words in English that have the same meaning, such as **auto** for *car* which has the cognate *automobile*.

baño
extraño
chaqueta
café
placer
estudiando
impresionante
botella
esfuerzo
recuperarse
estación
estómago
porche   proyecto
desastre
necesitar
gran
cantidad

1. bath, bathroom _____
2. bottle _____
3. coffee _____
4. disaster _____
5. effort _____
6. great _____
7. impressive _____
8. jacket _____
9. need _____
10. pleasure _____

11. porch _____
12. project _____
13. quantity _____
14. recuperate _____
15. station _____
16. stomach _____
17. strange _____
18. studying _____

Back to Basics: Coping with Verbs

The heart of the Spanish sentence is the verb. It changes endings according to the subject and time frame. Here is a quick review of three important tenses (groups of forms for particular time frames) that are used a lot in the beginning section of this book. (For a review of other tenses, see pages 77–81 and 140–145.)

- the infinitive: **hablar** *to speak* or *talk* / **comer** *to eat* / **vivir** *to live*
- the present participle (add **-ando** or **-iendo** to stem, similar to *-ing* word in English): **hablando** *speaking* or *talking* / **comiendo**, **viviendo** *eating, living*

Review of Present Tense Forms

Used for present or general actions. Translated as the simple present, *I speak*, or as the present progressive in English, *I am speaking*. There are three groups of regular verbs, with infinitives ending in **-ar**, **-er**, and **-ir**.

hablar (to speak)

hablo	*I speak*
hablas	*you speak*
habla	*he, she, it speaks,* or (formal) *you speak*
hablamos . .	*we speak*

habláis . . . . *you (all) speak*
hablan . . . . *they* or (formal) *you all speak*

comer (to eat)

como . . . . . *I eat*
comes . . . . . *you eat*
come . . . . . *he, she, it eats,* or (formal) *you eat*
comemos . . *we eat*
coméis . . . . *you (all) eat*
comen . . . . *they* or (formal) *you all eat*

vivir (to live)

vivo . . . . . . *I live*
vives . . . . . *you live*
vive . . . . . . *he, she, it lives,* or (formal) *you live*
vivimos . . . *we live*
vivís . . . . . *you (all) live*
viven . . . . . *they* or (formal) *you all live*

Another common group of verbs are called "stem-changing." They change the stem vowel in the present tense, except for the "we" and the third-person forms (he, she, it, they, and formal you). Another way to remember this is that the stem vowel (*e* or *o*) breaks under the weight of the stress. So *e* becomes *ie* or *i* when it is in the stressed syllable, e.g., *QUIE*-ro, *PI*-do. But the *e* does *not* break in the unaccented syllable: que-*RE*-mos. Some common examples include:

querer (ie) (to want)

quiero
quieres
quiere
queremos
queréis
quieren

poder (ue) (can, to be able)

puedo
puedes
puede
podemos
podéis
pueden

pedir (i) (to ask for)

pido
pides
pide
pedimos
pedís
piden

Review of Present Progressive Forms

The present progressive is not used as much in Spanish as it is in English. In Spanish, it is most often used only to tell what is happening exactly at the present moment, the equivalent of *I am eating right at this minute* (*as I speak to you on the phone*). You form the present progressive in Spanish by combining the present tense of **estar** with the present participle (**-ando** or **-iendo** form).

estoy hablando . . . . *I am speaking*
estás hablando . . . . *you are speaking*
está hablando . . . . . *he, she, it is speaking,* or (formal) *you are speaking*
estamos hablando . . *we are speaking*
estáis hablando . . . . *you (all) are speaking*
están hablando . . . . *they* or (formal) *you all are speaking*

The past participle (add **-ado** or **-ido** to the stem of the verb, sometimes similar to the *-ed* ending in English) is used as an adjective and to form the perfect tenses. The most common of the perfect tenses is the *present perfect*.

hablado . . . . *spoken* or *talked*
comido . . . . *eaten*
vivido . . . . *lived*

Review of Present Perfect Forms

The present perfect is used to express an action that has already been completed at the present moment. To form this tense in English we use the auxiliary *have* or *has* (which also indicates possession, e.g., *She has a car.*) Note that Spanish has a different verb for possession, **tener**, which is *never* used in forming the present perfect tense. Spanish uses **haber** with the past participle for the present perfect tense forms.

hablar (to speak; to talk)

he hablado	*I have talked*
has hablado	*you have talked*
ha hablado	*he, she, it has talked,* or (formal) *you have talked*
hemos hablado	*we have talked*
habéis hablado	*you (all) have talked*
han hablado	*they* or (formal) *you all have talked*

comer (to eat)

he comido	*I have eaten*
has comido	*you have eaten*
ha comido	*he, she, it has eaten,* or (formal) *you have eaten*
hemos comido	*we have eaten*
habéis comido	*you (all) have eaten*
han comido	*they* or (formal) *you all have eaten*

vivir (to live)

he vivido	*I have lived*
has vivido	*you have lived*
ha vivido	*he, she, it has lived,* or (formal) *you have lived*
hemos vivido	*we have lived*
habéis vivido	*you (all) have lived*
han vivido	*they* or (formal) *you all have lived*

HE COMIDO

WORKING WITH WORDS AND PATTERNS

- **gracias** ~ *Thank you very much* is **muchas gracias** (literally, *many graces*). To show that you are extremely grateful, you can say: **mil gracias** (similar to *thanks a million*, but more modest, since it refers to a thousand) or **muchísimas gracias** (the superlative form, meaning *many, many thanks*).

- **comida para llevar** ~ Notice on the package the words for *take-out food*, literally *food to carry*.

- **querido(a)** ~ A common form of endearment, **querido** is for a male and **querida** for a female. For a mixed group, you say **queridos**, e.g., **queridos amigos**. This is used as a greeting for postcards or letters to friends.

- **de vez en cuando** ~ This is an idiom, a phrase that means something different from the literal meaning of each of its words. You can translate it in different ways: *from time to time, now and then*, or *every once in a while*.

- **necesito** ~ Notice that it is not necessary to say **yo** since the personal pronouns are usually omitted in Spanish. The verb ending **-o** indicates that this means *I need*.

gracias thank you

necesito . . . I need . . .

querido(a) dear

para mí for me (for myself)

de vez en cuando from time to time

Un día para mí

A day for myself

WHAT YOU CAN LEARN Saying thank you, giving the most common term of endearment, telling what you need

PUTTING IT ALL TOGETHER (RESUMIÉNDOLO TODO). Fill in the blanks. (Answers on page 216.)

Eli toma un baño, lee, va de compras y echa una siesta. Su marido trae comida para (1) _____. Ella le dice: «(2) _____, querido,» y luego le dice: «de (3) _____ en cuando (4) _____ un día (5) _____ mí.»

Elly takes a bath, reads, goes shopping, and takes a nap. Her husband brings take-out food. She says, "Thank you, dear," and then thinks, "from time to time I need a day for myself."

WORKING WITH WORDS AND PATTERNS

- **relájese y rejuvenezca** ~ These and most of the words on the label are cognates. (See pages 4–5.) The word **celestial** is an exact cognate in English and Spanish, identical except for pronunciation. However, most cognate pairs have differences. Practice identifying them by finding the Spanish for these English words: *bath salts* _____, *herbs* _____, *luxurious* _____, *mixture* _____, *tranquilizing (soothing)* _____. The word **aceites** (*oils*) is not a cognate. Now you should be able to read the label.

- **ya voy** ~ To answer when someone is calling you in Spanish, use the verb **ir** (*to go*) and not the verb **venir** (*to come*), so literally you are saying "O.K., I'm going!" The word **ya** is an intensifier that means *already*, *now*, *at once*.

- **sólo** ~ The word **sólo** with a written accent mark means *only*. Without a written accent mark, the word **solo(a)** means *alone*.

- **queríamos** ~ The verb **querer** (*to want, to love*) is used in the imperfect tense here, and not in the preterite, because it describes a mental action. Mental and emotional actions in the past are usually in the imperfect tense.

KEY WORDS AND PHRASES

relájese y rejuvenezca relax and rejuvenate

nada nothing

¡Ya voy! I'm coming!, I'm on my way!

sólo queríamos we only wanted

¿Qué pasa? What's going on? What's the matter?

dónde estabas where you were

Eli toma un baño

Elly takes a bath

WHAT YOU CAN LEARN   Answering when someone calls you, asking what's the matter

PUTTING IT ALL TOGETHER (RESUMIÉNDOLO TODO). Fill in the blanks. (Answers on page 216.)

Eli lee una etiqueta que dice: «Relájese y rejuvenezca con un baño (1) _____ y celestial . . . » Ella está contenta, pero de repente escucha la voz de su hija Abril con un tono de urgencia. Eli corre, gritando, «¡Ya (2) _____!» Luego, les pregunta a Abril y a su pequeño amigo, (3) «¿Qué _____?» Los niños le responden, (4) «_____. Sólo (5) _____ saber dónde estabas.»

Elly reads a label that says "Relax and rejuvenate with a luxurious and celestial bath . . ." She's happy, but suddenly she hears her daughter April's voice (calling) in an urgent tone. Elly runs, shouting, "I'm coming!" Then she asks April and her little friend, "What's the matter?" The children answer, "Nothing. We only wanted to know where you were."

WORKING WITH WORDS AND PATTERNS

- **¡Hola!** ~ Remember: don't pronounce the **H** in Spanish. Say: ¡OH-la! Notice that exclamation points and question marks come before and after a statement, with the first one inverted. Spanish speakers feel that you need to know *before* you read something if it is an exclamation or question.

- **¿Qué te pasa?** *What's the matter?* ~ Literally: *What's happening to you?* The **te** is an indirect object meaning *to you*.

- **¿Estás cansada?** ~ The word **cansada** is the feminine form (since April is a girl). To a man or boy, you would say, **¿Estás cansado?**

- **me he pasado el día** ~ This is the present perfect tense formed by the verb **haber** plus the past participle, which in regular verbs ends in **-ado** or **-ido**. **He pasado** = *I have spent*. (The reflexive pronoun **me** is used here for emphasis but is not necessary.)

- **dando vueltas** ~ The form **dando** is a present participle of the verb **dar**, with **-ando** equivalent to *-ing* in English. Literally, **dar vueltas** means *to give turns*. You can extend the pattern with other verbs: **He pasado el día comiendo (trabajando, escribiendo cartas).** *I've spent the day eating (working, writing letters).*

KEY WORDS AND PHRASES

¡Hola! Hi!

me he pasado el día I've spent the day

¿Qué te pasa? What's the matter with you?

dando vueltas going around in circles (not getting anything done)

¿Estás cansada (cansado)? Are you tired?

DANDO
VUELTAS

Dando vueltas

Going around in circles

WHAT YOU CAN LEARN Greeting, asking if someone is tired, telling how you've spent your day

PUTTING IT ALL TOGETHER (RESUMIÉNDOLO TODO). Fill in the blanks. (Answers on page 216.)

El doctor Patterson le habla a su hija: «¡(1) _____, Abril! ¿Qué te (2) _____? ¿Estás (3) _____?» Abril le dice que sí porque ha pasado el (4) _____ dando (5) _____.

Dr. Patterson speaks to his daughter: "Hi, April! What's the matter with you? Are you tired?" April tells him that yes, she is, because she has spent the day going around in circles.

WORKING WITH WORDS AND PATTERNS

- **Tengo nueve años.** ~ *To be* _____ *years old* is one of the many expressions in which English uses the verb *to be* and Spanish the verb *to have*, **tener**. So, literally, in Spanish *you have 9* (or *22* or *60*) *years*. Some other examples: *I am hungry (thirsty, sleepy, in a hurry).* **Tengo** *(I have)* **hambre (sed, sueño, prisa).** (See page 4.)

- **realmente** ~ Make an adverb out of an adjective by adding **-mente** just as in English you add *-ly*: real + -ly = really, **real + -mente = realmente**. If the adjective ends in **-o(a)**, use the feminine **-a** ending: honest + -ly = honestly, **honesta + -mente = honestamente.**

- **edad** ~ This means *age* and is used in expressions like **¿Que edad tiene?** *How old is he* (or *she*)? or **Habla bien para su edad.** *He (or She) speaks well for his (or her) age.*

- **ayudarme a** ~ This verb and several others take **a** before an infinitive. The verbs for *to begin* (**empezar, comenzar**) are similar: **Las niñas empezaron (comenzaron) a cantar.** *The girls began to sing.*

KEY WORDS AND PHRASES

Tengo nueve años.
I'm nine years old.

tienes suficiente edad como para . . . you are old enough to . . .

realmente really

la mejor parte the best part

ayudarme a limpiar to help me clean (up)

4 El cumpleaños de Abril

April's birthday

WHAT YOU CAN LEARN   Telling how old you are, talking about being old enough for something

PUTTING IT ALL TOGETHER (RESUMIÉNDOLO TODO). Fill in the blanks. (Answers on page 216.)

Eli hace una fiesta para celebrar el (1) _____ de Abril. Los niños juegan y comen y Abril abre sus regalos. Después, los niños se van y Abril dice, «¡Realmente (2) _____ nueve años, Mami!» Entonces, Eli le explica cuál es la mejor parte de esto. Le dice, «¡(3) _____ suficiente (4) _____ como para (5) _____ a limpiar este desastre!»

Elly gives a party to celebrate April's birthday. The children play and eat, and April opens her presents. Afterwards, the children leave, and April says, "I'm really nine years old, Mom!" Elly explains to her what the best part of that is. She tells her, "You are old enough to help me clean up this disaster!"

WORKING WITH WORDS AND PATTERNS

- **No sé qué hacer.** ~ The verb **saber** (*to know*) is regular in the present tense except for the **yo** form, which is **sé**. (The accent mark is important to show this is not the reflexive pronoun **se**, which has a different meaning.) This pattern can be varied for other situations, for example, **No sé qué comer (comprar).** *I don't know what to eat (buy).*

- **ha estado** ~ This is the present perfect tense formed by the auxiliary verb **haber** and the past participle (**-ado**, **-ido**). Other examples: **Ha llegado (comido).** *She has arrived (eaten).* (See pages 6–7.)

- **así** ~ This word means *like*, *that*, or *so*. You can say *so so* if someone asks how you are doing.—**¿Cómo estás?—Así así, gracias.** It also occurs in popular phrases. **¡Así es la vida!** is the equivalent of *That's life!* **Así es.** *That's the way it is.*

- **toda la tarde** ~ This can be translated as *the whole afternoon*. The first two words have to agree with the time word, so *the whole day* would be: **todo el día.** Other variations: **toda la noche, todo el verano** *(the whole night, all summer long).*

- **Parece que alguien necesita . . .** ~ This can be a polite way of telling a child what to do. Instead of saying, *Put on your coat* or *Take a bath,* you can say: **Parece que alguien necesita un abrigo** (or **que alguien necesita tomar un baño**). **¡Tomar un baño!**

KEY WORDS AND PHRASES

No sé qué hacer. I don't know what to do.

Parece que . . . It seems that . . .

Ha estado así . . . (She) has been like that . . .

alguien necesita someone needs

toda la tarde all afternoon

¡PARECE QUE ALGUIEN NECESITA TOMAR UN BAÑO!

Alguien necesita una siesta

Someone needs a nap

WHAT YOU CAN LEARN   How to say "I don't know what to do," hinting that someone needs something, referring to a whole period of time

PUTTING IT ALL TOGETHER (RESUMIÉNDOLO TODO). Fill in the blanks. (Answers on page 216.)

Eli Patterson va de compras con su hija, y cuando regresan, Abril empieza a llorar. Eli le explica a su marido que Abril (1) _____ estado así (2) _____ la tarde. Le confiesa: «No (3) _____ qué hacer, Juan . . .» Juan Patterson responde: «(4) _____ que alguien (5) _____ una siesta.» Pero al final, ¡es Eli quien toma la siesta!

Elly Patterson goes shopping with her daughter, and when they return, April starts to cry. Elly explains to her husband that April has been unhappy all afternoon. She confesses to him: "I don't know what to do, John." John Patterson replies: "It seems that someone needs a nap." But in the end, it's Elly who takes the nap!

WORKING WITH WORDS AND PATTERNS

- **tengo (tener) que ir** *I have to go* ~ The expression **tengo que** + the infinitive of any verb is very useful for telling what you need to do. You can say: **tengo que salir/comer/ir al baño/ir al hotel** *(I have to leave/to eat/to go to the bathroom/to go to the hotel)* and many other things.

- **Ya casi llegamos.** *We're almost there.* ~ The literal translation: *Already almost we arrived.* The verb **llegar** means *to arrive, to get (someplace).* The word **ya** means *already* and **casi** *almost*; these never change form.

- **querido(a)** *dear* ~ A universal term of endearment. (See Comic #1)

- **no hay ningún lugar** *there's no place* ~ Literally, this means *there is not no place.* As in many other languages, the double negative is required in Spanish. It is not considered illogical but consistent.

- **¿Podemos usar . . . ?** *Can we use . . . ?* ~ Add a noun to the end and use this phrase to ask permission for using it, for example, **¿Podemos usar el teléfono (el auto/la piscina/las llaves)?** *Can we use the telephone (the car/the pool/the keys)?*

- **emergencia** ~ Some people consider this "Spanglish" and prefer to use the more traditional phrase, **un caso de urgencia**, or simply to say: **¡Es urgente!**

KEY WORDS AND PHRASES

algo que decirte
something to tell you

apenas vea as soon as I see (subjunctive for projection into the future)

el baño the bathroom

¡Ya! Ahí . . . All right, over there . . .

No puedo esperar.
I can't wait.

(la) confitería candy store

parar to stop

¡Es una emergencia! It's an emergency!

TENGO ALGO QUE DECIRTE.

6 Abril necesita el baño

April needs the bathroom

WHAT YOU CAN LEARN Expressing a need, telling someone you have an emergency, asking permission to use the bathroom or something else

PUTTING IT ALL TOGETHER (RESUMIÉNDOLO TODO). Fill in the blanks. (Answers on page 216.)

Eli y su hija Abril andan en su coche. Dice Abril, «Tengo que (1) _____ al baño.» Eli le dice, «Ya (2) _____ llegamos.» Abril insiste: «No puedo (3) _____.» Paran en una gasolinera y entran a la (4) _____. Eli le dice a la señora, «Perdón, ¿(5) _____ usar su baño? ¡Es una emergencia!» Mientras tanto, Abril se olvida de su problema y mira los dulces.

Elly and her daughter April are driving in their car. April says, "I have to go to the bathroom." Elly tells her, "We are almost home." April insists: "I can't wait." They stop at a gas station and go into the candy store. Elly says to the lady, "Excuse me, may we use the bathroom? It's an emergency!" Meanwhile, April forgets her problem and looks at the candies.

WORKING WITH WORDS AND PATTERNS

- **Mami** *Mommy* ~ Informal way of saying **madre** or **mamá** (*mother*).

- **¿Puedo usar el auto?** *May I use the car?* ~ This can be used to ask permission for using anything: **¿Puedo usar tu chaqueta, libro, lápiz?** *May I use your jacket, book, pencil?* **Auto** is only one way of saying *car*. In Mexico and most of Central America, many people say **el carro** and in some places they say **el coche**. In general, all of these words will be understood.

- **Voy a usar tu chaqueta roja.** *I'm going to use your red jacket.* ~ **Voy** is from the verb **ir** (*to go*) and is often used with **a** and an infinitive to talk about the future. **Voy a salir, comer, bailar.** *I'm going to leave, eat, dance.*

- **¿Dónde está(n) . . . ?** *Where is (are) . . . ?* ~ The plural (**están**) is used here with **llaves**. To ask where one thing is, do not use the **n**. **¿Dónde está el auto?** *Where is the car?*

- **en el bolsillo** ~ Notice that this can mean *in my pocket* because Spanish often uses the definite article (**el, la**) instead of the possessive when it is obvious who the owner is.

¿Puedo usar . . . ? May I use . . .?

¿Dónde están las llaves? Where are the keys?

Voy a usar . . . ¿está bien? I'm going to use . . . , is that O.K.?

en el bolsillo in the (my) pocket

7) En el bolsillo

In the pocket

WHAT YOU CAN LEARN   Asking permission to use something, asking where something is

PUTTING IT ALL TOGETHER (RESUMIÉNDOLO TODO). Fill in the blanks. (Answers on page 216.)

Eli pasea los perros y no encuentra una basura donde tirar la bolsa con sus «depósitos». Por eso, la mete en el (1) _____ de su chaqueta. Isabel entra y pregunta: «¿(2) _____ usar el auto?», y luego, «Voy a (3) _____ tu chaqueta roja, ¿(4) _____ bien?» Eli responde, «Sí, claro.» Isabel quiere saber dónde están las (5) _____ y Eli le dice, «¡En el bolsillo!» Desgraciadamente, Isabel mete su mano en el bolsillo.

Elly walks the dogs and can't find a garbage can to throw away the bag with their "deposits." So she puts it in the pocket of her jacket. Elizabeth comes in and asks, "May I use the car?" and then, "I'm going to use your red jacket, O.K.?" Elly replies, "Yes, of course." Elizabeth wants to know where the keys are, and Elly tells her, "In my pocket!" Unfortunately, Elizabeth puts her hand in the pocket.

WORKING WITH WORDS AND PATTERNS

- **hay** *there is (there are)* ~ This very common form does not change for singular or plural. **Hay una casa blanca.** *There's a white house.* **Hay tres casas.** *There are three houses.* **Hay** is especially useful for asking questions. **¿Hay café? ¿Hay agua? ¿Hay platos?** *Is there any coffee? Is there any water? Are there any plates?* Notice that the word *any* is not translated into Spanish.

- **tremendo(a)** *dreadful, terrible* ~ This means *tremendous* but often in the bad sense, whereas in English it usually means "really good," as when we say, "that's a tremendous stroke of luck."

- **por ninguna parte** Literally, this means *in no part*, meaning "nowhere." Spanish uses the double negative so that if a sentence starts out in the negative, it continues to be negative right to the end. In English, however, a double negative is avoided and that's why the best translation here is *anywhere*.

- **tener miedo a** *to be afraid of* ~ As is often the case, Spanish uses **tener** *(to have)* for an English expression that uses *to be*. In English we say *I am afraid of the dark*; in Spanish, **Tengo miedo a la oscuridad.** (Literally, *I have fear of the dark*.) When referring to being afraid of an action, Spanish uses **de** instead of **a**. **Tengo miedo de manejar.** *I'm afraid of driving.*

- **truenos** *thunder* ~ Notice that *thunder* is plural in Spanish. This is also true with the word for *business* (**los negocios**). On the other hand, *politics* is plural in English but singular in Spanish (**la política**).

- **Cuando Farley estaba con nosotros . . .** *When Farley [a dog they used to have] was with us . . .* ~ Here the imperfect tense of **estar** is used to describe past action. (See pages 77–78.)

- **solía esconderse** ~ This is the imperfect tense of the verb **soler**, which has no equivalent in English. It indicates that the action of the infinitive following it is habitual or customary. **Suelo estudiar con mis amigos.** (*I usually study with my friends.*)

KEY WORDS AND PHRASES

Hay una tormenta. There's a storm.

bueno well (all right)

No puedo encontrar a . . . I can't find . . .

Solía esconderse . . . He used to hide . . .

por ninguna parte anywhere

Tiene miedo a los truenos. He's afraid of thunder.

debajo del porche under the porch

8 La tormenta

The storm

WHAT YOU CAN LEARN   Saying there's a storm outside, talking about being afraid of something, saying you can't find someone (or something)

PUTTING IT ALL TOGETHER (RESUMIÉNDOLO TODO). Fill in the blanks. (Answers on page 216.)

Abril mira por la ventana. Le dice a Eli, «Mami, (1) _____ una tremenda (2) _____ afuera. ¡No puedo encontrar a Edgar por ninguna (3) _____!» Eli le explica que cuando el perro Farley estaba con ellos, (4) _____ esconderse (5) _____ del porche. Luego, Abril encuentra a Edgar.

April looks out the window. She says to Elly "Mom, there's a terrible storm outside. I can't find Edgar anywhere!" Elly explains to her that when their dog Farley was with them, he would usually hide under the porch. Then, April finds Edgar.

WORKING WITH WORDS AND PATTERNS

- **¡Qué fantástico!** ~ The word **qué** is used here for *how*. Many other words may follow: **¡Qué bonito (lindo, maravilla)!** *How pretty (lovely, marvelous)!*

- **No lo veo.** ~ Notice that **no** means *not* here and that the word order in a negative sentence is the reverse of English usage. Instead of *I do not see it*, this is literally: *Not it see I*, since the subject is given in the verb ending **o**.

- **un montón de** ~ In common speech this is used to mean *a lot of* or *many*, **un montón de libros, de problemas, de gente** *a bunch (or a lot) of books, problems, people*.

- **lo siento** ~ Literally, this means *I feel it*. So, to say *I'm very sorry*, you say **lo siento mucho** (*I feel it a lot*).

- **no veo nada** ~ Spanish uses the double negative, which is not viewed as illogical but rather as consistent (if you start out negating, then keep on with it). Literally, this sounds like *I don't see nothing*, but the English meaning is *I don't see anything*.

- **Tenías razón.** *You were right.* ~ This is the imperfect tense used to describe a past condition of being right. (See pages 77–78.) Like many English expressions that use the verb *to be*, this one translates to Spanish with the verb **tener**: *to be right* **tener razón** (literally, *to have reason*). (See page 4.)

(See pages 77–78.) (See page 4.)

KEY WORDS AND PHRASES

un puercoespín a porcupine

encima de ese árbol up in that tree

No lo veo. I don't see it.

Espera un minuto. Wait a minute.

yo tampoco me neither

el copo de ese abedul the top of that birch tree

ahí mismo right there (near you)

Lo siento. I'm sorry.

un viejo nido an old nest

No veo nada. I don't see anything.

un montón de hojas secas a bunch of dry leaves

Parece que tenías razón. It seems you were right.

de veras really (honestly, for sure)

los mayores grown-ups, older people

UN MONTÓN DE HOJAS SECAS.

9 Hay un puercoespín

There's a porcupine

WHAT YOU CAN LEARN   Expressing joy, saying you see something (or you don't), apologizing

PUTTING IT ALL TOGETHER (RESUMIÉNDOLO TODO). (Answers on page 216.)

Abril exclama: «¡Qué (1) _____!» Ve un puercoespín. Su padre Juan dice, «No lo (2) _____.» Su abuelo dice, «Yo (3) _____.» Creen que es un viejo nido o un montón de hojas secas. Abril insiste que lo ve, ¡de veras! Entonces, su abuelo ve el puercoespín; está en el copo de un abedul. Juan le pide perdón a su hija: «Lo (4) _____. Parece que tenías (5) _____, querida.» Abril le pregunta, «¿Como es que los mayores le creen a otros adultos . . . pero no me creen a mí?»

April cries out, "How wonderful!" She sees a porcupine. Her father, John, says, "I don't see it." Her grandfather says, "Me neither." April insists that she sees it, really! Then, her grandfather sees the porcupine; it's on the top of a birch tree. John apologizes to his daughter, "I'm sorry. It seems that you were right, dear." April asks him, "Why is it that you grown-ups believe other adults . . . but you don't believe me?"

WORKING WITH WORDS AND PATTERNS

- **Yo soy el primero.** ~ Since a boy is talking, he says **el primero**. To refer to a girl, it would be **la primera**. The subject pronouns are generally not used in Spanish, but here the **yo** (*I*) is used for emphasis.

- **en la fila** ~ Another common word for *line* (the kind that people wait in) is **cola**, which means **tail** (since a line of waiting people can curl around like an animal's tail).

- **yo sigo** ~ The verb **seguir** means *to follow* or *continue*, but this is the common way to say you are next (in line). The word **próximo(a)** is not used in this context, but occurs in phrases like **la próxima vez** (*next time*) or **el próximo mes** (*next month*).

- **Tú eres la última.** ~ Since this refers to a girl, it's in the feminine form. To refer to a boy it would be **Tú eres el último**.

- **el bus** ~ There are many Spanish words for *bus*, depending on the country, but the universal word that is understood everywhere is **el autobús**. For short, it is often called **el bus**.

KEY WORDS AND PHRASES

Yo soy el primero. I'm the first.

Tú eres la última. You're the last.

en la fila in line

Aquí viene el bus. Here comes the bus.

Yo sigo. I'm next (I follow).

SOY LA PRIMERA. ¿QUIEN ES EL ULTIMO?

10 En la parada de buses

At the bus stop

WHAT YOU CAN LEARN Telling who's first or last or next in line, announcing that a bus is coming

PUTTING IT ALL TOGETHER (RESUMIÉNDOLO TODO). (Answers on page 216.)

Los niños salen de la escuela y corren a la (1) _____ de buses. Un niño grita, «¡Yo soy el (2)_____ en la (3) _____!» Luego, le dice a Abril, «¡Tú eres la (4) _____!» Pero, al llegar, el bus para cerca de Abril y resulta que ella es la (5) _____ para subir.

The children leave school and run to the bus stop. One boy shouts, "I'm the first in line!" Then he says to April, "You're last!" But when the bus arrives, it stops near April and it turns out that she is the first to get on.

El español en tu vida

Spanish in your life

Practice what you've learned from Comics 1–10. (Answers on page 216.)

A. ¿ES USTED OBSERVADOR (O OBSERVADORA)?
(*Are you observant?*)

How observant are you? Can you tell the names in Spanish for the following objects which appeared in the life of the Pattersons in the preceding pages?

1. _____ _____ _____

2. _____ / _____

3. _____

4. _____

5. _____ / _____

6. _____ _____ _____

B. ¿QUÉ SE DICE? (*What do you say?*)

Imagine yourself in the following situations. Use the cues from the comics and fill in the blanks with the missing Spanish words.

1. Your thoughtful husband has just brought you some take-out food. **¿Qué se dice?**

2. You are calmly taking a bath when you hear your daughter screaming. **¿Qué se dice?**

3. It's your birthday, and you want to tell the world that you are nine years old. **¿Qué se dice?**

4. You see that your daughter is very crabby and your wife is at her wits' end. **¿Qué se dice?**

5. Your daughter needs to use the bathroom urgently so you go into a candy store. **¿Qué se dice?**

WORKING WITH WORDS AND PATTERNS

- **¿Tú crees que . . ?** ~ The informal *you* is used here. (The subject **tú** is not necessary and could be dropped, or it could also be used following the verb.) To someone you don't know very well, you would ask, **¿Cree usted que . . . ?**

- **Todos lo pasaron bien.** ~ The expression **pasarlo bien** (*to spend it well*) is a common way of saying *to have a good time*. **Siempre lo paso bien con mis amigos.** *I always have a good time with my friends.* In the comic the verb **pasar** is in the preterite because it is asking about a past completed action. *I had a good time yesterday* would be **Lo pasé bien ayer**.

- **De acuerdo a . . .** ~ Another way to say this is **según**.

- **recuperarse** ~ The **se** at the end of this infinitive shows it is a reflexive verb. This means it patterns with a reflexive pronoun that refers to the subject. **Mi amiga se recupera de la gripe.** *My friend is recovering from the flu.* **Yo me recupero lentamente de estos golpes.** *I recover slowly from these blows.*

- **de ella** ~ The word **ella** means *it* here because it refers to **fiesta** which is feminine. If it referred to the masculine word **accidente**, *it* would be translated as **él**.

KEY WORDS AND PHRASES

¿Tú crees que . . . ?
Do you think that . . .

Todos lo pasaron bien.
Everybody had a good time.

De acuerdo a . . .
According to . . .

la medida de the measure of

que toma recuperarse de ella [the time] it takes to recover from it

11 Las chicas hacen una fiesta

The girls have a party

<u>WHAT YOU CAN LEARN</u>   Asking for someone's opinion, giving an opinion, saying you had a good time

PUTTING IT ALL TOGETHER (RESUMIÉNDOLO TODO). (Answers on page 216.)

Isabel y Carlota (1) _____ una fiesta. Después, todos sus amigos se van y entonces Isabel le pregunta a su amiga, «Carlota, ¿tú (2) _____ que todos lo (3) _____ bien?» Carlota le responde, «De (4) _____ a mi experiencia, la medida de una buena fiesta es la longitud de tiempo que toma (5) _____ de ella.»

Elizabeth and Candace have a party. Afterwards, all their friends leave and then Elizabeth asks her friend, "Candace, do you think that everyone had a good time?" Candace answers her, "According to my experience, the measure of a good party is the length of time it takes to recover from it."

WORKING WITH WORDS AND PATTERNS

- **¿Los puedo acompañar?** ~ The pronoun **los** for *you* (referring to a mixed group) comes first, so the literal translation is *You may I accompany?* However, it is also common to put the **los** at the end of the infinitive: **¿Puedo acompañarlos?** In this case, the word order is similar to English. (See the last note.)

- **¡Claro que sí! ¡Cómo no!** ~ These are expressions of approval and encouragement, like *of course!* Both have the same meaning, and there are even two others with similar meanings: **desde luego, por supuesto.**

- **¡Sería fantástico!** ~ The conditional tense is used here (with **-ía** endings attached to the infinitive) to express how something *would be* if it were to happen. (See pages 80–81.)

- **Estoy bromeando.** ~ This is the present progressive verb tense of **bromear** (*to joke*, *fool around*). It's formed by adding **-ando** or **-iendo** (equivalent to *-ing*) to the verb and using forms of **estar** as an auxiliary. It's used to emphasize something happening at that exact moment in time. (See page 6.)

- **demasiado** ~ This useful word by itself means *too much*. In front of a plural noun, it means *too many*, such as **demasiados cocineros** (*too many cooks*) or **demasiadas preguntas** (*too many questions*).

- **Me gusta desconcertarlos.** ~ Literally, this means *It pleases me to upset* (or *rattle*) *them* but the meaning of **me gusta** is *I like*.

KEY WORDS AND PHRASES

Parece divertido. It seems like fun (entertaining).

demasiado que hacer too much to do

¿Los puedo acompañar? May I go along with you?

¡Claro que sí! ¡Cómo no! But of course! Why not?

¡Sería fantástico! It would be fantastic!

¡Qué pena! Too bad! What a shame!

Casi nos pilla. She almost caught us.

de vez en cuando from time to time

Estoy bromeando. I'm joking.

Me gusta desconcertarlos. I like to upset them.

12 A la playa
To the beach

Asking to go along with someone, expressing approval of a suggestion, declining an invitation

PUTTING IT ALL TOGETHER (RESUMIÉNDOLO TODO). (Answers on page 216.)

Isabel y sus amigos están para salir cuando Eli les pregunta, «¿Van a la playa?» Isabel le contesta que sí. Entonces, Eli les dice, «Parece (1) _____. ¿Los puedo (2) _____?» Todos le responden con un entusiasmo forzado «¡(3) _____ que sí! ¡Cómo no!» Pero Eli dice, «Sólo estoy bromeando. Tengo (4) _____ que hacer.» Los jóvenes se van y Eli piensa, «De vez en cuando me (5) _____ desconcertarlos un poco.»

Elizabeth and her friends are about to leave when Elly asks them, "Are you going to the beach?" Elizabeth answers that they are. Then Elly says, "It sounds like fun. May I go along with you?" Everyone replies with forced enthusiasm, "But of course!" "Naturally!" But Elly says, "I am only kidding. I have too much to do." The young people leave, and Elly thinks to herself, "From time to time I like to shake them up a bit."

WORKING WITH WORDS AND PATTERNS

- **me siento** ~ This is the reflexive verb **sentirse**. You use it with adjectives to describe how you feel, **me siento bien (mal, nerviosa, emocionada)** *I feel good (bad, nervous, excited)*. Change the reflexive pronoun to match the subject: **Carlos se siente nervioso. Nosotros *nos* sentimos bien. ¿Tú *te* sientes deprimida, Margarita?** *Carlos feels nervous. We feel good. Do you feel depressed, Margarita?*

- **Siento mi estómago un poco más liviano.** *I feel my stomach (is) a little bit lighter.* ~ Here Elly uses the verb **sentir** which is not reflexive because she is not describing herself, but talking about a thing (her stomach, in this case) different from herself.

- **un poco, unos pocos** ~ Use **un poco** to say *a little bit*, **unos pocos** to say *a few*. Notice that in the Hispanic world, people measure their weight in kilograms (kilos), not pounds. (1 kilo = 2.2 lbs.)

- **he perdido, he estado, no ha sido, he bajado** ~ All of these verbs are in the present perfect tense, used to tell about actions that have been completed at the present moment. (See pages 6–7.)

- **tan bien que** *so good that* ~ Use **tan . . . que** for comparisons: **tan mal (feliz, preocupado) que . . .** *so bad (happy, worried) that . . .*

- **Voy a hacer algo.** *I'm going to do something.* ~ To speak about the future you can use the verb **ir** + an infinitive: **Voy a comer** *I'm going to eat*, **Vamos a caminar** *We are going to walk*, **¿Vas a volver?** *Are you going to return?* (See page 80.)

- **me gusta** ~ The verb **gustar** means *to please*. Literally, **me gusta** means *it pleases me*, but it is the equivalent of *I like it* in English. When talking about more than one thing you like, use **me gustan** *(they please me)* *I like them.* **Me gustan las naranjas.** *I like oranges.*

KEY WORDS AND PHRASES

Sé por qué. I know why.

He estado tratando de . . . I have been trying to . . .

Me siento delgada. I feel thin.

No ha sido fácil. It hasn't been easy.

más liviano lighter

He bajado de peso. I have lost weight.

He perdido . . . kilos. I have lost . . . kilos.

tan bien so good

algo que realmente me gusta something I really want to

WHAT YOU CAN LEARN Telling someone that you feel good, talking about losing weight, saying you like something

PUTTING IT ALL TOGETHER (RESUMIÉNDOLO TODO). (Answers on page 216.)

Una mañana Eli se levanta y se dice, «¡Hoy me (1) _____ realmente bien!» Ella sabe por qué. Se siente bien por que se siente (2) _____. Sube a la pesa y se exclama, «¡Sí, he (3) _____ unos pocos kilos! ¡No ha sido fácil pero la verdad es que he bajado de (4) _____! ¡Me siento tan bien que voy a hacer algo que (5) _____ gusta!» Luego, va derecho a la cocina y se pone a preparar pasteles y galletitas.

One morning Elly gets up and says to herself, "Today I feel really good!" She knows why. She feels good because she feels thin. She gets on the scale and exclaims, "Yes, I have lost a few kilos! It hasn't been easy but the truth is that I have lost weight! I feel so good that I'm going to do something that I like!" Then she goes straight to the kitchen and gets down to baking cakes and cookies.

WORKING WITH WORDS AND PATTERNS

- **Impresionante, ¿no?** ~ To make a statement into a question you can add a confirmation tag like **¿no?**, **¿no es verdad?**, or **¿verdad?**

- **cuando pintó éstos** ~ The verb **pintar** is in the preterite tense here to show a completed action in the past. (See pages 76–77.)

- **¿Le gusta . . . ? ¿Viene acá . . . ?** ~ Notice that the gentleman uses the formal usted forms **(le, viene)** since he is speaking with someone he doesn't know. The common expression **a menudo** means *frequently, often, many times.*

- **¿Le importaría compartir una mesa . . . ?** ~ The conditional here adds a tone of politeness. (See pages 80–81.)

- **Deberías sentirte halagada.** *You should feel flattered.* ~ Once again the conditional softens a statement and is more polite. Here Elly's friend uses it so that she doesn't sound too bossy when she gives advice. Using the conditional for politeness is especially common with the verbs **deber**, **poder**, and **querer**. **¿Podrías salir conmigo esta noche?** *Could you go out with me tonight?* **¿Querrías dar una vuelta?** *Would you want to take a walk?*

- **tipo** ~ This is a common slang term for *guy* that sometimes is just a little bit pejorative.

- **jovencitas** ~ The diminutive ending (**-citas**) adds a slight flavor of being small and dainty, something like "cute young things."

KEY WORDS AND PHRASES

Impresionante, ¿no?
Impressive, isn't it?

cuando pintó éstos
when he painted these

¿Viene acá a menudo?
Do you come here often?

a la hora del almuerzo
at lunchtime

¿Le importaría compartir una mesa . . . ? Would you mind sharing a table . . .?

He quedado de . . . con alguien. I've arranged to . . . [meet, etc.] someone.

Deberías sentirte halagada. You should feel flattered.

para un tipo for a guy

un par de jovencitas
a pair of youngsters

En la galería de arte

At the art gallery

WHAT YOU CAN LEARN Talking about art, inviting someone out, refusing an invitation

PUTTING IT ALL TOGETHER (RESUMIÉNDOLO TODO). (Answers on page 216.)

Eli va a la (1) _____ de arte. Un anciano se le acerca y le pregunta, «(2) _____, ¿no?» Le habla un poco del artista, y luego le pregunta, «¿Viene acá a (3) _____?» Eli le responde que viene a veces a la hora del (4) _____. Entonces, el señor revela su intención: «¿Le importaría (5) _____ una mesa en la cafetería?» Eli le dice que no. «He quedado de verme con alguien.» Después, su amiga le dice que debe sentirse halagada.

Elly goes to the art gallery. An elderly gentleman approaches her and asks, "Impressive, isn't it?" He talks a bit about the artist and then asks her, "Do you come here often?" Elly replies that she sometimes comes at lunchtime. Then the gentleman reveals his intentions: "Would you mind sharing a table in the cafeteria?" Elly says no. "I have made an arrangement to get together with someone." Later a friend tells her she should feel flattered.

WORKING WITH WORDS AND PATTERNS

- **Me alegro de que estés en casa.** ~ If someone tells you some good news, you can simply say, **Me alegro** (*I'm glad*). If you want to say that you are glad that something is the way it is, then you have to use a subjunctive verb form after **Me alegro de que**. That is why Elly says **estés** instead of the normal present tense **estás**. After an expression of emotion with a change of subject, a subjunctive is used in Spanish. (See pages 140–142 for information and use of the subjunctive.)

- **¿Le puedes llevar esto a Carola . . . ?** ~ In Spanish the indirect pronoun is stated even when you mention the name of the person referred to. To an English speaker, this seems redundant, since it translates like this: *Can you take this to her to Carol?* But it is good Spanish to use both. **Pepe *les* dio los dulces a los niños.** *Pepe gave [to them] the candies to the children.*

- **por favor** ~ This is not used as often as *please* is used in English, but it always sounds polite, so it is a good idea to use it when asking for a favor. In everyday slang, people sometimes shorten it to **¡porfa!**

- **¡Está lloviendo!** ~ The word for *rain* is **lluvia** and the verb *to rain* is **llover**. April uses the present progressive tense (see page 6) to emphasize that it is raining right now.

KEY WORDS AND PHRASES

Me alegro de que estés en casa. I'm glad that you're home.

¿Le puedes llevar esto a Carola . . . ? Could you take this to Carol?

al otro lado de la calle on the other side of the street

por favor please

¡Está lloviendo! It's raining!

ESTÁ LLOVIENDO

15 Una caminata bajo la lluvia

A walk in the rain

WHAT YOU CAN LEARN   Asking someone to deliver something for you, saying that it's raining

PUTTING IT ALL TOGETHER (RESUMIÉNDOLO TODO). (Answers on page 216.)

Una tarde, Abril charla con sus amigos bajo la lluvia y luego camina lentamente a casa. Su mamá la saluda, «¡Abril! Me (1) _____ de que estés (2) _____ casa. ¿(3) _____ puedes llevar esto a Carola al otro (4) _____ de la calle, por favor?» Abril le responde, «¡Pero mamá! ¡Está (5) _____!»

One afternoon, April chats with her friends outside in the rain and then walks slowly home. Her mother greets her, "April, I'm glad you're home. Can you please take this to Carol on the other side of the street?" April answers, "But, Mom! It's raining!"

WORKING WITH WORDS AND PATTERNS

- **¡Tienes un paraguas!** ~ It's easy to remember the word for umbrella since it is made up of two smaller words: **para** (*for*) and **aguas** (*waters*). It's **un aparato para aguas** (*an appliance for waters*), **un paraguas**.

- **tan pequeño** ~ This adjective (descriptive word) ends in **-o** because it describes the umbrella (**paraguas**) which is masculine. To talk about a small cap (**gorra**) you say **una gorra pequeña** because the word is feminine.

- **Lo sé.** ~ In English we simply say "I know" when someone tells us something we are already familiar with. In Spanish that does not sound complete, so you say **lo sé**, literally, *I know it*. **Sé** is the irregular **yo** form of the verb **saber** (*to know*).

- **Lo compré.** *I bought it.* ~ This is the preterite tense to express a completed action in the past. (See pages 76–77.) The word **lo** means *it* and is the direct object. Notice that the word order in Spanish is different from the English and the equivalent of *it* goes in front of the verb, not after it.

- **Cuanto más chico el paraguas . . .** ~ The adjective **chico(a)** is synonymous with **pequeño(a)**. Both mean *small*. This is the first part of a cause-effect comparison (the cause). Literally, *How much more small the umbrella* or, in plain English: *The smaller the umbrella . . .*

- **más cerca la chica** ~ The word **chica** means small (when referring to something feminine) but it also means *girl*, which is the meaning here. This is the second part of the cause-effect comparison: *. . . the closer the girl!*

KEY WORDS AND PHRASES

¡Tienes un paraguas! You have an umbrella!

Es tan pequeño. It's so small.

Lo sé. I know.

por eso because of that (for that reason)

Lo compré. I bought it.

Cuanto más chico . . . más cerca . . . The smaller . . . the closer . . .

16 El paraguas pequeño

The little umbrella

WHAT YOU CAN LEARN   Remembering the word for *umbrella*, describing something as small, saying that you know (something), making a cause and effect comparison

PUTTING IT ALL TOGETHER (RESUMIÉNDOLO TODO). (Answers on page 216.)

Miguel y su novia Deana caminan bajo la lluvia. Deana le dice, «¡Tienes un (1) _____! ¡Pero es tan (2) _____!» Miguel confiesa, «Lo (3) _____. ¡Por eso (4) _____ compré!» Entonces, Miguel se dice a sí mismo, «¡Cuanto más chico el paraguas, más (5) _____ la chica!»

Michael and his girlfriend Deanna are walking in the rain. Deanna says to him, "You have an umbrella! But it is so small!" Michael confesses, "I know. That's why I bought it!" Then Michael says to himself, "The smaller the umbrella, the closer the girl!"

WORKING WITH WORDS AND PATTERNS

- **Tienes razón.** ~ Like so many other expressions in Spanish, this one uses **tener** (*to have*) to express something that in English is said with the verb *to be*. Other examples are **tener sueño** (*to be sleepy*), **tener sed** (*to be thirsty*). For a list of these expressions, see page 4.

- **se trata de** ~ Use this expression to tell what something is about. For example, when talking about a book or movie, **¿De qué se trata?** *What's it about?* **Se trata de un triángulo amoroso.** *It's about a love triangle.*

- **Hay que . . .** ~ You may want to express some general rule or suggest a course of action. In that case, use **hay que** + an infinitive. **Hay que relajarse de vez en cuando.** *You have [One has] to relax from time to time.* **Hay que correr para llegar a tiempo.** *You have [One has] to run to get there on time.*

- **con las manos en la masa** ~ Literally, this means *with their hands in the dough*, as though someone were trying to taste the pastry before it's baked.

- **¡No tocar!** ~ The infinitive is often used with **no** in front of it for a negative command. The words **por favor** are implied, so the meaning is *Please don't touch!*

KEY WORDS AND PHRASES

Tienes razón. You are right.

cuando se trata de . . . when it's a matter of . . .

Hay que . . . One must . . . (It's necessary to . . .)

pillar to catch (someone guilty or evasive)

con las manos en la masa in the act, red-handed (literally, with their hands in the dough)

venta de pasteles bake sale (literally, sale of pastries)

CON LAS MANOS EN LA MASA.

Con las manos en la masa

Red-handed

WHAT YOU CAN LEARN Telling someone he or she is right, expressing a general rule or suggesting a course of action

PUTTING IT ALL TOGETHER (RESUMIÉNDOLO TODO). (Answers on page 216.)

Eli sube la escalera y (1) _____ los dos perros desobedientes que están dormidos en la cama de sus amos. Entonces, le dice a su marido, «Tienes (2) _____, Juan. Cuando se (3) _____ de disciplinar a los animales, ¡hay (4) _____ pillarlos con las manos en la (5) _____!» Luego, Eli ve que Juan está comiendo los pasteles reservados para una venta.

Elly goes up the stairs and catches the two disobedient dogs that are asleep on their masters' bed. Then she says to her husband, "You are right, John. When it comes to disciplining animals, you must catch them red-handed!" Then Elly sees that John is eating the pastries put aside for a bake sale.

WORKING WITH WORDS AND PATTERNS

- **llevarse bien** ~ Literally, *to carry themselves well*, but you say it to describe two people who get along well with each other: **se llevan bien**. Use this expression with the reflexive pronoun. **Nos llevamos bien.** *We get along well.* **Me llevo bien con mi jefe.** *I get along with my boss.*

- **valer la pena** ~ Here the verb is in the preterite to talk about the past. (See preterite forms, pages 76–77.) In the present, say **Vale la pena**. *It's worth it.* If you are referring to something in the plural, such as *piano lessons*, put the verb in the plural: **¿Las lecciones de piano? Sí, valen la pena.**

- **hermanita** ~ Adding diminutive endings, such as **-ito**, **-ita**, **-itos**, **-itas**, conveys the idea of small size or of affection. **Tomasito** *dear little Tomás*, **amiguitas** *dear friends* (female).

- **volverse** ~ Use the verb **volver** with the reflexive pronoun to express the idea of changing from one thing to another. **Poco a poco nos volvemos más organizados.** *Little by little, we are becoming more organized.* **Con tantos cursos, te vuelves más inteligente, ¿no es verdad?** *With so many courses, you are getting smarter, aren't you?*

- **cuánto más . . . , más . . . se vuelve** *The _____er (he/she) gets), the _____er (he/she) becomes.* ~ Literally, *how much more _____, the more _____ he or she turns into.* Use this formula to make direct comparisons. **Cuánto más viejo nuestro perro, más gordo se vuelve.** *The older our dog gets, the fatter he becomes.* **Cuánto más ricos, más arrogantes se vuelven.** *The richer they get, the more arrogant they become.*

KEY WORDS AND PHRASES

llevarse bien to get along well (together)

¡Valió la pena! It was worth it! (It was worth the effort!)

hermanita little sister (dear sister)

cuánto más vieja the older (she gets)

más extraña se vuelve the stranger she becomes

18 Ahora se llevan bien

Now they get along well

WHAT YOU CAN LEARN   Saying that something was worth the effort, using a diminutive for affection, making direct comparisons

PUTTING IT ALL TOGETHER (RESUMIÉNDOLO TODO). (Answers on page 216.)

Isabel y su hermano Miguel juegan a Monopolio. Eli los mira y ve que se (1) _____ bien. En su imaginación recuerda que antes no era así, y ella grita: «Sí ¡valió la (2) _____!» Luego, Miguel observa, «No sé, (3) _____, pero (4) _____ más vieja, más extraña (5) _____ vuelve.»

Elizabeth and her brother Michael are playing Monopoly. Elly looks at them and sees that they're getting along well. In her imagination she remembers that it wasn't like this before, and she shouts: "Yes, it was worth the trouble!" Then Michael remarks, "I don't know, little sister, but the older she gets, the stranger she becomes."

WORKING WITH WORDS AND PATTERNS

- **¡Hola, chico!** ~ Use words like **chico(a)**, **amigo(a)**, **compañero(a)** to add an affectionate tone when talking with a friend. Certain countries have special affection words for this purpose, such as **che** in Argentina and Uruguay or **'mano(a)** (short for **hermano[a]**) in Mexico. Here, of course, the affection is being used for an ulterior purpose that the dog senses.

- **perrito lindo** ~ The use of the diminutive ending **-ito** is the equivalent of saying "good little doggie."

- **Ven aquí.** ~ Use this informal command form for friends and children (or pets).

- **¿no crees?** ~ You can say this after making a statement to confirm your opinion with the person you're talking to. In English, we have a wide variety of expressions for this, e.g., *isn't it?*, *don't you think?*, *can't they?*, and so forth. In Spanish there are fewer common ones.

- **cuando les van a dar un baño** ~ Don't be fooled by Spanish word order which is often just the reverse of what it is in English. In literal translation, the phrase reads like this: *when to them they are going to give a bath*. The **les** (*them*) goes in front of the whole verb, not after it as in English. In this Spanish construction, the subject, equivalent of *they*, is impersonal and is the equivalent of the passive voice in English: *when they are going to be given a bath.*

KEY WORDS AND PHRASES

¡Hola, chico! Hello, buddy (pal, dear)!

perrito lindo sweet lovely doggie

Ven aquí. Come here. (**tú** form)

Es increíble, ¿no crees? It's incredible, don't you think?

parecen saber seem to know

cuando les van a dar un baño when they are (somebody is) going to give them a bath

Bañando el perro

Giving the dog a bath

WHAT YOU CAN LEARN   Saying "come here," expressing affection, confirming an opinion

PUTTING IT ALL TOGETHER (RESUMIÉNDOLO TODO). (Answers on page 216.)

El perro Edgar está rascándose cuando le habla Juan muy dulcemente, «¡Hola, (1) _____! ¿Cómo está mi (2) _____ lindo? (3) _____ aquí.» Edgar se huye, pero Juan lo agarra y lo lleva a la bañera. Mientras lo bañan, Juan le dice a Eli, «Es increíble, ¿no (4) _____? ¡Los perros siempre parecen saber cuando (5) _____ van a dar un baño!»

Edgar the dog is scratching himself when John speaks to him very sweetly, "Hello, buddy! How is my good little doggie? Come here." Edgar runs away, but John grabs him and carries him to the bathtub. While they bathe him, John says to Elly, "It's unbelievable, don't you think? Dogs seem to know when they are going to be given a bath."

WORKING WITH WORDS AND PATTERNS

- **preparando un asado** ~ The Spanish word **barbacoa** is a false cognate which in some places refers to meat steamed with spices. What Canadians and Americans call *barbecue* is called an **asado** in Mexico, a roasted dinner usually prepared outside on a grill. The phrase **asar la carne** means *to roast* (or *barbecue*) *the meat*.

- **limpiar, pulir, quitar polvo** ~ In Spanish the infinitive is often used to describe general actions that are in process of completion. English uses the *-ing* form of the verb (present participle).

- **hace falta** ~ The pattern **hace falta** + an infinitive is used to tell what must be done. **Hace falta hablar con el gerente.** *One must [It is necessary to] speak with the manager.* **Nos hace falta dormir.** *It's necessary that we go to sleep. (We must sleep.)*

- **No funciona.** *It doesn't work.* ~ This refers to machines that don't function. The English word *function* can be used to remember it.

- **Estamos listos.** ~ Use the verb **estar** to describe conditions. Now John and Elly are ready (in the condition of being ready). The propane bottle is in the condition of being empty, **la botella está vacía.**

- **Lo siento. He quedado con . . . para . . .** ~ Try to remember this formula to refuse an invitation in a courteous way. *I'm sorry. I made plans with . . . to . . . .*

KEY WORDS AND PHRASES

limpiar, pulir, quitar polvo cleaning, polishing, dusting (taking away dust)

Hace falta rasparla. It's necessary to scrape it.

El encendedor no funciona. The lighter doesn't work.

una pieza nueva a new part (for a machine)

¡Espera! Wait!

Estamos listos. We are ready.

He quedado con . . . I have made plans (arranged) with . . .

Me quedo a dormir. I am staying overnight (to sleep).

¡ESPERA!

20 Preparando un asado

Preparing a barbecue

WHAT YOU CAN LEARN Learning practical housekeeping terms, explaining what needs to be done, declining an invitation politely

PUTTING IT ALL TOGETHER (RESUMIÉNDOLO TODO). (Answers on page 216.)

Juan está preparando un asado, limpiando, puliendo y (1) _____ polvo. Entonces, observa que hace (2) _____ raspar la parrilla. Además, tiene que salir a comprar una (3) _____ nueva. Los dos tardan todo el día, y finalmente (4) _____ listos. Pero su hija mayor Isabel les explica, «Lo siento. Pero he (5) _____ con unos amigos para ir a comer pizza.» Su hija pequeña Abril también tiene otros planes. Eli y Juan salen a comer hamburguesas y papas fritas.

John is preparing a barbecue, cleaning, polishing, and dusting. Then he notices that the grill has to be scraped. Besides, he has to go buy a brand new part. Both of them spend the whole day like this, and finally they are ready. But their older daughter Elizabeth explains to them, "I'm sorry. I have arranged with some friends to go out to eat pizza." Their younger daughter April also has other plans. Elly and John go out to eat hamburgers and French fries.

WORKING WITH WORDS AND PATTERNS

- **materiales de arte, papel para envolver** ~ In Spanish you can't use a noun or gerund to modify another noun the way you can in English (art supplies, wrapping paper), so you often connect two nouns with a preposition. Other examples: **el reloj de oro** *the gold watch*, **las noticias de la mañana** *the morning news.*

- **¿Qué les parece (limpiar) ahora?** ~ To make a polite suggestion, use this expression with the appropriate infinitive. To your friend who drove you to the party, **¿Qué te parece salir ahora?** To your talkative assistant, **¿Qué le parece trabajar ahora?**

- **Estamos esperando que empiecen las noticias.** *We are waiting for the news to start.* ~ Literally, this is *we are waiting that the news will start*. When referring to a future action in the secondary part of a sentence, use the subjunctive (**empiecen**) for projection into the future. (See pages 140–142.)

- **Me alegra que . . .** ~ The verb **alegrar** means *to make happy*. This expression always takes a verb in the subjunctive mode (see pages 140–142) which is why it is followed by **se interesen** (and not by **se interesan**). It makes John happy that his children are interested in what is happening in the world and it is as though the color of his emotion is projected into the verb that follows.

- **lo que** ~ Use **lo que** for the word *what* when it is not asking a question: **lo que nos interesa**, **lo que vemos en la pantalla** *what interests us, what we see on the screen.*

KEY WORDS AND PHRASES

materiales de arte, papel para envolver
art supplies, wrapping paper

¿Qué les parece (limpiar) ahora?
What do you think about cleaning up now?

Me alegra que . . .
It makes me happy that . . .

lo que está sucediendo
what is happening

las noticias de la tarde
the evening news

Watching the news

WHAT YOU CAN LEARN   Suggesting politely that it's time to do something, talking about a news program

PUTTING IT ALL TOGETHER (RESUMIÉNDOLO TODO). (Answers on page 216.)

Isabel y Abril juegan con materiales (1) _____ arte. Su padre Juan entra en el cuarto y les pregunta, «¿Qué les (2) _____ limpiar ahora?» Isabel le responde, «Bien, Papi, solo estamos (3) _____ que empiecen las noticias.» A Juan le (4) _____ mucho que sus hijas se interesen en (5) _____ está sucediendo en el mundo. Pero, en realidad, las niñas se interesan en el programa ¡porque han pegado bigotes y cuernos a la pantalla!

Elizabeth and April are playing with art supplies. Their father John enters the room and asks them, "What do you think about cleaning up now?" Elizabeth answers him, "Fine, Dad, we are only waiting until the news comes on." It makes John very happy that his children are interested in what is happening in the world. But, in reality, the girls are interested because they have stuck a moustache and horns on the screen!

El español en tu vida

Spanish in your life

Practice what you've learned from Comics 11–21. (Answers on page 216.)

A. BUSCANDO LAS PALABRAS CLAVES (*Looking for the key words*)

Look at the following comics. Two key words are missing in each. Can you write them in?

1.

2.

3.

4.

5.

6.

B. ¿CUÁL ES LA PREGUNTA? (*What's the question?*)

Look at the comics below. Judging from the answers given, choose the correct question from the list and write the corresponding letter in.

1.

2.

3.

4.

5.

Preguntas (*Questions*)

A. ¿Le puedes llevar esto a Carola, por favor?
B. ¿Los puedo acompañar?
C. ¿Qué les parece limpiar ahora?
D. ¿Tú crees que todos lo pasaron bien?
E. ¿Le importaría compartir una mesa en la cafetería?

WORKING WITH WORDS AND PATTERNS

- **tomar el almuerzo ~** You can use the verb **tomar** to talk about eating breakfast, lunch, or a snack. For supper, use the verb **cenar**. **Tomo el desayuno a las ocho. Tomo el almuerzo a las dos y a veces tomo una merienda por la tarde. Ceno tarde, a las nueve de la noche.** *I eat breakfast at eight. I eat lunch at two, and at times I have a snack in the afternoon. I eat supper at nine o'clock at night.*

- **¿Qué estás haciendo? ~** You can use the simple present tense and ask, **—¿Qué haces?** *What are you doing?* But to emphasize asking about what is happening at this very moment, use this form, the present progressive tense. It is made up of the verb **estar** plus the present participle of the action verb, which ends in **-ando** or **-iendo**. (See page 6.)

- **Yo les di de comer. ~** Use the idiom **dar de comer** to talk about giving someone something to eat. Here **dar** is in the preterite to refer to the past. (See pages 76–77.)

- **hace** + *time expression ~* This useful construction means *ago*, but it comes before rather than after the time expression since, literally, it means: *it makes (so many) days or months or years*—**hace diez años, hace dos semanas, hace mucho tiempo** *ten years ago, two weeks ago, a long time ago.*

(See page 6.)

(See pages 76–77.)

KEY WORDS AND PHRASES

tomar el almuerzo to eat lunch

lanzar to throw, throwing

jadeo, babeo, gemido pant, slobber, moan (sounds made by the dogs)

¿Qué estás haciendo? What are you doing?

Yo les di de comer. I gave them (something) to eat.

hace unos minutos a few minutes ago

VOY A TOMAR EL ALMUERZO.

El abuelo toma el almuerzo

Grandpa eats his lunch

WHAT YOU CAN LEARN   Talking about meals, asking what someone is doing, making a time reference to the past

PUTTING IT ALL TOGETHER (RESUMIÉNDOLO TODO). (Answers on page 216.)

El abuelo sale al jardín para (1) _____ su (2)_____. Los dos perros lo miran y hacen sonidos. Él se siente mal y entra a buscarles comida. Eli lo ve y le pregunta, «¿Qué estás (3) _____, papá?» Entonces, le informa, «Yo les di de (4) _____ a los perros (5) _____ sólo unos minutos.»

Grandpa goes out to the garden to eat his lunch. The two dogs look at him and make noises. He feels bad and goes inside to find food for them. Elly sees him and asks, "What are you doing? I fed the dogs just a few minutes ago."

WORKING WITH WORDS AND PATTERNS

- **Prepárense . . .** ~ The plural command (addressed to radio listeners) uses the present subjunctive form (see pages 140–142). Since it is a reflexive verb, the **se** is tacked on to the end, literally, *Prepare yourselves*.

- **a rocanrrolear** ~ Here's the Spanish version of *to rock and roll*.

- **¿Cómo te puedes concentrar . . . ?** ~ The **te** is here because *to concentrate* is a reflexive verb in Spanish: **concentrarse** (*to concentrate [oneself]*). Asking a question like this is a polite way of suggesting a change in behavior.

- **Lo voy a tener que bajar . . .** ~ Put **lo**, the equivalent of *it* (the object pronoun), either way at the front as it is here (*It I am going to have to lower*), or tack it on to the infinitive: **Voy a tener que bajarlo.** *I am going to have to lower it.*

- **No estoy haciendo . . . estoy estudiando.** ~ Use **estoy** with the **-ando** or **-iendo** form of the action verb to tell what you are doing right at this moment. This is called the present progressive tense (see page 6).

KEY WORDS AND PHRASES

principales top (most important) ones (here referring to songs)

¿Cómo te puedes concentrar . . . ? How can you concentrate . . .?

esta bulla this racket (loud and confusing noise)

Lo voy a tener que bajar . . . I'm going to have to lower it

cielito darling (literally, little sky or little heaven)

hacer tareas to do homework

No estoy haciendo tareas. I'm not doing homework.

Estoy estudiando . . . I'm studying . . .

Escuchando y estudiando

Listening and studying

WHAT YOU CAN LEARN Suggesting a change of behavior, telling what you are doing at this very moment

PUTTING IT ALL TOGETHER (RESUMIÉNDOLO TODO). (Answers on page 216.)

Abril lee mientras mira televisión y (1) _____ un grupo de música rock. Su mamá entra y le pregunta, «¿Cómo te puedes concentrar con esta (2) _____?» Entonces, le advierte, «(3) _____ voy a tener que bajar un poco.» Abril insiste, «¡Mami! ¡No estoy haciendo (4) _____! ¡De veras!» Eli se va y Abril sonríe y se dice a si misma: «Estoy (5) _____ . . .»

April is reading while she watches television and listens to a rock group. Her mother comes in and asks her, "How can you concentrate with this racket?" Then she warns, "I'm going to have to lower it a little." April insists, "Mom! I'm not doing homework! Honestly!" Elly leaves, and April smiles and thinks to herself, "I'm studying . . ."

WORKING WITH WORDS AND PATTERNS

- **Pensando en mi hermano.** ~ When you mean that you have someone on your mind, use **pensar en**. **Pienso en María Teresa.** *I'm thinking about María Teresa.* When you are asking someone's opinion, use **pensar de**. **¿Qué piensas de la nueva doctora?** *What do you think of the new* [woman] *doctor?*

- **echar de menos** ~ Use this idiom to say you miss somebody. (Literally, it means *to throw [someone] in less*.) In most of Latin America, another way to say the same thing is **extrañar** (literally, *to strange*). **¿Echas de menos a tus primos? Sí, los extraño mucho.** *Do you miss your cousins? Yes, I miss them a lot.*

- **yo también** ~ Notice that in English we tend to say, *Me too*, but in Spanish you have to use **yo**, which is the equivalent of *I*. It's like saying, *I also*.

KEY WORDS AND PHRASES

pensando en thinking about

¿Sabes una cosa . . . ? (Do you) know something . . . ?

a veces at times, sometimes

echo de menos I miss

yo también me too

Pensando en mi hermano

Thinking about my brother

WHAT YOU CAN LEARN Saying you miss somebody, seconding an opinion that's just been stated

PUTTING IT ALL TOGETHER (RESUMIÉNDOLO TODO). (Answers on page 216.)

El perro y el conejo corren por la casa, haciendo mucha bulla y atacándose. De repente, Isabel le dice a su amiga, «¿(1) _____ una cosa, Dora? A (2) _____ realmente (3) _____ de (4) _____ a mi hermano . . . » Dora le da la razón, «Sí, (5) _____ también.»

The dog and rabbit run through the house, making a racket and attacking each other. Suddenly, Elizabeth comments to her friend, "Know something, Dora? At times I really miss my brother . . ." Dora agrees with her, "Yes, me too."

WORKING WITH WORDS AND PATTERNS

- **¡Feliz Día del Padre!** ~ Use the word **feliz** to wish people a happy holiday: **Feliz Día de la Madre (Navidad, Pascua, Día de las Gracias, Día de la Independencia).** *Happy Mother's Day (Merry Christmas, Happy Easter, Thanksgiving, Independence Day).*

- **¿Podría hablar con . . . ?** ~ After greeting someone with **Hola** or **Buenos días,** use this phrase to ask to speak to someone on the phone. The verb **poder** is in the conditional, which makes it very polite. (See pages 80–81.)

- **recién hecho** ~ The word **recién** is a shortened form of **recientemente** (*recently*) that is useful in many expressions: **recién llegados** *newcomers,* **recién casados** *newlyweds,* **recién nacido** *newborn.*

- **¡Por supuesto!** ~ There are several expressions for expressing agreement like this: **Desde luego, Cómo no, Naturalmente, Claro que sí.** All of these mean approximately the same thing.

- **¿Alguien sabe por qué . . .** ~ The word **porque** means *because,* but when it is two separate words and the **qué** has an accent mark (**por qué**), it means *why.*

KEY WORDS AND PHRASES

¡Feliz Día del Padre! Happy Father's Day

¿Podría hablar con . . . ? May I speak with . . . ?

¡Por supuesto! Of course!, Certainly.

café recién hecho fresh-brewed coffee

¡Qué extraño! How strange!

¿Alguien sabe por qué . . . ? Does anyone know why . . . ?

El teléfono está descolgado

The telephone is off the hook

WHAT YOU CAN LEARN   Wishing people a happy holiday, asking for someone on the telephone, expressing agreement

PUTTING IT ALL TOGETHER (RESUMIÉNDOLO TODO). (Answers on page 216.)

Abuelo se despierta cuando suena el teléfono. La voz de su nieto le dice, «¡Hola, abuelo! ¡(1) _____ Día del Padre! ¿(2) _____ hablar con Papi?» Abuelo se pone los dientes y los anteojos y responde, «¡Por (3) _____!» Luego baja la escalera. Llega a la cocina y ve el café (4) _____ hecho. Eli ve el teléfono descolgado y piensa, «¡Qué extraño!» Entonces, pregunta, «¿Alguien sabe (5) _____ qué está descolgado el teléfono?»

Grandpa wakes up when the telephone rings. Then his grandson's voice says (to him), "Hello, Grandpa. Happy Father's Day! Could I speak with Dad?" Grandpa puts his teeth in and his glasses on and answers, "Of course!" Then he goes down the staircase. He gets to the kitchen and sees the fresh-brewed coffee. Elly sees the telephone off the hook and thinks, "How strange!" Then she asks, "Does anyone know why the telephone is off the hook?

WORKING WITH WORDS AND PATTERNS

- **¡No lo quiero hacer!** *I don't want to do it!* ~ When you use *it* as the direct object of an action, put the Spanish pronoun (**lo** or **la**) in front of the whole verb. The word order is very different from the English: **No lo quiero hacer** (literally, *Not it I want to do*). Another correct way is to put the **lo** or **la** at the very end and attach it to the infinitive. **No quiero hacerlo.**

- **¡Lo odio!** ~ The verb **odiar** is not a cognate of *to hate*, but it is similar to the adjective *odious*, which means *hateful*, so that's a good way to remember it.

- **estúpido . . . torpe . . . idiota . . .** ~ April uses these strong words to insult her project, but you can also use them to insult people. Be careful, however. The word **estúpido(a)** is stronger than its cognate *stupid* in English. If you are fooling around and want to tell a friend, *Don't be stupid*, say **No seas tonto(a)** or **No seas bobo(a)**. **Tonto** and **bobo** mean *foolish* or *silly*.

- **seguir haciendo** ~ You can use the verbs **seguir** or **continuar** instead of **estar** in the present progressive tense. (See page 6.)

- **¡Me rindo!** ~ This is the reflexive verb **rendirse**, which is a stem-changing verb; that's why it has an **i** instead of an **e**. (See page 6.) If you are talking about yourself and someone else, say **Nos rendimos.** (*We give up.*)

- **Lo hice. Lo terminé.** ~ Use the preterite tense as April does here to express a completed action in the past. (See pages 76–77.)

- **Estar de ánimo** ~ Another way to say this is **estar de humor**. A useful expression is **estoy de buen (mal) humor** *I am in a good (bad) mood*.

KEY WORDS AND PHRASES

¡No quiero hacer . . . ! I don't want to do . . . !

Tengo que encontrar . . . I have to find . . .

¡Es demasiado! It's too much!

¡Lo odio! I hate it!

estúpido . . . torpe . . . idiota . . . stupid . . . crude . . . idiotic . . .

seguir haciendo to continue doing

¡Me rindo! I give up! I surrender.

corte . . . pegar . . . cut . . . pasting . . .

Listo, lo hice. Lo terminé. Ready, I did it. I finished it.

estar de ánimo to be in the mood

26 Abril termina su proyecto

April finishes her project

WHAT YOU CAN LEARN   Complaining about a job, expressing dislike, three words to use as insults

PUTTING IT ALL TOGETHER (RESUMIÉNDOLO TODO). (Answers on page 216.)

Abril llora porque tiene que hacer un proyecto para la escuela y no lo quiere hacer. Ella se queja, «¡Es (1) _____! ¡Lo (2) _____! Estúpido . . . (3) _____ . . . idiota . . . ¡No es (4) _____! ¡Me rindo!» Pero, después de un rato, se calma y se pone a cortar y pegar. Finalmente, mira su trabajo y piensa, «Listo, lo terminé. Todo lo que necesitaba era (5) _____ de ánimo . . .»

April is crying because she has to do a project for school and she doesn't want to do it. She complains, "It's too much! I hate it! Stupid . . . crude . . . idiotic . . . It's not fair! I give up!" But, after a while, she calms down and starts to cut and paste. Finally, she looks at her work and thinks, "(All) Ready, I did it. All I needed was to be in the mood . . ."

WORKING WITH WORDS AND PATTERNS

- **Besándose en el coche.** ~ Use **se** when talking about two people doing something to each other. **Mis amigos latinos se abrazan cuando se encuentran.** *My Latino friends hug each other when they meet.* **Esos niños siempre se ayudan con sus tareas.** *Those boys always help each other with their homework.* This is called the *reciprocal reflexive.*

- **llevar . . . tanto tiempo** ~ You can use this handy formula to tell how long you have been someplace: **llevar** (present tense) + time quantity. **Llevo trece años en la misma casa.** *I have been in the same house for thirteen years.* **Llevamos dos horas en este restaurante.** *We've been in this restaurant for two hours.* **¿Cuánto tiempo llevas estudiando español?** *How long have you been studying Spanish?* (Notice that you use the present tense of **llevar** but the meaning is in the present perfect [progressive] in English.)

- **empañarse** ~ Use this reflexive verb with the reflexive pronoun in front of it. **Mis anteojos se empañan cuando hace frío.** *My glasses get blurry when it's cold out.*

- **¡No se puede limpiar!** ~ This is a useful construction to talk about what can't be done. **No se puede** + infinitive. **¡Ssst! No se puede hablar en el cine.** *Shhh! You can't talk in the movie theater.* **Miren, ¡aquí no se puede fumar!** *Look, you can't smoke here.*

- **Sabías donde estaba.** *You knew where I was.* ~ These verbs are in the imperfect because they are describing a mental act and a state or condition in the past. (See pages 77–79.)

KEY WORDS AND PHRASES

Llevamos aquí tanto tiempo . . . We have been here so much time (so long)

se han empañado have gotten blurry

¡No se puede limpiar! It can't be cleaned!

rasca scrape

al menos at least

Sabías donde estaba. You knew where I was.

27 Besándose en el coche

Kissing in the car

WHAT YOU CAN LEARN   Saying how much time has passed, telling what can't be done

PUTTING IT ALL TOGETHER (RESUMIÉNDOLO TODO). (Answers on page 216.)

Isabel y su novio Antonio están (1) _____ en el coche. Es invierno. (2) _____ tanto (3) _____ en el coche que las ventanas se han empañado. Isabel dice, «¡No se (4) _____ limpiar! Se han congelado.» Los dos rascan y de repente se asoma la cara del papá de Isabel. Ella lo acompaña a la casa y le indica, «¡Al menos (5) _____ donde estaba!»

Elizabeth and her boyfriend Anthony are kissing in the car. It's winter. They have been in the car so long that the windows have clouded up. Elizabeth says, "It can't be cleaned! They've frozen!" The two of them scrape, and suddenly the face of Elizabeth's father appears in the window. She accompanies him to the house and comments, "At least you knew where I was!"

WORKING WITH WORDS AND PATTERNS

- **¿No les parece . . .** ~ This is Latin American usage. The **les** (*to you*) refers to **ustedes**. You can use this construction with many descriptive words, for example: **¿No les parece lindo (cómico, extraño)?** *Don't you think it's lovely (funny, strange)?*

- **vitrina** ~ This word is used in Latin America to mean the same thing as **escaparate**, *store window* or *a glass showcase*.

- **¿Qué estás haciendo . . . ? La estoy mirando . . .** ~ Use the present progressive to ask or talk about actions that are happening right at this minute. (See page 6.)

- **cuando era pequeño(a)** ~ In this case **pequeño(a)** refers to being young. Another way to evoke a childhood memory is to say, **cuando era niño(a)**.

- **¡Cómo me gustaría . . . !** ~ You can use this with many different infinitives to express your wishes. **¡Cómo me gustaría aprender a bailar! ¡Cómo nos gustaría vivir en el campo!** *How I would like to learn how to dance! How we would like to live in the country!*

- **de nuevo** ~ This means the same thing as **otra vez**.

KEY WORDS AND PHRASES

los escaparates the store windows

¿No les parece . . . ? Doesn't it seem to you . . . ?

una vitrina bellamente decorada a beautifully decorated shop window

¿Qué estás haciendo? What are you doing?

desde la altura correcta from the correct height

Así es como recuerdo . . . That's the way I remember . . .

cuando era pequeño when I was little

¡Cómo me gustaría . . . ! How I would like . . . !

de nuevo once again

¡Súbeme! Lift me up!

CUANDO ERA PEQUEÑO

The store windows at Christmas

WHAT YOU CAN LEARN Asking for agreement on an opinion, recalling a childhood memory, saying what you would like

PUTTING IT ALL TOGETHER (RESUMIÉNDOLO TODO). (Answers on page 216.)

Miguel pasea con su novia Deana, su amigo Gordo y su familia. Todos miran los (1) _____ y Gordo pregunta, «Chicos, ¿no les (2) _____ esta una vitrina bellamente decorada?» Miguel se agacha y explica, «Así es como (3) _____ ver los escaparates cuando era (4)_____. ¡Cómo me gustaría ver todo de (5) _____desde la perspectiva de un niño!» Luego, el hijo de Gordo le pide, «Papi, ¡súbeme!»

Michael is strolling with his fiancée Deanna, his friend Gordon and Gordon's family. Everyone is looking at the Christmas shop windows and Gordon asks, "Guys, don't you think that this window is beautifully decorated?" Michael squats down and explains, "This is how I remember seeing the store windows when I was little. How I would like to see everything again from a child's perspective!" Then Gordon's son asks him, "Daddy, lift me up!"

WORKING WITH WORDS AND PATTERNS

- **el cajero automático** *ATM* or *cash machine* ~ **Cajero** also means *cashier* or *teller*.

- **¡La-na la-na la!** ~ April is singing **¡lana!** (*wool!*) which in many places of Latin America is slang for *money*, like *dough* in English.

- **Esto representa . . .** ~ Use **esto** when referring to a situation or idea. In this case John talks about the situation of getting money from the machine.

- **una gran cantidad** ~ Notice that you say **gran** (instead of **grande**) when you put the word in front of any noun, masculine or feminine: **un gran hombre, una gran ciudad** *a great man, a great city*. If you put it afterwards, use **grande** and it means *large* or *big*: **un hombre grande, una ciudad grande** *a large* (or *grown-up*) *man, a big city*.

- **Lo sé.** ~ In English we just say *I know*, but in Spanish it seems incomplete, so they say **lo sé**, literally, *I know it*.

- **Hemos estado . . .** ~ Use the present perfect tense to describe an action that has just been completed. (See pages 6–7.)

- **estar en la cola** *to be in line* ~ **Hacer cola** means *to stand* (or *to wait*) *in line*. The word **cola** refers to the tail of an animal because often a line of people curves around in a similar way. A less common way of saying *in line* is **en la fila**.

- **como una hora** ~ To make a rough time estimate, you can put **como** or **más o menos** in front of the time expression. **¿Por cuánto tiempo? Como cinco días.** *For how long? Around five days.* **Vamos a tener que esperar más o menos veinte minutos.** *We'll have to wait about twenty minutes.*

KEY WORDS AND PHRASES

gratis gratis, free of charge

una gran cantidad a great amount (quantity)

esfuerzo effort

Lo sé. I know (it).

Hemos estado en la cola. We have been in line.

como una hora about (around, more or less) an hour

29 El cajero automático

The money machine

WHAT YOU CAN LEARN   Talking about being in line, giving a rough time estimate

PUTTING IT ALL TOGETHER (RESUMIÉNDOLO TODO). (Answers on page 216.)

Abril y su padre Juan hacen (1) _____ para usar el cajero automático. Abril se alegra cuando su padre recibe el dinero y canta «¡(2) _____ . . . ! ¡La-na! ¡Lana! ¡La!» Juan le explica que no es gratis. «(3) _____ representa una gran cantidad de (4) _____», le dice. Abril responde que lo sabe porque han estado esperando allí (5) _____ una hora.

April and her father John are waiting in line to use the cash machine. April is glad when her father gets the money and sings out, "Money, money! Dough, dough dough! ¡La, la, la!" John explains to her that it isn't free of charge. "This represents a great amount of effort," he says. April answers that she knows because they have been waiting there for about an hour.

WORKING WITH WORDS AND PATTERNS

- **arreglar** ~ This useful verb means *to fix* in the sense of repair, but it also can mean *to arrange* or *to put in order*. **¿No vas a arreglar la casa para la fiesta? Mi tío tiene que arreglar sus documentos antes de viajar.** *Aren't you going to arrange the house for the party? My uncle has to put his documents in order before traveling.*

- **¿Cuánto tiempo te vas a quedar . . . ?** *How long are you going to stay . . . ?* ~ You can use the verb **quedarse** to talk about staying at some place. Since it is reflexive, you have to remember to use the correct reflexive pronoun. **Siempre nos quedamos en el hotel en el centro.** *We always stay at the hotel downtown.* **Me voy a quedar con mi primo para la boda.** *I'm going to stay with my cousin for the wedding.*

- **Míralo.** ~ This is a handy way to get someone's attention: **¡mira!**, the familiar command form of **mirar**, but with **lo** (*it*) attached to the end. For the formal command, you would say, **¡Mírelo usted!**

- **Mientras me necesiten.** ~ Use the present subjunctive when projecting action into the future because the future is always uncertain. (See pages 140–142.) Grandpa will stay as long as he is needed (literally, *as long as they need me*) and who knows how long that will be? That's why the verb here is **necesiten** and not the usual present tense form **necesitan**.

- **buscar** ~ This verb means *to seek*, *to search for*, or *to look for*. In Spanish you don't add any word to mean *for* after it. **Buscamos a Carlitos.** *We are looking for Charlie.*

KEY WORDS AND PHRASES

¿Cuánto tiempo te vas a quedar . . . ? How long are you going to stay . . .?

Míralo de esta manera. Look at it (in) this way.

Mientras me necesiten. As long as I'm needed.

¿Qué estás buscando? What are you looking for?

para romper to break

Grandpa fixes things

WHAT YOU CAN LEARN   How to ask people how long they are staying, asking what someone is looking for

PUTTING IT ALL TOGETHER (RESUMIÉNDOLO TODO). Fill in the blanks. (Answers on page 216.)

Abril mira a su abuelo mientras él arregla varias cosas en la casa. Le pregunta, «¿Cuánto tiempo te vas a (1) _____ con nosotros, abuelo?» El contesta, «Míralo de esta (2) _____. (3) _____ me necesiten.» Más tarde, Isabel le pregunta a Abril, «¿Qué estás (4) _____?» y ésta responde, «Algo para (5) _____.»

April watches her grandpa while he fixes several things in the house. She asks him, "How long are you going to stay with us, Grandpa?" He replies, "Look at it this way. As long as I am needed." Later, Isabel asks April, "What are you looking for?" and she answers, "Something to break."

El español en tu vida

Spanish in Your Life

Practice what you've learned from Comics 22–30. (Answers on page 216.)

A. EQUIVALENTES INSTANTÁNEOS (*Instant Equivalents*)

Look at the following comics and the phrases that accompany them.
Then write the Spanish equivalent that belongs in each comic.

1. What are you doing?/only a few minutes ago

2. It's impossible!/Honest! (Truly!)

3. I really miss/me too

4. It's not fair!/I give up!

5. We've been here so long/It can't be cleaned!

6. I know./in line

B. ¿QUÉ FALTA AQUÍ? (*What's missing here?*)

Look at the comics below. Write the important word that is missing
in each one in the blank.

1.

2.

3.

C. EN CASA CON LOS PATTERSON (*At home with the Pattersons*)

Examine the drawing below. Label all the objects you can with their Spanish names.
This is based on comics 1–30.

1. _____

2. _____

3. _____

4. _____

5. _____

6. _____

7. _____

8. _____

9. _____

10. _____

11. _____

12. _____

13. _____

14. _____

15. _____

Moderate Level

Before You Read (Comics 31–55)

Do you want to move your Spanish up a notch? Are you ready for longer and more complex conversations between characters? Read the "moderate" group of comic strips in which the Pattersons and their friends often talk about past events, future plans, and what they would do in various situations. Check your grasp of details after each comic strip with the *Putting It All Together* exercise—but now without the English translations at hand (you'll find them in the appendices, if you need help). Then see if you have understood the main point or points by doing the new exercise called *Did You Get It? (¿Comprendiste?)*. Finally, test your memory with the exercises in the sections called **El español en tu vida** that appear intermittently.

But wait a moment! Before beginning, look over the following learning aids and review the preterite and imperfect past tenses, so you can communicate about the past. Learn the future and conditional to extend your range of discourse. This will help develop your reading comprehension and fluency.

Good luck! ¡**Buena suerte!** And enjoy yourself! **Y, ¡que te diviertas!**

Learn the Links

Here are more small words that appear often and link ideas. Learn them now.

ahí, allí . . . . *there, over there*
con . . . . *with*
cosa, cosas . . . . *thing, things*
ese, esa . . . . *that* (refers to masc. or fem.)
esos, esas . . . . *those* (refers to masc. or fem.)
este, esta . . . . *this* (refers to masc. or fem.)
estos, estas . . . . *these* (refers to masc. or fem.)
hasta . . . . *until, up to*
hay/no hay . . . . *there is, there are/there isn't, there aren't*
hoy . . . . *today*
mi, mis . . . . *my*
otro, otra . . . . *another, other* (refers to masc. or fem.)
para . . . . *for, to, in order to*
pero . . . . *but*
por . . . . *for, by, during, through*
su, sus . . . . *his, her, their, your* (formal)
tanto, tanta . . . . *so much* (refers to masc. or fem.)
tantos, tantas . . . . . *so many* (refers to masc. or fem.)

Back to Basics: Using the Preterite, Imperfect, Future, and Conditional

The heart of the Spanish sentence is the verb, and it changes endings according to the subject and time frame. Here is a quick review of four important tenses and moods (groups of forms for particular time frames) that are used a lot in the moderate section of this book. (For a review of other tenses, see pages 5–7 and 139–145.) Read it through and use it as reference when you read the comic strips.

Speaking About the Past with the Preterite and the Imperfect

Whereas English has only one past tense, Spanish has two: (1) the *preterite* for expressing past actions viewed as completed, and (2) the *imperfect* for describing past actions that extended over an indefinite period of time or for expressing repeated or habitual action. The choice between these two depends on the point of view of the speaker.

As a general rule, use the *preterite* for simple, completed actions (I *went* to the store, I *bought* some bread) and the *imperfect* for describing an action that was going on (I *was walking* through the park when suddenly . . .) or for habitual action in the past (When I *lived* in Costa Rica, I *used to go* to the beach every day). Compare:

- **preterite (simple completed actions):** *Lavé* y *doblé* la ropa de Abril y la *dejó* amontonada. *I washed and folded April's clothing and she left it all piled up.*
- **imperfect (description, extended or habitual actions):** *Caminaba* por el parque cuando de repente . . . *I was walking through the park when suddenly . . .* **Cuando *vivía* en Costa Rica, *iba* a la playa todos los días.** *When I lived in Costa Rica, I would go to the beach every day.*

Telling time or age in the past is always in the *imperfect* since this is description of a condition that does not have a definite completion. Also, mental and emotional actions are very often expressed in the imperfect since they are really descriptions of conditions.

- **imperfect (time, age, and mental or emotional conditions in the past):** *Eran* las seis cuando llegaron nuestros amigos. *It was six o'clock when our friends came.* **Cuando *tenía* dieciséis años, fui a mi primera fiesta.** *When I was sixteen years old, I went to my first party.* **¡*Quería* mostrar mi anillo de compromiso!** *I wanted to show off my engagement ring!* **Ambos *éramos* estudiantes** . . . **Yo *estaba* loco por ti . . .** *We were both students . . . I was crazy about you . . .*

Review of Regular Preterite Tense Forms

The *preterite* is used for expressing completed past actions and translated as the simple past, e.g., **hablé** = *I spoke* or *I talked.*

hablar (to speak)

hablé	*I spoke*
hablaste	*you spoke*
habló	*he, she, it,* or *(formal) you spoke*
hablamos	*we spoke*
hablasteis	*you (all) spoke*
hablaron	*they* or *(formal) you all spoke*

comer (to eat)

comí	*I ate*
comiste	*you ate*
comió	*he, she, it,* or *(formal) you ate*
comimos	*we ate*
comisteis	*you (all) ate*
comieron	*they* or *(formal) you all ate*

vivir (to live)

viví	*I lived*
viviste	*you lived*
vivió	*he, she, it,* or *(formal) you lived*
vivimos	*we lived*
vivisteis	*you (all) lived*
vivieron	*they* or *(formal) you all lived*

Review of Regular Imperfect Tense Forms

The *imperfect* is used for describing past actions and conditions and often translated

with *used to + infinitive*, with a form of *to be +
the present participle*, or with the simple past,
e.g., **hablaba** = *I used to speak, I used to talk* or
I was speaking, I was talking or *I spoke, I talked.*

hablar (to speak; to talk)

hablaba	*I was speaking*
hablabas	*you were speaking*
hablaba	*he, she, it was speaking, or (formal) you were speaking*
hablábamos	*we were speaking*
hablabais	*you (all) were speaking*
hablaban	*they or (formal) you all were speaking*

comer (to eat)

comía	*I was eating*
comías	*you were eating*
comía	*he, she, it was eating, or (formal) you were eating*
comíamos	*we were eating*
comíais	*you (all) were eating*
comían	*they or (formal) you all were eating*

vivir (to live)

vivía	*I was living*
vivías	*you were living*
vivía	*he, she, it was living, or (formal) you were living*
vivíamos	*we were living*
vivíais	*you (all) were living*
vivían	*they or (formal) you all were living*

Review of Irregular Preterite Tense Forms

There are quite a few common verbs that are
irregular in the preterite. The following appear
in the comic strips in this group. Since they are
very much used, they are worth learning. Notice

that **ir** (*to go*) and **ser** (*to be*) have the same form
in the preterite.

ir, ser (to go, to be)

fui	*I was*
fuiste	*you were*
fue	*he, she, it was, or (formal) you were*
fuimos	*we were*
fuiste	*you (all) were*
fueron	*they or (formal) you all were*

estar [u-stem] (to be)

estuve	*I was*
estuviste	*you were*
estuvo	*he, she, it was, or (formal) you were*
estuvimos	*we were*
estuvisteis	*you (all) were*
estuvieron	*they or (formal) you all were*

poder [u-stem] (to be able)

pude	*I was able (I could)*
pudiste	*you were able (you could)*
pudo	*he, she, it was able (could), or (formal) you were able (could)*
pudimos	*we were able (we could)*
pudisteis	*you (all) were able (you could)*
pudieron	*they or (formal) you all were able (could)*

poner [u-stem] (to put)

puse	*I put*
pusiste	*you put*
puso	*he, she, it, or (formal) you put*
pusimos	*we put*

pusisteis . . . . *you (all) put*
pusieron . . . . *they or (formal) you all put*

tener [u-stem] (to have)

tuve . . . . *I had*
tuviste . . . . *you had*
tuvo . . . . *he, she, it, or (formal) you had*
tuvimos . . . . *we had*
tuvisteis . . . . *you (all) had*
tuvieron . . . . *they or (formal) you all had*

venir [i-stem] (to come)

vine . . . . *I came*
viniste . . . . *you came*
vino . . . . *he, she, it, or (formal) you came*
vinimos . . . . *we came*
vinisteis . . . . *you (all) came*
vinieron . . . . *they or (formal) you all came*

decir [i-stem] (to say or tell)

dije . . . . *I said*
dijiste . . . . *you said*
dijo . . . . *he, she, it or (formal) you said*
dijimos . . . . *we said*
dijisteis . . . . *you (all) said*
dijeron . . . . *they or (formal) you all said*

hacer [i-stem] (to do or make)

hice . . . . *I did*
hiciste . . . . *you did*
hizo . . . . *he, she, it or (formal) you did*
hicimos . . . . *we did*
hicisteis . . . . *you (all) did*
hicieron . . . . *they or (formal) you all did*

Review of Irregular Imperfect Tense Forms

The imperfect tense has only three irregular verbs: **ser**, **ir**, and **ver**. They are very common and useful and thus well worth learning. All of them are used at different moments in the comic strips included in this book.

ser (to be)

era . . . . *I was*
eras . . . . *you were*
era . . . . *he, she, it was, or (formal) you were*
éramos . . . . *we were*
erais . . . . *you (all) were*
eran . . . . *they or (formal) you all were*

ir (to go)

iba . . . . *I was going*
ibas . . . . *you were going*
iba . . . . *he, she, it was going, or (formal) you were going*
íbamos . . . . *we were going*
ibais . . . . *you (all) were going*
iban . . . . *they or (formal) you all were going*

ver (to see)

veía . . . . *I was seeing*
veías . . . . *you were seeing*
veía . . . . *he, she, it was seeing, or (formal) you were seeing*
veíamos . . . . *we were seeing*
veíais . . . . *you (all) were seeing*
veían . . . . *they or (formal) you all were seeing*

Review of Past Progressive Forms

The *past progressive* is not used as much in Spanish as in English, but it does occur at times. It is most often used to emphasize what was happening exactly at a particular moment. Notice it is similar to the present progressive. (See page 6.) It is formed by combining the imperfect of **estar** with the present participle (**-ando** or **-iendo** form).

hablar (to speak; to talk)

estaba hablando	*I was speaking*
estabas hablando	*you were speaking*
estaba hablando	*he, she, it was speaking,* or (formal) *you were speaking*
estábamos hablando . . .	*we were speaking*
estabais hablando	*you (all) were speaking*
estaban hablando	*they* or (formal) *you all were speaking*

Review of Future and Conditional Forms

The *future* tense is used to express actions that will take place in the future or to express possibility or probability in the present.

- **Mañana iremos a la playa.** *Tomorrow we will go to the beach.*
- **¿Donde estarán los niños?** *Where can the children be?*

The *conditional* tense (or mood) is used to express conjecture, what would happen under certain circumstances, to express possibility or probability in the past, or to show politeness or courtesy.

- **En tu lugar, no compraría el auto.** *In your place, I wouldn't buy the car.*
- **Me prometieron que llegarían a tiempo.** *They promised me they would come on time.*
- **¿Estarían contentos de recibir la invitación?** *Could they have been happy to receive the invitation?*
- **¿Podrías prestarme tu abrigo?** *Would you be kind enough to lend me your coat?*

Both tenses, the future and the conditional, add endings to the whole infinitive.

FUTURE TENSE

hablar (to speak; to talk)

hablaré	*I will talk*
hablarás	*you will talk*
hablará	*he, she, it,* or (formal) *you will talk*
hablaremos	*we will talk*
hablaréis	*you (all) will talk*
hablarán	*they* or (formal) *you all will talk*

comer (to eat)

comeré	*I will eat*
comerás	*you will eat*
comerá	*he, she, it,* or (formal) *you will eat*
comeremos	*we will eat*
comeréis	*you (all) will eat*
comerán	*they* or (formal) *you all will eat*

vivir (to live)

viviré	*I will live*
vivirás	*you will live*
vivirá	*he, she, it,* or (formal) *you will live*
viviremos	*we will live*
viviréis	*you (all) will live*
vivirán	*they* or (formal) *you all will live*

CONDITIONAL TENSE (OR MOOD)

hablar (to speak; to talk)

hablaría	*I would talk*
hablarías	*you would talk*
hablaría	*he, she, it,* or (formal) *you would talk*
hablaríamos	*we would talk*
hablaríais	*you (all) would talk*
hablarían	*they* or (formal) *you all would talk*

comer (to eat)

comería	*I would eat*
comerías	*you would eat*
comería	*he, she, it,* or (formal) *you would eat*
comeríamos	*we would eat*
comeríais	*you (all) would eat*
comerían	*they* or (formal) *you all would eat*

vivir (to live)

viviría	*I would live*
vivirías	*you would live*
viviría	*he, she, it,* or (formal) *you would live*
viviríamos	*we would live*
viviríais	*you (all) would live*
vivirían	*they* or (formal) *you all would live*

NOTE: In the future and the conditional there are several irregular verbs, such as **tener** and **poder**, that change the infinitive and add a **d** before adding the endings (**tendré**, **tendrás**, **tendrá**, etc., **podría**, **podrías**, **podría**, etc.).

WORKING WITH WORDS AND PATTERNS

- **¿Vas a usar eso . . . ?** *Are you going to wear that?* ~ You can use **llevar** or **traer** in place of **usar** in this expression, since all three verbs mean *to wear*.

- **de nuestro pueblo** ~ **Pueblo** has several different meanings. Here it means *the people of the nation*, so you can talk about the **pueblo mexicano** (the Mexican people) or the **pueblo canadiense** or **estadounidense** (the Canadian people or the people of the United States). Another common meaning is *town* (in contrast to a city, **ciudad**).

- **que lucharon** ~ Express completed past actions with the preterite. Here the regular verb **luchar** (*to fight*) is in the preterite, referring to the men and women who fought in the war which occurred some time ago. (See page 77.) Notice that to say *who* or *that* most of the time you can use **que**.

- **por nosotros** ~ When you are trying to choose between **por** or **para**, always choose **por** if the meaning is "for the sake of," as it is in this case.

- **¿Por qué hay tan pocos?** ~ The word **poco** means *a little* and **un poco** means *a little bit*. In the plural, **pocos** or **pocas** means *few*. You choose the ending of course to match what you are referring to. If you are looking at a plate with only two enchiladas, you could ask, **¿Por qué hay tan pocas?**

KEY WORDS AND PHRASES

¿Vas a usar eso . . . ? Are you going to wear that?

el desfile the parade

con gran orgullo with great pride

Aquí viene. Here he comes.

de nuestro pueblo of our country

que lucharon por nosotros who fought for us

¿Por qué hay tan pocos? Why are there so few (of them)?

Grandpa marches in the parade

WHAT YOU CAN LEARN Asking people what they are going to wear, expressing pride, expressing past completed actions with the preterite

PUTTING IT ALL TOGETHER (RESUMIÉNDOLO TODO). Fill in the blanks. (Answers on page 216.)

Es el Día de Conmemoración, Día de los veteranos, y el Abuelo se pone el sombrero y la chaqueta. Abril le pregunta, «¿Vas a (1) _____ eso en el (2) _____, abuelo?» El le responde, «Con gran (3) _____.» Abril espera con su familia y su mamá le dice, «Aquí viene tu abuelo. Estos son los hombres y mujeres de nuestro pueblo que lucharon (4) _____ nosotros.» Luego Abril le pregunta, «Mami, ¿por qué hay tan (5) _____?»

DID YOU GET IT? (¿COMPRENDISTE?) Choose the most appropriate ending for the statement. (Answer on page 216.)

El abuelo de Abril siente orgullo porque . . . (a) luchó en la Segunda Guerra Mundial. (b) participó en muchos desfiles en el pasado. (c) tiene muchas chaquetas que puede usar.

WORKING WITH WORDS AND PATTERNS

- **que me serví una taza** ~ To mention a completed action in the past, use the preterite: **serví** *I served* (See page 77.) The **me** here in front of the verb means *to me* or *to myself*.

- **la dejé** ~ To say *it* in this context, use **la** and not **lo** because **taza** (*cup*) is a feminine noun.

- **mientras veía las noticias** ~ To describe a scene in the past, use the imperfect: **mientras veía** *while I was watching . . .* (See pages 77–78.) This sets the stage or background for the actions that are expressed in the preterite.

- **la sala de estar** ~ If you want to remember this word for *living room* or *family room*, think of *salon*, as in a *beauty salon* and **estar** as the verb for *being* in the sense of everyday existence and changing from one condition or state to another. Literally, this is the *being salon*.

- **aquí abajo** ~ Here, the words are in the opposite order from the English equivalent *down here*. This is often the case with Spanish and English equivalents, as in these examples: **mucho ir y venir**, *a lot of coming and going*, **blanco y negro**, *black and white*.

KEY WORDS AND PHRASES

¡Qué extraño! How strange!

que me serví una taza that I served myself a cup

La dejé . . . I left it . . .

mientras veía las noticias while I was watching the news

la sala de estar the living room or family (rec) room

¿Alguien sabe qué hago . . . ? Does anybody know what I'm doing . . .?

32 El abuelo olvidadizo

Forgetful grandpa

PUTTING IT ALL TOGETHER (RESUMIÉNDOLO TODO). Fill in the blanks. (Answers on page 216.)

El abuelo está en la cocina y de repente se dice a sí mismo, «¡Qué (1) _____! ¡Yo sé que me (2) _____ una taza de café!» Luego, recuerda, «¡Ah sí! (3) ¡_____ dejé en la (4) _____ _____ _____ mientras (5) _____ las noticias!» Baja la escalera, recoge una revista y entonces se da cuenta de que se ha olvidado de por qué está allí.

DID YOU GET IT? (¿COMPRENDISTE?) Choose the most appropriate ending for the statement. (Answer on page 216.)

El abuelo ya es viejo y empieza a tener problemas con . . . (a) el café. (b) la memoria. (c) las noticias.

WORKING WITH WORDS AND PATTERNS

- **Mantenga limpia . . .** ~ Signs with commands on them use the **Ud.** formal command forms in Spanish which are in the present subjunctive. (See pages 140–142.)

- **Tus manos están congeladas.** ~ Use the verb **estar** (and not **ser**) to describe the state or condition of something. **Tus manos están frías (calientes).** *Your hands are cold (warm).*

- **¿Dónde está(n) . . . ?** ~ This is one of the most useful patterns, especially when traveling. Use it without the **-n** to ask where one thing is, and with the **-n** for the plural. **¿Dónde está la playa? ¿Dónde están los autos para alquilar?** *(Where is the beach? Where are the rental cars?)*

- **Quería mostrar . . .** ~ Use the imperfect for describing personal or emotional states in the past, such as wanting to do something. (See pages 77–78.)

- **anillo de compromiso** ~ The word **compromiso** is a false cognate because it looks like *compromise* but it doesn't mean that; it means *commitment* or *engagement*. Nouns cannot modify other nouns in Spanish (as they do in English) so that is why you have to use the **de**, literally, *ring of engagement*. If you want to say *They are engaged*, use the adjective with **estar** to express the condition of being engaged: **Están comprometidos.**

KEY WORDS AND PHRASES

Mantenga limpia . . .
(sign) Keep (our city) clean

Gracias por colaborar
(sign) Thanks for cooperating

están congeladas are icy cold (frozen)

¿Dónde están tus guantes? Where are your gloves?

Quería mostrar . . . I wanted to show . . .

mi anillo de compromiso my engagement ring

33 Caminando bajo la nieve

Walking in the snow

WHAT YOU CAN LEARN   Telling someone that his or her hands are cold, asking where something is, describing past personal or emotional states with the imperfect

PUTTING IT ALL TOGETHER (RESUMIÉNDOLO TODO). Fill in the blanks. (Answers on page 216.)

Miguel ya está comprometido y habla por teléfono con su novia Deana. Ella camina bajo la (1) _____, toma un bus y llega a la casa de Miguel. El le toma las manos y observa que están (2) _____. Le pregunta, «¿Dónde (3) _____ tus (4) _____?» Deana le responde, «¡Quería mostrar mi (5) _____de compromiso!»

DID YOU GET IT? (¿COMPRENDISTE?) Choose the most appropriate ending for the statement. (Answer on page 216.)

Deana no se puso los guantes porque . . . (a) los dejó en su casa. (b) tenía que ir en el bus. (c) quería mostrar su anillo.

WORKING WITH WORDS AND PATTERNS

- **el tiempo local** *the local weather* ~ In Spanish, the same word for *time*, **tiempo**, is used for *weather*. To ask about the weather, say **¿Qué tiempo hace?** (Literally, this means *What weather is it making?*) To say that there's freezing rain or snow, say: **Hay lluvias heladas. Hay nieve.**

- **que te mandó la abuela** ~ Notice that in a descriptive clause in Spanish, the subject usually comes at the end, very different from English word order. Compare: *the raincoat that grandmother sent*/**el impermeable que mandó la abuela.** The verb is in the preterite to express a completed action. (See pages 76–79.)

- **¿Me lo podrías prestar?** ~ There is no Spanish verb for *to borrow*, so use this phrase with the verb that means *to lend* (**prestar**) if you want to borrow something. Notice that the verb **poder** is in the conditional tense, which makes it very polite.

- **Ya me las arreglaré.** ~ Use this idiom if you want to tell someone that you can manage, that you don't need any help. The verb is **arreglar** *to arrange* or *fix*, and here it is in the future tense. (See pages 80–81.) Literally, it means *I will now arrange them* (*things*) *for myself.* To say, *The children managed it*, say: **Los niños ya se las arreglaron.**

- **¡Vaya!** ~ You can say this to express amazement or surprise, something like, "*Wow!* or "*Oh, my God!*" It is the present subjunctive command form of the verb **ir** and literally means *Go!*

- **Se le metió . . . en su cabecita.** ~ This is the **se** *for passive voice* construction. As often happens in Spanish, the subject is at the end of the sentence: **un poco de sentido común** and the verb comes at the beginning: **meterse** (*to put itself in*). Literally, it states: *A little bit of common sense puts itself into her little head.* In this case, the diminutive of **cabeza** (**cabecita**) indicates the small size of a child's head and the affection the mother feels for her daughter.

KEY WORDS AND PHRASES

lluvias heladas freezing rain

el impermeable the raincoat

que te mandó la abuela that grandmother sent you

¿Me lo podrías prestar? Could you lend it to me?

¡No importa! I don't care (Who cares?)

Ya me las arreglaré. I'll make do. (I'll manage.)

¡Vaya! How about that? (Wow!, Go on! Look at that!)

¡Esto sí que es algo notable! This sure is something remarkable!

se le metió un poco de sentido común a little bit of common sense entered

34 El impermeable

The raincoat

WHAT YOU CAN LEARN   Talking about winter weather, asking to borrow something, expressing amazement

PUTTING IT ALL TOGETHER (RESUMIÉNDOLO TODO). Fill in the blanks. (Answers on page 216.)

Abril escucha el pronóstico del (1) _____ en la radio. Dicen que va a haber (2) _____ _____ para las próximas 24 horas. Abril habla con su mamá de un (3) _____ que les mandó la abuela. Le pregunta, «¿Me lo (4) _____ _____?» Eli se lo da, y Abril sale afuera. Eli está asombrada y piensa, «¡(5) _____! ¡Esto sí que es algo notable!»

DID YOU GET IT? (¿COMPRENDISTE?) Choose the most appropriate ending for the statement. (Answer on page 216.)

Eli está contenta. Cree que a su hija se le metió en la cabeza un poco de sentido común. En realidad, a Abril se le metió en la cabeza . . . (a) el deseo de pasarlo bien en la lluvia helada. (b) el miedo de salir cuando hace mal tiempo. (c) un buen impermeable mandado por su abuela.

WORKING WITH WORDS AND PATTERNS

- **¿Lo pasaste bien . . . ?** *Did you have fun?* ~ Literally, *Did you spend (pass) it well?* This question is in the **tú** form of the preterite tense. To answer, you can say, **Sí, lo pasé muy bien** or **No, no lo pasé bien.** Or, like Elizabeth, you can respond with one positive word: **¡Estupendo!** (*Splendid!*)

- **Jugamos vóleibol.** *We played volleyball.* ~ **Jugamos** and Elizabeth's other actions are in the preterite tense, used for narrating completed actions. The **nosotros** (*we*) forms are the same in the preterite as the present tense forms for regular **-ar** and **-ir** verbs (**nadamos, nos subimos, tomamos**) and it's only through context that we know they are preterite here. In contrast, **-er** verbs in the **nosotros** form have a different preterite, as we see when Elizabeth says **corrimos**, different from the present **corremos**. (See pages 76––79 on the preterite.) In standard Spanish, the verb **jugar** takes **a** before a sport and the definite article is used: **jugamos al vóleibol**, but it is sometimes omitted in everyday speech.

- **Todos nos subimos a unas canoas.** *We all climbed into some canoes.* ~ The reflexive verb **subirse** has various meanings: *to get on, go up, climb (get) into.*

- **Nos fuimos a la isla de picnic.** *We went to Picnic Island.* ~ Remember that the irregular verb **ir** (*to go*) has the same forms as the verb **ser** (*to be*): **fui, fuiste, fue, fuimos, fuisteis, fueron.** This means that **fuimos** could mean *we went* or *we were.* The context here guides you to the correct meaning: *we went.* In the same way, you see later on that the form **fue** means *it was*, not *it went*: **Fue un día fantástico** (*It was a fantastic day*).

- **no pudiste venir** *you couldn't come* ~ The verb **poder** (*to be able*) is a **u**-stem irregular in the preterite (**pude, pudiste, pudo, pudimos, pudisteis, pudieron**).

- **Una sabe que se está poniendo vieja cuando . . .** *You know that you're getting old when . . .* ~ **Una** (or **Uno** if a man is speaking) is often used in Spanish for this kind of general statement, which in English is often said as *One knows that she* (or *he*) *is getting old when . . . .*

KEY WORDS AND PHRASES

pasarlo bien to have a good time

corrimos (correr) de vuelta we ran back

en la playa at the beach

asar castañas to roast chestnuts

nadamos (nadar) we swam

¡Estoy . . . agotado(a)! I'm exhausted (wiped out)!

luego then, later

¡Qué pena . . . ! What a shame . . . !

It was a fantastic day!

WHAT YOU CAN LEARN Recounting a series of outdoor activities, asking if someone had a good time, expressing exhaustion or extreme tiredness

PUTTING IT ALL TOGETHER (RESUMIÉNDOLO TODO). Fill in the blanks. (Answers on page 216.)

Isabel llega a casa después de pasar el día en la playa. Su mamá le pregunta, «¿Lo (1) _____ bien?» Isabel responde, «¡Estupendo!» y cuenta las actividades que hizo con sus amigos: «Jugamos vóleibol y nadamos . . . nos (2) _____ a la Isla de Picnic . . . caminamos a las rocas y (3) _____ fotos y de ahí corrimos de vuelta al parque . . . (4) _____ un día fantástico, Mami. ¡Estoy totalmente (5) _____! ¡Qué pena que no pudiste venir!» Luego, Eli le asegura que ella también ha tenido días fantásticos.

DID YOU GET IT? (¿COMPRENDISTE?) Choose the most appropriate ending for the statement. (Answer on page 216.)

Eli piensa que ahora prefiere recordar los buenos momentos más que revivirlos porque ella se pone . . . (a) vieja. (b) fantástica. (c) enferma.

WORKING WITH WORDS AND PATTERNS

- **cariño** ~ This is a common term of endearment in certain places, such as Spain and Argentina, and can be used for a woman or a man without change.

- **Creo que los colgué . . .** *I believe (that) I hung them up* ~ Use the verb **colgar** to talk about hanging something up on a hook or a hanger (or the telephone on its cradle), but remember to write it as **colgué** in the preterite tense. This verb is regular but the **u** is added to preserve the hard sound **g** since without it, the **g** (before an **e** or an **i**) would have a soft sound (like an English **h**).

- **lo que vi en la tele** *what I saw on T.V.* ~ Use **lo que** for *what* when making a statement (and **qué** for *what* when asking a question). The word **tele** is short for **televisión**.

- **se metió dentro/cuando se puso los guantes** *slipped inside/when he put on his gloves* ~ Many English verb-adverb combinations (like *slip into* or *put on*) are expressed in Spanish with reflexive verbs. **Una araña se metió dentro** translates literally as: *a spider put itself inside . . .* Use the reflexive verb **ponerse** for *to put on* clothing (literally, *I put to myself*) and remember that it has a slightly irregular **u**-stem preterite: **Me puse el abrigo. Nos pusimos la gorra porque nevaba.** *I put on my coat. We put on our hats because it was snowing.* (See pages 78–79.)

- **¡Le mordió ASI!** *It bit him LIKE THIS!* ~ The verb **morder** is a stem-changing verb, but that doesn't affect the preterite forms. **Ese perro muerde. Ayer ese perro mordió a un niño.** *That dog bites. Yesterday that dog bit a boy.*

- **Se le hinchó . . . el dedo.** *His finger swelled up (got swollen) . . .* ~ Use the reflexive verb **hincharse** when talking about something getting swollen and the indirect object pronoun (here, **le**) to show which person it is happening to.

- **¿Encontró tu madre los guantes . . . ?** ~ Keep typical Spanish word order in mind when asking a question: verb/subject/object. In English we use a form of the word *do* in questions and the typical word order is different. Compare: *Did your mother find the gloves?* (*Did*/subject/verb/object)

KEY WORDS AND PHRASES

cariño sweetheart (used for man or woman)

¿Has visto . . . ? Have you seen . . . ?

los guantes de jardinería the gardening gloves

Un tipo colgó . . . de un clavo. A guy hung up . . . on a nail.

una araña a spider

se metió dentro de uno de los dedos slipped into one of the fingers

ponerse los guantes to put on his (her) gloves

morder (ue) to bite

Se le hinchó tanto . . . His (Her) finger swelled up so much . . .

saltando encima de ellos jumping on top of them

WHAT YOU CAN LEARN   Telling a story with reflexive verbs, typical word order for questions in Spanish

PUTTING IT ALL TOGETHER (RESUMIÉNDOLO TODO). (Answers on page 216.)

Eli busca sus guantes de jardinería. Juan le dice, «Creo que los colgué en el garaje.» Eli va al garaje y Abril empieza a contarle (1) _____ vio en la tele. Cuenta Abril, «Un tipo colgó así los guantes de un clavo y una (2) _____ se metió dentro de uno de los dedos. Y luego cuando (3) _____ _____ _____ guantes, ¡le mordió ASI! (4) _____ _____ _____ tanto el dedo que tuvo que ir al hospital.» Después, en el jardín Juan le pregunta a Abril, «¿(5) _____ _____ _____ los guantes?», y Abril dice que sí, «¡Y está saltando encima de ellos!»

DID YOU GET IT? (¿COMPRENDISTE?) (Answer on page 216.)

Después de escuchar lo que vio Abril en la tele, Eli . . . (a) decidió limpiar muy bien el garaje. (b) quería ayudar a Juan a plantar flores. (c) tenía miedo de ponerse los guantes.

WORKING WITH WORDS AND PATTERNS

- **¿Por qué le estás enseñando a Abril . . . ?** *Why are you teaching . . .?* ~ Notice that in Spanish you include the indirect object pronoun even when you mention the name of the person, so literally you are asking, *Why are you teaching to her to April . . . ?* It may seem redundant to English speakers, but it is correct Spanish usage. Observe the next three sentences in this comic and you will see the same thing.

- **a hacer cosas como ésta** *to do things like this* ~ The **a** is here because the verb **enseñar** (and other verbs, such as **aprender**, **comenzar**, **empezar**) always have **a** after them when they are followed by an infinitive. **Aprendí a bailar salsa.** *I learned to dance salsa.* **Empezaron a correr.** *They began to run.*

- **No lo sé.** *I don't know.* ~ Notice that in Spanish it is common to add **lo** for *it* to make the idea seem more complete when someone admits he or she doesn't know something.

- **Estoy preocupada por . . .** ~ This useful phrase can be followed by many different nouns: **Estoy preocupada por la economía (la salud de mi hermana, tu falta de respeto, la amenaza de la guerra).** *I'm worried about the economy (my sister's health, your lack of respect, the threat of war).*

KEY WORDS AND PHRASES

¿Por qué le estás enseñando a Abril . . . ? Why are you teaching April . . .?

Papi le enseñó a Miguel . . . Daddy taught Michael . . .

Miguel me enseñó a mi . . . Michael taught me . . .

y yo le enseñé a Abril. and I taught April.

pasa de una generación a otra . . . pass on from one generation to the next . . .

sus leyendas their legends

Estoy preocupada por . . . I'm worried about . . .

"¡ TE VOY A QUITAR EL CALCETÍN !"

③⑦ Costumbres familiares

Family customs

WHAT YOU CAN LEARN   Asking people why they are doing something, expressing your worries or concerns

PUTTING IT ALL TOGETHER (RESUMIÉNDOLO TODO). (Answers on pages 216–217.)

Isabel saca unos calcetines de un cajón y (1) _____ _____ a su hermanita Abril a doblarlos y a ponerlos en las perillas de puerta como broma. (Entonces si alguien quiere entrar, va a tener problemas.) Eli las ve y le pregunta a Isabel, «¿Por qué (2) _____ _____ _____ a Abril a hacer cosas como ésta?» «No lo sé» le responde, «Papi le enseñó a Miguel, Miguel (3) _____ _____ _____ _____ y yo le enseñé a Abril.» Eli se dice a sí misma que otra gente pasa de una generación a otra sus juegos, sus (4)_____, y su lengua. Juan le pregunta qué pasa y ella contesta, «Estoy (5) _____ _____ nuestra cultura.»

DID YOU GET IT? (¿COMPRENDISTE?) (Answer on page 217.)

Eli está preocupada por la cultura de su familia porque sus hijas . . . (a) no tienen mucha comunicación con sus padres. (b) están aprendiendo tradiciones frívolas. (c) nunca quieren jugar juntas.

MODERATE LEVEL

95

WORKING WITH WORDS AND PATTERNS

- **deshacerse de** *To get rid of* ~ Literally, this reflexive verb means to *undo yourself* (*myself, himself, herself, ourselves*, etc.) *from* (something) or *rid yourself of it*. Use it with the appropriate reflexive pronouns. **Voy a deshacerme de mi antiguo carro.** *I'm going to get rid of my old car.* **Ellas se deshicieron de ese negocio que no les rendía nada.** *They got rid of that business that wasn't making any money for them.*

- **ya es hora de** + infinitive . . . *It's about time to . . .* ~ Add an infinitive to this useful phrase to announce that it is time to do something. Literally it means *Already it is the hour to . . .* **Ya es hora de arreglar las cuentas. ¡Ya es hora de divertirnos un poco!** *It's about time to settle the accounts. It's about time to have a little fun!* This idiom is also used frequently in the past with the imperfect of **ser**: **¡Ya era hora de empezar ese proyecto!** *It was about time to start that project!*

- Learning vocabulary ~ One way to acquire vocabulary is to make lists of cognates, such as **reciclaje**, **reciclar** (*recycling, to recycle*) and *near cognates*. A near cognate is a Spanish word similar to a word in English that is not used much but which gives a clue to the meaning. For example, **recipiente** means *container*, and it is similar to the word *receptacle*. So, add it to your cognate list like this: **recipiente** (*receptacle*) *container*.

- **basura, cajas, clavos, tapas, tarros** . . . *garbage, boxes, nails, tops, jars* (or *cans*) ~ To learn words that are not cognates, try associating them with images. Practice memorizing basic household vocabulary by drawing lines from the pictures in the comics to the margin and labeling the items in Spanish. For example, in the last frame, label **cajas**, **botellas**, and **tarros**.

KEY WORDS AND PHRASES

¿Qué estás haciendo? What are you doing?

deshaciéndome de todos estos recipientes getting rid of all these containers

Ya es hora de deshacernos de . . . It's about time to get rid of . . .

toda la basura all the garbage

botar to throw away

para guardar clavos for storing (keeping) nails

tapas tops (for bottles, cans, or boxes)

una caja . . . un tarro a box . . . a jar (or can or pot)

WHAT YOU CAN LEARN   Talking about household items, announcing that it's time to do something, learning vocabulary by association and visualization

PUTTING IT ALL TOGETHER (RESUMIÉNDOLO TODO). (Answers on page 217.)

Juan está llevando un montón de (1) _____ de plástico cuando Eli le pregunta, «Juan, ¿qué (2) _____ _____ ?» Juan explica y luego opina, «Ya es (3) _____ _____ _____ de toda la basura . . . » Eli le pregunta, «¿De veras que vas a (4) _____ todas esas botellas?» Juan responde que no porque son buenas para guardar clavos. Después, deciden guardar muchas otras cosas. Abril le comenta a su padre, «Creía que (5) _____ _____ _____ todas estas cosas, Papi.» Contesta Juan, «Lo hicimos. Las reciclamos de un lugar de la casa a otro . . . »

DID YOU GET IT? (¿COMPRENDISTE?) (Answer on page 217.)

Juan y Eli no botaron muchas cosas porque . . . (a) ya estaban muy cansados de trabajar. (b) querían guardarlas para sus hijos. (c) comprendieron que podían usarlas.

El español en tu vida

Spanish in your life

Practice what you've learned from Comics 31–38. (Answers on page 217.)

A. ¿QUÉ SE DICE? (*What do you say?*)

Imagine yourself in the following situations. Use the cues from the comics and fill in the blanks with the missing Spanish words.

1. You fixed yourself a cup of coffee but suddenly you can't find it. **¿Qué se dice?**

2. Your friend's hands feel cold and she isn't wearing gloves. **¿Qué se dice?**

3. You had a wonderful day but now are completely exhausted. **¿Qué se dice?**

4. You saw something great on T.V. and wonder if your mom knows about it. **¿Qué se dice?**

5. You're doing something wrong but don't know why. **¿Qué se dice?**

B. ¿CUÁL ES LA PREGUNTA? (*What's the question?*)

Look at the following selections from the comics. Each one has an answer in it. Can you remember the missing question and write it in?

1.

2.

3.

4.

5.

WORKING WITH WORDS AND PATTERNS

- **acabar de** + infinitive *to have just . . .* ~ A simple way to talk about an action just completed is to use **acabar de** in the present tense followed by the infinitive of your choice. John could have used the present perfect tense of the verb **tirar** instead: **Eli, ¿has tirado todos los bombones a la basura justo en este momento?** But this second version is longer and more cumbersome. Use **acabar de** + infinitive for actions that have just been completed: **Acabo de llegar.** *I have just arrived.* **Acabamos de comer.** *We have just eaten.* **Mis tíos acaban de regresar de su viaje.** *My aunt and uncle have just returned from their trip.*

- **Estaban en . . . desde hace tiempo.** *They'd been in . . . for quite some time.* ~ Use the imperfect and **desde hace tiempo** to refer to an action extending over a period of time in the past which has now come to an end. **Vivíamos en esa casa desde hace tiempo cuando decidimos venderla.** *We'd been living in that house for some time when we decided to sell it.* **Estudiaban español desde hace tiempo antes de viajar a Perú.** *They had studied Spanish for quite a while before traveling to Peru.*

- **No necesitamos las calorías o las grasas.** *We don't need the calories or the fat.* ~ Use the handy verb **necesitar** to express what you need or don't need. **Necesito un café cargado. No necesito chocolates.** *I need a strong (cup of) coffee. I don't need chocolates.*

- **Considéralo . . . Guárdame . . .** *Consider it . . . Save me . . .* ~ To tell a friend or loved one to do something, use the intimate command form (which for regular **-ar** or **-er** verbs just means dropping the **r** of the infinitive). If there's an object following the action, then add it onto the end (**-lo**, **-me**).

KEY WORDS AND PHRASES

¿Acabas de tirar . . . a la basura? Have you just thrown . . . in the garbage?

desde hace tiempo for quite a while

en la alacena in the cupboard

una caja entera sin abrir an entire unopened box

fuerza de voluntad willpower

que se sobrepone a which wins out over

Guárdame. Save me.

los rellenos de cerezas the cherry-filled ones

39

Bombones a la basura

Candies to the garbage can

WHAT YOU CAN LEARN   A simple way of expressing just-completed actions, how to make reference to an extended time period in the past, telling a friend to do something

PUTTING IT ALL TOGETHER (RESUMIÉNDOLO TODO). (Answers on page 217.)

Eli tira una caja entera de chocolates sin abrir a la basura y Juan la ve. Le pregunta, «Eli . . . ¿ (1) _____ _____ _____ todos los bombones a la basura?» Eli explica: «Estaban en la (2) _____ desde (3) _____ _____ y realmente (4) _____ _____ las calorías o las grasas. Considéralo un acto de fuerza de voluntad . . . » Juan decide que Eli tiene razón, pero más tarde ve que ella está comiendo los chocolates y le dice, «(5) _____ los rellenos de cerezas.»

DID YOU GET IT? (¿COMPRENDISTE?) (Answer on page 217.)

Las acciones de Eli demuestran que ella . . . (a) no tiene deseos de comer bombones. (b) está preocupada por su apariencia. (c) no tiene mucha fuerza de voluntad.

WORKING WITH WORDS AND PATTERNS

- **¡Ay!** ~ For expressing emotion, use **¡Ay!** It's more or less the equivalent of *Oh!*, *Oh my goodness!*, or *Oh, heck!*

- **Son las seis.** ~ To tell someone what time it is, use **son las** . . . plus the number corresponding to the hour: **Son las cinco, las ocho, etcétera.** The exception to this is with *one o'clock*, in which case you say: **Es la una.**

- **hora de . . .** + infinitive ~ Spanish has different ways of translating the English word *time*. Sometimes **tiempo** is used, as in **No queremos perder tiempo**. *We don't want to waste any time.* But when *time* refers to a precise moment, generally **hora** is used. **Es hora de . . . comer (salir, comprar un nuevo carro).** *It's time to . . . eat (leave, buy a new car).* **¿Qué hora es?** *What time is it?*

- **Lo siento.** ~ This is the standard way to apologize. It means *I'm sorry*, but literally it is *I feel it.*

- **Estamos cerrando . . . Estábamos mirando . . .** ~ Use the progressive tenses (**estar** + the **-ando** or **-iendo** form of the verb) to emphasize something being done at an exact moment. In the first example, the present tense of **estar** is used: *We are closing . . .* In the second case, the imperfect of **estar** is used for reference to the past: *We were looking (browsing) . . .* To say to a clerk that you are just browsing right now, say **Sólo estoy mirando.**

- **¿Podríamos entrar? ¿Por favor?** ~ Use **poder** in the conditional when you want to be very polite. Adding the **¿Por favor?** *Please?* makes it even more polite.

¡Ay! Mis pies me están matando . . . Oh my! My feet are killing me . . .

Son las seis. It's six o'clock.

hora de cerrar la tienda time to close the store

¿Podríamos entrar? May we come in?

tantas cosas hermosas so many beautiful things

¿Las puedo ayudar en algo? May I help you with something?

40

Sólo estábamos mirando

We were only looking

WHAT YOU CAN LEARN How to complain about foot pain, asking for permission to come in, saying that you're just browsing

PUTTING IT ALL TOGETHER (RESUMIÉNDOLO TODO). (Answers on page 217.)

La compañera de trabajo de Eli se queja: «¡Ay! ¡Mis pies (1) _____ _____ _____!» Ella mira su reloj y anuncia, «(2) _____ _____ seis.» Eli dice, «(3) _____ _____ _____ la tienda.» Dos señoras tocan a la puerta. «¿(4) _____ _____?» preguntan, «¿Por favor?» La compañera responde, «Lo siento, estamos cerrando . . . » Pero las señoras entran de todas formas y dicen, «Ustedes tienen tantas cosas (5) _____.» Lo miran todo y demoran un buen rato, pero no compran nada. Al final, dicen, «Sólo estábamos mirando . . . »

DID YOU GET IT? (¿COMPRENDISTE?) (Answer on page 217.)

Las dos señoras que entran en la tienda son . . . (a) amables. (b) desconsideradas. (c) sinceras.

WORKING WITH WORDS AND PATTERNS

- **tarea** ~ Besides *homework*, you can use this word for *task* or *job*. *Housework* is often called **tareas del hogar** or **tareas de la casa**. Another common word for *homework* from school is **los deberes**.

- **¡Cómo que me carga . . . !** ~ This is slang, so use it only when you are talking informally. Add an **-n** when complaining about something plural: **¡Estas reglas me cargan!** *These rules annoy me!*

- **refunfuño** ~ This word comes from the verb **refunfuñar**, meaning *to grumble*, *growl*, or *mutter angrily*. Say it aloud a few times and you will see that it is somewhat onomatopoetic because its sound suggests its meaning.

- **No veo la hora de . . .** + infinitive ~ Use this idiom when you are very enthusiastic about something and can hardly wait for it. Literally, it means *I don't see the time to . . .* **¡No veo la hora de nadar (montar a caballo, asistir al concierto)!** *I can't wait to swim (go horseback riding, attend the concert)!*

- **no tendré que hacer . . .** ~ Notice that the verb **tener** has an irregular form for the future tense: **tendré**, **tendrás**, **tendrá**, etc.

KEY WORDS AND PHRASES

¡Odio esta cosa! (odiar)
I hate this thing! (to hate)

¡Cómo que me carga completamente! Like, it totally annoys me!

Estoy atascada aquí dentro. I'm stuck here inside.

¡No es justo! It's not fair!

¡Refunfuño! Grumbling!

No veo la hora de terminar . . . I can hardly wait to finish . . .

los fines de semana weekends

no tendré que hacer I won't have to do

TRABAJAR ES REFUNFUÑAR.

41 Haciendo la tarea para la escuela *Doing homework*

WHAT YOU CAN LEARN   Expressing anger and dislike, saying you can hardly wait for something

PUTTING IT ALL TOGETHER (RESUMIÉNDOLO TODO). (Answers on page 217.)

Isabel está muy enojada. Entra en la c_____
No quiere hacer su tarea para la escu_____
_____ completamente! ¡Es un día _____
dentro . . . ¡No es justo!» Eli la escu_____
friega. Isabel le dice «¿Sabes? No (4_____
terminar mis estudios. Así . . . no (5_____
El perro guiña el ojo.

DID YOU GET IT? (¿COMPRENDISTE?) (Ansv_____

Obviamente, Isabel no tiene razón en s_____
para la escuela van a continuar por r_____
tuvieron que trabajar mucho en la escu_____
hacer cosas desagradables a veces.

WORKING WITH WORDS AND PATTERNS

- **acabar de** + infinitive = *to have just . . .* ~ This useful phrase can be combined with the verb of your choice to talk about what you have just done: **Acabo de cocinar una buena cena.** *I have just cooked a good supper.* **Acabamos de volver.** *We have just returned.* Notice that the present tense of **acabar** is used and the result is similar to the present perfect tense in English.

- **lavé . . . doblé . . . limpié . . . recuperé** *I washed . . . I folded . . . I cleaned . . . I recovered* ~ Use the preterite to recount a series of completed actions, in this case by adding the ending **-é** to the verb roots since all of these are regular **-ar** verbs.

- **hay más (menos) . . . que antes** ~ Use this formula to make comparisons with an earlier time. **Hay más nieve que antes. Hay menos autos que antes.** *There's more snow than before. There are fewer cars than before.*

- **la dejó amontonada** ~ When referring to something that is feminine (in this case, **la ropa**) say **la** for *it* (not **lo**). Literally, **amontonado(a)** means *piled up* or *heaped up*, in **montones** (**piles**), but the general meaning is *messy, scattered around.*

- **quién habrá inventado . . .** ~ The verb **inventar** is in the future perfect tense which is used here to express doubt or possibility. A good translation would be: *Who could possibly have invented . . . ?*

KEY WORDS AND PHRASES

acabo de bañar y escobillar I've just washed and brushed

están afuera they are outside

revolcándose en la tierra rolling around on the ground

doblé la ropa I folded the clothing

la dejó amontonada she left it piled (heaped) up

más deshechos que antes more junk than before

los tres kilos que bajé the three kilos that I lost (went down)

me pregunto I wonder (literally, I ask myself)

Mucho que hacer

A lot to do

WHAT YOU CAN LEARN   Telling what you have just done, talking about doing housework

PUTTING IT ALL TOGETHER (RESUMIÉNDOLO TODO). (Answers on page 217.)

Eli mira a los perros que están (1) _____ revolcándose en la tierra. Ella piensa, «¡Fantástico! (2) _____ _____ bañar y escobillar a los dos perros . . . Lavé y (3) _____ _____ _____ de Abril y la dejó amontonada . . . Limpié el garaje y ahora hay más (4) _____ que antes. Y parece que recuperé los tres kilos que bajé. (5) _____ _____ quien habrá inventado la frase «La futilidad del **hombre**.»

DID YOU GET IT? (¿COMPRENDISTE?) (Answer on page 217.)

Eli piensa en todo el trabajo que acaba de hacer y le parece . . . (a) de gran importancia. (b) totalmente insignificante. (c) fantástico y divertido.

WORKING WITH WORDS AND PATTERNS

- **ropa de verano** *summer clothes* . . . **una chaqueta de verano** *a summer jacket* ~ Vary this pattern for the other seasons: **ropa de invierno** *winter clothes*, **una chaqueta de primavera** *a spring jacket*. In Spanish, nouns cannot modify other nouns as they do in English, so that is why you need the prepositional phrase with **de** or another prepositional phrase. Other examples are **el reloj de oro** *the gold watch*, **los libros para la escuela** *the schoolbooks*.

- **de su talla** ~ **Su** means *his*, *her*, *your* (if you are using the formal **usted**), or *their*. Use different pronouns to match the person being referred to. **Estos son de mi (nuestra, tu) talla.** *These are my (our, your) size*. Notice that **de** *(of)* is necessary so literally, you are saying, *These are of my (our, your) size.* When the word *size* refers to the general quality of largeness or smallness (and not to which number you wear in clothing), use **tamaño**. **Oye, recibiste un paquete hoy.** *Hey, you received a package today.* **Ah, ¿sí? ¿De qué tamaño?** *Oh, really? How big? (Of what size?)*

- **¿Qué le parece?** *What do you think of it?* ~ Use this common idiom for asking someone's opinion. Literally, it means *What does it seem like to you?* Later, Elly employs a variation of the same idiom with the informal *you* to John: **¿No te parece?** *Don't you think so? (Doesn't it seem like it to you?)*

- **le quedan anchos** *they are big on him* (Literally, *to him they stay large*) ~ Vary this helpful idiom to suit the circumstances. **La camisa me queda grande (chica).** *The shirt is big (small) on me.* **Los pantalones te quedan largos.** *The slacks are long on you.*

- **la camisa rayas** ~ In some places they say **la camisa rayas** or **la camisa con rayas**.

- **el chaleco color crema** ~ Change this useful pattern for describing various colors: **los zapatos color café, la bolsa color durazno, el vestido color arena**, *the coffee-colored shoes, the peach-colored purse, the sand-colored dress.*

- **¿Estuve yo allí?** *Was I there?* ~ Notice that the preterite is used here because John thinks of the shopping in the store as a whole event that is now completed.

KEY WORDS AND PHRASES

¿Puedo ayudarlos?
May I help you?

pantalones cortos, calcetines shorts, socks

estos son de su talla
these are (in) his size

Nos llevamos esto. We'll take this. (Literally, *we carry this with us.*)

la camisa (or **con**) **rayas**
the striped shirt

el chaleco color crema
the cream-colored vest

firme aquí sign here

Estoy encantada con . . .
I'm delighted with . . .

WHAT YOU CAN LEARN   Offering to help someone, talking about clothing, varying idioms to suit the situation

PUTTING IT ALL TOGETHER (RESUMIÉNDOLO TODO). (Answers on page 217.)

Eli y Juan entran en una tienda de ropa para hombres. El dependiente los saluda, «¿(1) _____ _____ ?» Eli le contesta, «Sí, mi marido necesita ropa (2) _____ _____.» Ella selecciona algunas prendas en su (3) _____ y Juan se las prueba. Eli lo mira y dice, «La camisa está bien . . . Los pantalones cortos (4) _____ _____ anchos.» Después, se llevan varias cosas, pagan y salen de la tienda. Eli dice que está encantada con las compras y le pregunta a Juan, «¿No (5) _____ _____?» Juan responde, «No sé. ¿Estuve yo allí?»

DID YOU GET IT? (¿COMPRENDISTE?) (Answer on page 217.)

Parece que cuando Juan y Eli van de compras . . . (a) Eli participa más que Juan. (b) Juan participa más que Eli. (c) los dos participan igualmente.

WORKING WITH WORDS AND PATTERNS

- **Estaban peleándose.** ~ Use **se** when talking about others doing something *to each other*. This is called the reciprocal reflexive. **Se besaban. No se hablaban.** *They were kissing each other. They weren't talking to each other.*

- **una simple «peleíta»** *a simple little fight* (*squabble*) ~ The word **pelea** (*fight*) is used here in the diminutive to make it sound small and of little consequence.

- **hembra . . . macho** *female . . . male* ~ **Hembra** is used to refer to animals or to people, but **macho** generally is used only to refer to animals. For people, use **varón** for *male*. **¿Qué tuvieron Teresa y Alejandro, ¿varón o hembra?** *What did Theresa and Alexander have, a girl or a boy (baby)?* **¡Qué linda mascota! ¿Es macho o hembra?** *What an attractive pet! Is it a male or a female?* The word **macho** can also be applied to men with the meaning of *he-man* or *very manly*, and it is the root for **machista**, which means *male chauvinist*. **Jorge es muy machista.** *George is a real male chauvinist.*

- **probablemente** *probably* ~ add **-mente** to change an adjective to an adverb (**-mente** = *-ly*). This is always added to the feminine form, so **rápido(a)** becomes **rápidamente**.

- **¿ . . . tú pelearías por mí?** *. . . would you fight for me?* ~ Use the verb in the conditional to ask about a possible or hypothetical action, like this one. (See pages 80–81.)

- **Supongo que me tardé mucho en contestar.** ~ The verb **tardar** + **mucho en** + an infinitive is a useful idiom for talking about someone taking a long time for something. **Los niños tardaron mucho en empezar el partido.** *The children took a long time to start the game.*

KEY WORDS AND PHRASES

vuelta . . . y más vueltas . . . tossing and turning (literally, turn and more turns)

yo tampoco me neither

dos sapos estaban peleándose two toads were fighting with each other

por una hembra for a female

Seguro que andaba por ahí. (It's) certain that she was going around there.

todos los machos all males

que me tardé mucho en contestar that I took a long time to answer

44 En la cama con insomnio

In bed with insomnia

WHAT YOU CAN LEARN Describing a fight, asking about a hypothetical action, saying that you (or someone) waited too long to do something

PUTTING IT ALL TOGETHER (RESUMIÉNDOLO TODO). (Answers on page 217.)

Juan y Eli tienen insomnio y dan (1) _____ y más vueltas en la cama. Juan le cuenta a Eli algo extraño que vio, «Dos sapos estaban peleándose en el patio. Y no era una simple "peleíta" . . . » Eli opina, «(2) _____ era por una (3) _____.» Juan responde que no vio a ninguna. Eli le pregunta, «Juan, ¿tú (4) _____ por mí?» Pasan unos minutos y Eli le da en la cara con una almohada. Juan piensa, «Supongo que (5) _____ _____ mucho en contestar.»

DID YOU GET IT? (¿COMPRENDISTE?) (Answer on page 217.)

Eli está desilusionada. Pensaba que Juan iba a decirle . . . (a) Soy muy macho y eres mi hembra. (b) Sí, pelearía por ti. (c) No me gustan las peleas.

WORKING WITH WORDS AND PATTERNS

- **¿Me puedes dar dinero para . . . ?** *Can you give me money for . . . ?* ~ Use this question to ask for money in a nice way, adding words to explain what the money is needed for. It's even more polite if you put **poder** in the conditional: **podrías.** (See pages 80–81.)

- **¿Qué más puedo comer?** *What else can I eat?* ~ Literally, this means *What more can I eat?* Notice that the English word *else* does not really exist in Spanish.

- **¿Tenemos algo de queso?** *Do we have any cheese?* ~ Literally, *do we have something of cheese?* Like *else*, the word *any* doesn't exist in Spanish.

- **No me gustan de esa clase.** *I don't like that kind.* (Literally, *the ones of that kind are not pleasing to me*) ~ To say *that kind* or *that type*, use the phrase **de esa clase.**

- **¿No tenemos nada que sea rápido y fácil y que a mí me guste?** *Don't we have anything that's fast and easy and that I like?* ~ Here's a perfect example of the subjunctive after a negative word (**nada**, *nothing*). One of the three concepts that requires the subjunctive is *doubt or unreality*, so here the subjunctive forms must be used. That's why you say **sea** instead of **es** and **guste** instead of **gusta.** (See pages 140–142.)

- **Toma.** ~ Use the informal command for people you know well: simply drop the **-r** from the infinitive of regular **-ar** and **-er** verbs. **Compra papas fritas. Come tu ensalada.** *Buy French fries (fried potatoes). Eat your salad.* The **-ir** verbs (**escribir**) are the same as the **-er**: **Escribe las cartas.** *Write the letters.*

KEY WORDS AND PHRASES

tu misma yourself

¿cómo qué? Like what?

pan, queso, apio, manzana, pasas bread, cheese, celery, apple, raisins

Eso significa que tengo que . . . This means I have to . . .

¿Qué tal una . . . ? How about a . . . ?

¿ . . . nada que sea rápido y fácil . . . ? . . . anything that's fast and easy . . . ?

Toma. Take (it).

¿Qué hago para el almuerzo?

What do I make for lunch?

WHAT YOU CAN LEARN   Asking for money, talking about food for lunch

PUTTING IT ALL TOGETHER (RESUMIÉNDOLO TODO). (Answers on page 217.)

Isabel está para salir a la escuela cuando llama a Eli, «Mamá, ¿(1) _____ _____ _____ dinero para el almuerzo?» Eli le dice, «¿Por qué no te haces algo (2) _____ _____ . . . ? ¿un sándwich?» Isabel pregunta, «¿Dónde está el pan? ¿Tenemos (3) _____ _____ _____?» Luego, Eli le sugiere varias otras cosas: apio, una manzana, una (4) _____ de granola, un pudín, pero no (5) _____ _____ a Isabel. Por fin, Eli se rinde y le da a Isabel dinero para comprar el almuerzo.

DID YOU GET IT? (¿COMPRENDISTE?) (Answer on page 217.)

Eli le da dinero a Isabel para el almuerzo porque . . . (a) no hay comida en la casa. (b) es imposible encontrar comida que le guste. (c) sabe que sirven muy buena comida en la cafetería.

WORKING WITH WORDS AND PATTERNS

- **el bienestar físico ~** The word **bienestar** is literally *well-being*, and in Spanish the opposite is **malestar** (literally, *bad being* or *ill being*) but in English we could translate it as *indisposition*, *malaise*, or *uneasiness*.

- **hablemos sobre ~** To suggest that everyone talk about something, say **Hablemos sobre . . . (la música, el tiempo, los viajes).** *Let's talk about . . . (music, the weather, travel).* To suggest *not* talking about something, say **No hablemos sobre . . . (la política, los desastres, el trabajo).** *Let's not talk about . . . (politics, disasters, work).* This is the **nosotros** form of the present subjunctive of **hablar** and any other verb can be used in a similar way: **Bailemos. Comamos. No escribamos cartas.** *Let's dance. Let's eat. Let's not write letters.*

- **Nuevos datos muestran que . . .** *New data shows that . . .* ~ The English word *data* is treated as though it is singular, but in Spanish the word is **datos** and is treated as plural, meaning *items* or *bits of information*. That's why the verb **muestran** is plural.

- **Recuerden su régimen para vigilar su salud.** *Remember your diet to safeguard your health.* ~ The word **régimen** is a synonym of the cognate **dieta**, which is used earlier in the comic strip. The form **recuerden** is the present subjunctive command for **ustedes**, used to address the radio listeners.

- **que me han parado por beber y conducir . . .** ~ The verb **parar** means *to stop* (your movement) or *to stop* (someone from doing something). **Paré cuando llegué a la calle. El policía me paró.** *I stopped when I reached the street. The policeman stopped me.* There are two verbs that mean *to drive*: **conducir (zc)** and **manejar.** You can use either one, but the first is used more in Spain and the second more in Latin America. Notice that, besides **beber**, there is also another word for *to drink* (used earlier in this comic strip): **tomar. Eli tomó (bebió) mucha agua antes de salir — ¡mala idea!**

KEY WORDS AND PHRASES

nuestro informe sobre
. . . our report about . . .

Hablemos sobre dietas.
Let's talk about diets.

a pesar de . . . in spite of . . .

Recuerden su régimen.
Remember your diet.

por lo menos de 6 a 8 vasos de agua at least 6 to 8 glasses of water

Esta es la primera vez
. . . This is the first time . . .

que me han parado por . . . that they've stopped me for . . .

WHAT YOU CAN LEARN   Understanding some terms related to health and diets, suggesting that everyone talk, saying it's the first time that something has happened to you

PUTTING IT ALL TOGETHER (RESUMIÉNDOLO TODO). (Answers on page 217.)

Eli está escuchando la radio en la librería. La voz de la radio anuncia, «Ese fue nuestro informe sobre el (1) _____ _____. Ahora (2) _____ _____dietas. A pesar de la amplia información existente, el público no consume suficientes verduras . . . para vigilar su (3) ____. Tomen por lo menos de 6 a 8 (4) _____ _____ _____ cada día.» Eli bebe mucha agua. Después, sube al auto para regresar a casa. Siente urgencia de ir al baño y empieza a correr. Un policía la para y le da una multa. Eli piensa, «Esta es (5) _____ _____ _____ en mi vida que me han parado . . . »

DID YOU GET IT? (¿COMPRENDISTE?) (Answer on page 217.)

Eli dice al final que la han parado por beber y conducir. Esto muestra que Eli . . . (a) tomó mucho alcohol durante la tarde. (b) no sabe conducir un coche. (c) todavía tiene su sentido de humor.

WORKING WITH WORDS AND PATTERNS

- **La cena . . . es a las seis.** ~ The manner in which Elly is speaking is quite formal, probably because she is a little bit nervous about leaving her family to eat by themselves. Usually, you don't have to say **a la que voy** unless you are writing something formal. It's clear what dinner you are speaking about. Use **a las . . .** with whatever number is needed to tell the time at which something is occurring. **El concierto (la película, la fiesta) es a las siete y media.** *The concert (the movie, the party) is at seven-thirty.* If it is at one o'clock, say **a la una**.

- **Sólo tienes que ponerla . . .** ~ This is a gentler way of telling someone what to do than the command forms. Here the intimate **tú** form is used just as if you are describing the actions. Elly uses this again later when she says, **la metes en el microondas . . . las revuelves y luego las calientas . . .**

- **en el horno a 175 grados hasta que esté hervida** *in the oven at 175 degrees until it's boiled* ~ In Spain and Latin America the Celsius system is used, so 175 degrees is in Centigrade. The clause **hasta que esté hervida** is in the subjunctive since it is a projection into the future, which to the Spanish mind is always unknown and therefore uncertain. The verb **estar** which would usually be **está**, becomes **esté**. (See pages 140–142.)

- **Pon la verdura congelada.** ~ The word **pon** is the irregular familiar command form of the verb **poner**. There are only a few of these— **pon, ven (venir), di (decir), sal (salir)**, etc.—and they are used a lot.

KEY WORDS AND PHRASES

La cena a la que voy es a las seis. The dinner I'm going to is at six o'clock.

Sólo tienes que ponerla . . . You only have to put it . . .

en el microondas . . . en el horno in the microwave . . . in the oven

Pon la verdura en un plato cubierto Put the vegetable in a covered dish

la metes . . . las revuelves . . . las calientas you put it in . . . you stir them . . . you heat them

de nuevo again

panecillos . . . ensalada fresca . . . buns, rolls (literally, *little breads*) . . . fresh salad

de postre hay . . . for dessert there is . . .

Está bien . . . ¡de verdad! It's all right . . . Really!

47 La mamá sale de noche

Mom goes out for the evening

WHAT YOU CAN LEARN Telling what time your appointment is, talking about food for supper, a gentle way of giving instructions

PUTTING IT ALL TOGETHER (RESUMIÉNDOLO TODO). (Answers on page 217.)

Eli se prepara para salir. Luego, le da instrucciones a su familia, «La cena a la que voy es (1) _____ _____ _____, Juan, por lo que les he dejado todo preparado. Hay una (2) _____ _____ . . . Sólo tienes que ponerla en el microondas y luego en el horno . . . (3) _____ la verdura congelada en un plato cubierto y . . . las revuelves y las calientas de nuevo. Compré (4) _____ y hay ensalada fresca y de (5) _____ hay . . . » Isabel la interrumpe, «Está bien, mamá . . . ¡De verdad!» Eli se va. Todo el mundo se mira unos a otros. Luego salen a comer comida rápida.

DID YOU GET IT? (¿COMPRENDISTE?) (Answer on page 217.)

Eli prepara todo y sale a su cena, pero ella no sabe que su esposo y sus hijas . . . (a) prefieren comer comida rápida. (b) no pueden operar el microondas. (c) no tienen tiempo para seguir instrucciones.

El español en tu vida

Spanish in your life

Practice what you've learned from Comics 39–47. (Answers on page 217.)

A. ¿QUÉ SE DICE? (*What do you say?*)

Imagine yourself in the following situations. Use the cues from the comics and fill in the blanks with the missing Spanish words.

1. You and your friend were browsing in a shop in Mexico and the sales clerk offers to help you just as you're leaving. **¿Qué se dice?**

2. You are very angry because you have to do something that you hate. **¿Qué se dice?**

3. You have just cooked a good dinner, and you read a note saying everyone will be out. **¿Qué se dice?**

4. You're selling clothing in a store, and some prospective customers walk in. **¿Qué se dice?**

5. You like apples but not the kind you are being offered. **¿Qué se dice?**

B. IMAGENES SIN PALABRAS (*Pictures without words*)

Look at the following selections from the comics. Select the best description of what the people are probably thinking. **¿En qué estarán pensando?** *What could they be thinking about?*

1. Juan estará pensando . . . _____ (a) ¿Por qué tiré ropa a la basura? (b) ¿Dónde están los chocolates? (c) ¿Cuándo vamos a limpiar la casa?

2. Eli y su compañera estarán pensando . . . _____ (a) ¡Ya es hora de volver a casa! (b) ¡Vamos a tener una buena conversación! (c) ¡Qué señoras más amables!

3. Eli estará pensando . . . _____ (a) Mi hija es muy inteligente. (b) Los jóvenes no comprenden muchas cosas. (c) Es importante hacer las tareas para la escuela.

4. Juan estará pensando . . . _____ (a) ¿Qué chaqueta voy a usar mañana? (b) ¿Por qué no hay paz en el mundo?(c) ¿Cómo puedo contestar esa pregunta?

5. Eli estará pensando . . . _____ (a) ¡Necesito tomar agua! (b) ¡Quiero ir al baño! (c) ¡Tengo que comprar los medicamentos!

WORKING WITH WORDS AND PATTERNS

- **para mí** ~ Vary this expression to refer to someone else's opinion: **para ti**, **para él**, **para ella**, **para usted**, **para nosotros**, **para ustedes** *in your opinion, in his opinion, in her opinion, in your* (formal) *opinion, in our opinion, in your* (plural) *opinion*

- **Ésta es la que más me gusta.** ~ Literally, *this one is that which most to me is pleasing*. Notice that *this one* is feminine here because it refers to **la estación**.

- **hemos visto** ~ Use the present perfect tense to talk about an action seen as complete at this moment. This compound tense uses **haber** and the past participle, which in this case is irregular (**visto**). (See pages 142–143.)

- **más de 20** *more than 20* ~ Usually you say **más que** for *more than*, except when a number follows (in an affirmative sentence), in which case you say **más de**. **Maite estudia** *más que* **su hermano. Sigue** *mas de* **tres cursos**. *Maite studies more than her brother. She's taking more than three courses.*

- **Me imagino que podríamos decir . . .** *I imagine (that) we could say . . .* ~ Use the reflexive verb **imaginarse** to talk about what you imagine.

KEY WORDS AND PHRASES

para mí in my opinion

esta época del año this time (period of time) of the year

de todas las estaciones of all the seasons

Ésta es la que más me gusta. This is the one I like most.

Hemos visto un montón de otoños. We have seen a lot of falls.

Hay menos sabandijas. There are fewer bugs.

¡ PARA MÍ, LA PRIMAVERA ES LO MÁXIMO!

48 Una caminata en el bosque

A walk in the woods

WHAT YOU CAN LEARN   Expressing an opinion, talking about autumn, telling what you like best

PUTTING IT ALL TOGETHER (RESUMIÉNDOLO TODO). (Answers on page 217.)

Es otoño y Eli y Juan caminan por el bosque. Eli opina, «(1)_____ _____, Juan, esta época del año es celestial. El aroma, los colores, los mercados, la (2) _____ _____ _____. De todas las estaciones, ¡creo que ésta es (3) _____ _____ _____ _____ _____!» Dice Juan, «(4) _____ _____ que podríamos decir que estamos en el otoño de nuestras vidas.» Eli contesta que es una buena analogía y Juan precisa, «Sí, para empezar, hay menos (5) _____ . . .»

DID YOU GET IT? (¿COMPRENDISTE?) (Answer on page 217.)

Juan hace una analogía que compara el otoño con . . . (a) esta época de sus vidas. (b) los colores y la frescura del viento. (c) un bosque lleno de sabandijas.

WORKING WITH WORDS AND PATTERNS

- **algo para hacernos recordar** ~ Vary this pattern for other occasions: **algo para hacernos reír** (**llorar, pensar, pasarlo bien**) *something to make us laugh (cry, think, have a good time)*

- **Un hombre llamado . . . en la guerra.** ~ Use the preterite for narrating completed actions and the imperfect for descriptions when you tell a story in the past the way Elly tells the story of John McCrae here in frames 4 and 5. Notice the verbs: **escribió . . . que crecían . . . había . . . murieron . . .** *wrote . . . that were growing . . . there were . . . died . . . .* The two in the preterite express completed actions and the two in the imperfect describe the scene. (See pages 76–80.)

- **ni siquiera** ~ Say this useful idiom any time you want the idea of *not even.* —**¿Así que vas a ganar la competición de natación?** —**¿Yo? ¡Ni siquiera sé nadar!** *So, you're going to win the swimming competition? Me? I don't even know how to swim!*

- **Ya lo sé . . .** *I (already) know that . . .* ~ Use this phrase any time you want to reassure someone that you understand exactly what he or she has said to you.

- **para no olvidar** *in order not to forget* ~ This common phrase written on the box of the man selling poppies is often expressed in English in the old-fashioned way as *Lest we forget.*

KEY WORDS AND PHRASES

algo para hacernos recordar something to make us remember

que crecían en los campos de Flandes that were growing in the fields of Flanders

Había cruces que marcaban las tumbas. There were crosses that marked the graves.

¿Por qué tengo que llevar . . . ? Why do I have to wear . . . ?

Ni siquiera estoy muy segura de . . . I'm not even very sure about . . .

Y ésa, creo yo, es la mejor razón de todas. And that, I believe, is the best reason of all.

Comprando amapolas

Buying poppies

WHAT YOU CAN LEARN   Talking about things that make us remember, telling a story with the preterite and imperfect, asking why you have to do something,

PUTTING IT ALL TOGETHER (RESUMIÉNDOLO TODO). (Answers on page 217.)

Es el Día de la Conmemoración en Canadá cuando la gente compra amapolas en honor de los veteranos que lucharon en las guerras pasadas. Abril le pregunta a su mamá por qué venden amapolas y Eli le explica que es un símbolo, algo (1) _____ _____ _____. Luego, le cuenta la historia de John McCrae, el canadiense que escribió la bella poesía sobre las amapolas que (2) _____ en los campos de Flandes. Abril le pregunta, «¿(3) _____ _____ _____ _____ llevar una amapola? (4) _____ _____ estoy muy segura de lo que es una guerra.» Eli responde, «(5) _____ _____ _____ . . . Y ésa . . . es la mejor razón de todas.»

DID YOU GET IT? (¿COMPRENDISTE?) (Answer on page 217.)

Eli cree que es importante llevar una amapola para . . . (a) sentirse feliz. (b) contribuir dinero. (c) no olvidar.

WORKING WITH WORDS AND PATTERNS

- **¡Me siento tan feliz de . . . !** ~ Vary this useful idiom to state why you are happy. **¡Me siento tan feliz de estar en casa (verlos a ustedes, terminar este proyecto)!** *I feel so happy to be home (to see all of you, to finish this project)!* But be careful if there is a change of subject in the second part of the sentence because in that case you must use the subjunctive. **¡Me siento tan feliz de que llueva hoy!** *I feel so happy that it's raining today!* (See pages 140–142.)

- **Así que tratamos de llenar el espacio.** *So we tried to fill the space.* ~ Use **tratar de** + an infinitive to express someone trying to do something. **Traté de llamarte por teléfono.** *I tried to call you on the telephone.* **Trataron de comprar boletos pero no pudieron.** *They tried to buy tickets but couldn't.*

- **por lo que quedamos fuera de acción** *with the result that we became inactive* ~ Literally, this would be *for which (reason) we remained out of action.*

- **uno dejó de funcionar** ~ Use **dejar de** + an infinitive to talk about stopping doing something. **El año pasado dejé de fumar.** *Last year I stopped smoking.* **Dejaron de llamarnos.** *They stopped calling us.*

- **La oficina iba a explotar.** *The office was going to explode/***Le iba a decir que había sido horrible . . .** *I was going to tell him that it had been horrible . . .* ~ The imperfect of **ir** is useful to talk about an action that *was going to happen.* John was afraid the office *was going to explode.* Elly *was going to tell* John her day had been horrible (but didn't when she heard that his had been worse). **Íbamos a entrar cuando cerraron la puerta.** *We were going to enter when they closed the door.*

- **doña Teresa** ~ There is no equivalent for this title of respect that is sometimes given to an older lady and used before her first name (not the last name). It is something like saying *"Dear old Mrs. Teresa."* The masculine equivalent is **don**, as in **don José** or **don Miguel**.

KEY WORDS AND PHRASES

¡Me siento tan feliz de . . . ! I'm so happy to . . . !

pela que pela "peeling away" *(indicates the sound of peeling potatoes)*

No vino a una cita. (She) didn't show up (come) for her appointment.

El sistema . . . se cayó. The system . . . crashed. (Literally, fell down.)

Me salté el almuerzo. I skipped lunch.

Uno dejó de funcionar. One (of them) stopped working.

falló broke down (failed)

niños llorones crying children

en la sala de espera in the waiting room

Mi silla dental se atascó. My dental chair got stuck.

Un día pesado en el trabajo

A hard day at work

WHAT YOU CAN LEARN Stating why you feel happy, recounting the day's activities with the preterite and imperfect, using **iba** (and related forms) to talk about what was going to happen

PUTTING IT ALL TOGETHER (RESUMIÉNDOLO TODO). (Answers on page 217.)

Juan llega a casa muy cansado y exclama, «¡Ooohhh! ¡Me siento (1) _____ _____ _____ _____ en casa! La señora Martínez no vino a una (2) _____ de tres horas . . . así que tratamos de llenar el espacio con otros pacientes . . . Luego el sistema de la computadora . . . se cayó . . . me salté el almuerzo . . . Tenemos dos esterilizadores y uno (3) _____ _____ _____ . . . Había tanta tensión entre el personal que pensé que la oficina (4) _____ _____ _____ . . . Doña Teresa dejó a sus niños llorones . . . y uno de ellos rompió una lámpara . . .» Luego, le pregunta a su esposa, «¿Y cómo (5) _____ tu día?» Eli le responde, «Estupendo.»

DID YOU GET IT? (¿COMPRENDISTE?) (Answer on page 217.)

En realidad, Eli acaba de pasar un día . . . (a) excelente. (b) muy malo. (c) normal.

WORKING WITH WORDS AND PATTERNS

- **Anoche me di un baño y me acosté.** ~ Use the reflexive verbs **darse** (to give oneself) and **acostarse** (to put oneself to bed) to describe taking a bath and going to bed, which means you have to use the appropriate reflexive pronouns. Literally, this phrase would be: *Last night I gave myself a bath and I put myself to bed . . .*

- **la noche anterior** the previous night ~ Use **anoche** for *last night*, and you can use this phrase to say *the night before last*, or you can say **anteanoche**. To say *the night before that*, use the phrase included in Elizabeth's thoughts in the 5th frame: **Y la noche antes de ésa.**

- **dormir . . . dormirse** to sleep . . . to fall asleep ~ Use the verb **dormir** to talk about *sleeping* and the reflexive verb **dormirse** to talk about *falling asleep* or *going to sleep*. **Los niños *durmieron* ocho horas.** *The children slept for eight hours.* **Los niños *se durmieron* a la medianoche.** *The children fell asleep at midnight.*

- **cuando se está estudiando** when you are studying (when one is studying) ~ Use **se** for the impersonal reference about what "one" or "a person" is doing. (In North America "you" is normally used for this impersonal reference.) **Aquí se come bien.** *Here you eat well. (Here one eats well.)*

KEY WORDS AND PHRASES

Anoche me di un baño y me acosté. Last night I took a bath and went to bed.

con sábanas limpias with clean sheets

no paré de dar vueltas I didn't (couldn't) stop tossing and turning

lo mismo pasó the same thing happened

dormir de noche to sleep at night

y tan fácil dormirse cuando . . . and so easy to fall asleep when . . .

51 Durmiéndose en la biblioteca

Falling asleep in the library

WHAT YOU CAN LEARN Talking about getting ready for bed, saying that the same thing happened before, talking about sleeping and falling asleep

PUTTING IT ALL TOGETHER (RESUMIÉNDOLO TODO). (Answers on page 217.)

Isabel está en la biblioteca, tratando de estudiar. Piensa, «Anoche me di un baño y (1) _____ _____ en una cómoda cama con (2) _____ limpias . . . Pero no paré de dar vueltas hasta la medianoche. (3) _____ _____ _____ la noche anterior. Y la noche antes de ésa.» En este momento Isabel casi se duerme, pero se despierta bruscamente. Luego, ella se pregunta, «¿Por qué es tan difícil (4) _____ de noche? ¿Y tan fácil (5) _____ cuando se está estudiando?»

DID YOU GET IT? (¿COMPRENDISTE?) (Answer on page 217.)

El problema de Isabel es que . . . (a) duerme demasiado de noche. (b) se duerme cuando estudia. (c) no quiere leer en la biblioteca.

WORKING WITH WORDS AND PATTERNS

- **¡Ésa sí que fue . . . !** *That sure (indeed, really) was . . .* ~ Use this phrase when you want to state an opinion about something very emphatically or enthusiastically. Vary according to circumstances. In this case the first word is **Ésa** because it refers to **fiesta**, a feminine word, but if you are talking about a soccer game, **partido**, then the first word must be masculine: **¡Ése sí que fue un buen partido!** *That indeed was a good game!* If you are talking about apples, **manzanas**, then the first word must be feminine and plural: **¡Ésas sí que son manzanas deliciosas!** *Those really are delicious apples!*

- **cierto** ~ This is one way to express agreement. Some other ways, which have the general meaning of *Right, For sure, That's true*, are the following: **De veras, De acuerdo, Correcto, Ya lo creo, Vale.**

- **Hablé con los González . . .** ~ To refer to a married couple like "the Smiths" or "the Andersons," in Spanish you say **los** along with the last name: **los Díaz, los Rivera, los Fuentes, los Cintrón. . . .** You do not pluralize the last name.

KEY WORDS AND PHRASES

¡Ésa sí que fue una linda fiesta! That was definitely a wonderful party!

cierto right, that's for sure

Hablé con los González . . . los Reyes . . . los Zurita. I spoke with the Gonzalezes, the Reyes, and the Zuritas.

aunque fuera de una sola even if it were only one

Una fiesta de Navidad

A Christmas party

WHAT YOU CAN LEARN Saying it was a great party, talking about the Smiths and the Joneses, saying you'd like to remember

PUTTING IT ALL TOGETHER (RESUMIÉNDOLO TODO). (Answers on page 217.)

Juan y Eli van a una elegante fiesta de Navidad. Comen, beben y hablan con la gente. Después, Eli dice, «¡(1) _____ _____ _____ _____ una linda fiesta!» Juan contesta, «Cierto . . . Hablé con los González, (2) _____ _____, los Reyes, (3) _____ _____ y los Arce . . . » y luego menciona varios otros matrimonios. Eli está impresionada con esta lista y exclama, «¡Fantástico!» Entonces, Juan confiesa, «Sólo (4) _____ _____ _____ _____ de las conversaciones, aunque fuera de (5) _____ _____ . . . »

DID YOU GET IT? (¿COMPRENDISTE?) (Answers on page 217.)

Para Juan, las conversaciones en la fiesta no eran . . . (a) numerosas (b) interesantes (c) memorables

WORKING WITH WORDS AND PATTERNS

- **¡Mira! ¿Ves eso?** ~ You can say this phrase to catch someone's attention and get him or her to look at something. If the person is someone you don't know very well, use the formal: **¡Mire Ud.! ¿Ve eso?**

- **las Navidades, la Navidad** *Christmastime (Christmas holidays), Christmas* ~ Christmas can be singular or plural, if it is thought of as the whole period of celebration. To say *Merry Christmas*, you can say: **¡Feliz Navidad!** or **¡Felices Navidades!**

- **una época** ~ The word **época** is handy for talking about a period of time. **En mi época, las cosas eran diferentes. Vivimos en la época de la tecnología.** *In my time, things were different. We live in the era of technology.*

- **regalar** ~ The verb **regalar** means *to give a gift*, or *to give free of charge*. **Le regalaron muchas cosas lindas.** *They gave her many lovely things.* **Me regaló dos boletos para el partido.** *He gave me (without charging me anything) two tickets to the game.*

- **goce . . . placer . . .** ~ These words are close in meaning, expressing the idea of enjoyment, joy, pleasure.

- **tratando de ayudar** ~ Use the common idiom **tratar de** + an infinitive when you want to say you are trying to do something. **Estoy tratando de aprender español (encontrar regalos, leer el periódico).** *I'm trying to learn Spanish (find gifts, read the newspaper).*

KEY WORDS AND PHRASES

¡Mira, papi! ¿Ves eso?
Look, Daddy! Do you see that?

«despierta niña» (a toy called) "Wake up, little girl"

un trineo con cohetes
a sled with rockets

una cámara de verdad
a real camera

una época para regalar
a time for giving

un goce . . . en dar a los demás a joy in giving to others

que supera . . . cualquier otro placer
that is greater than any other pleasure

o no habrá nadie a quien regalarle or there will be no one to give to

tratando de ayudar
trying to help

Haciendo compras para la Navidad *Shopping for Christmas*

WHAT YOU CAN LEARN

Getting someone to look at something, telling people what you want, explaining the spirit of Christmas

PUTTING IT ALL TOGETHER (RESUMIÉNDOLO TODO). (Answers on page 217.)

Juan y Eli están haciendo compras con Abril en una gran tienda. Abril le toca el brazo a su padre y le dice, «¡(1) _____, Papi! ¿Ves eso? ¡Lo quiero para las (2) _____!» Luego, le señala otras cosas que quiere recibir. Juan le explica a Abril que ahora es una (3) _____ _____ _____ . . . que hay un goce especial en dar a los demás que supera con mucho (4) _____ _____ _____. Abril lo escucha y entonces dice, «Pero alguien tiene que recibir o no habrá nadie a quien regalarle . . . Bueno . . . yo sólo (5) _____ _____ _____ ayudar . . . »

DID YOU GET IT? (¿COMPRENDISTE?) (Answers on page 217.)

Abril explica, con cierta lógica, que una parte esencial de las Navidades es . . . (a) tener personas que quieran recibir regalos. (b) tener personas que quieran dar regalos. (c) tener tiendas donde vendan trineos, cámaras y relojes.

WORKING WITH WORDS AND PATTERNS

- **Oye Isabel.** *Listen, Elizabeth.* ~ Use **oye** to catch the attention of a friend or companion. It is actually the intimate command form of the verb **oír** *to hear*. The formal command of this verb, **¡Oiga!**, is very useful to catch the attention of strangers on the street or in a public place. It is not impolite and means something like, *Could you please help me?*

- **la Víspera de Año Nuevo** ~ Literally this means *the Night before the New Year*. Another very common way of saying *New Year's Eve* is **Nochevieja** (literally, *Old Night*). This is similar to **Nochebuena** *Christmas Eve* (literally, *Good Night*).

- **¡Te ves fantástica!** ~ Use the reflexive verb **verse** (*to be seen*) when talking about how someone looks or appears. **Los muchachos se ven cansados.** *The boys look (appear) tired.* **¿Me veo bien con esta camisa?** *Do I look good in this shirt?*

- **¡Dios mío!** *My goodness! (Good heavens!)* ~ Literally, this means *My God!* but it doesn't have the slightest hint of offense or lack of respect. Use it freely to express surprise or concern.

- **Eso es asunto de ellos.** ~ Use **eso** whenever you are referring to an idea or situation. To say that *it's none of our business*, say literally, *It's an issue* (or *concern*) *of them* (*him, her*). **Es asunto de ellos (de él, de ella).** *It's their (his, her) business.*

KEY WORDS AND PHRASES

Es la Víspera de Año Nuevo. It's New Year's Eve.

Se supone que . . . It's assumed that . . .

ustedes dos están «involucrados» con . . . the two of you are involved with . . .

Nos conocemos desde que éramos niños. We've known each other since we were children.

¡Te ves fantástica! You look terrific (fantastic)!

Están comprometidos con . . . They are engaged to . . .

Esto podría descarrilar sus otras relaciones. This could wreck their other relationships.

Eso es asunto de ellos. That's their business.

¡ES LA VÍSPERA DE AÑO NUEVO!

Going out with an old boyfriend

WHAT YOU CAN LEARN   Complimenting a friend on how he or she looks, saying you've known someone since you were children, saying that's none of your (our) business

PUTTING IT ALL TOGETHER (RESUMIÉNDOLO TODO). (Answers on page 217.)

Isabel se viste y su hermanita Abril le pregunta, «Oye Isabel . . . ¿vas a salir con Antonio?» «Sí,» responde Isabel, «¿Hay algo malo en eso?» Abril dice, «Oh, no . . . sólo que es la (1) _____ de Año Nuevo y se supone que ustedes dos están "involucrados" con otras personas . . . » Isabel explica, «Antonio y yo (2) _____ _____ _____ que éramos niños . . . » Suena el timbre. Entra Antonio, mira a Isabel, y le dice, «¡Hola, tú! (3) ¡_____ _____ _____!» Los dos salen. Abril exclama, «¡Dios mío! ¡Esto podría descarrilar sus otras (4) ____!» Eli le dice, «Bueno, (5) _____ _____ _____ de ellos.» Pero sus padres dan saltos de alegría.

DID YOU GET IT? (¿COMPRENDISTE?) (Answers on page 217.)

Realmente, Eli y Juan creen que un romance entre Isabel y Antonio . . .
(a) sería algo muy bueno. (b) sería algo muy malo. (c) es asunto de ellos.

WORKING WITH WORDS AND PATTERNS

- **cuando tenía 16** *when I was 16* ~ Always use the imperfect and not the preterite when telling someone's age in the past because this is description and not action, and the flow of time is thought of as a continuum. Basic rule: imperfect for description in the past, preterite for completed action. (Notice the preterite forms **fui** and **duró** that follow immediately to express completed actions.)

- **Como logré que mis padres no supieran.** *How I managed (it) that my parents didn't find out.* ~ Here's a case where the past subjunctive (**supieran**) is used because it follows an expression of will or influence (**logré**) and the word **que** (*that*). (See pages 140–142.)

- **¿Te acuerdas (de) . . . ?** *Do you remember . . .?* ~ Use either the verb **recordar** or the verb **acordarse de** to talk about remembering. If you use the latter, be sure to make it reflexive. It is kind of like asking, *Do you have the memory (of) . . . ?* Both of these verbs are stem-changing. (See page 6.)

- **Me sorprende que te acuerdes . . .** *I'm surprised that you remember . . .* ~ The present subjunctive (**te acuerdes**) occurs here after an expression of emotion and the word **que** (*that*). (See pages 140–142.)

- **Nos casamos.** ~ Use the reflexive verb **casarse** to talk about *getting married*. Notice the word **casa** inside it. It is like taking a house (**casa**) onto yourselves. **Fernando y Marilú se casaron en Cancún.** *Ferdinand and Mary Lou got married in Cancun.* **Tomás y yo nos casamos hace muchos años.** *Thomas and I got married many years ago.* Notice that you can add **con** (*with*) to the verb. **Tere, ¿cuándo te casaste con Gerardo?** *Terry, when did you get married to Gerald?*

- **Hemos visto . . . Hemos sobrevivido . . . Hemos descubierto . . .** *We have seen . . . We have survived . . . We have discovered . . .* ~ Use the present perfect tense to talk about what you've seen, done, and learned. (See page 6.)

KEY WORDS AND PHRASES

que duró toda la noche that lasted the whole night

¡Qué refriega! What a blast! (Literally, What a scrubbing!)

Al año siguiente nos casamos. The next year we got married.

«Nido de cuervos» the "Crow's Nest" *(the name of a nightclub)*

Lo pusimos en un canasto. We put him in a basket.

¡Bendito! Good heavens! (Literally, Blessed one!)

tan significativas como . . . as significant as . . .

ninguno de los dos neither one of *(the two of)* us

quedar(se) despierto stay awake

ronquido *(sound)* snore

En la cama con recuerdos

In bed with memories

WHAT YOU CAN LEARN   Reliving memories with the preterite and imperfect, talking about what you've seen and learned with the present perfect

PUTTING IT ALL TOGETHER (RESUMIÉNDOLO TODO). (Answers on page 217.)

Eli y Juan estan en la cama, charlando. Juan recuerda, «Cuando (1) _____ 16, fui a mi primera fiesta que duró toda la noche! . . . » Luego, Eli le pregunta a su marido, «¿ (2) _____ _____ _____ nuestro primer Año Nuevo juntos, Juan?» Juan contesta, «Ambos (3) _____ estudiantes . . . Yo estaba loco por ti . . . » Los dos siguen recordando. Juan dice, «Al año siguiente (4) _____ _____ . . . » Finalmente Juan declara, «Pero ahora, después de casi 25 años juntos, (5) _____ _____ que esas celebraciones de toda la noche no son tan significativas como una tranquila noche juntos.» Luego, Juan oye un ronquido y apaga la lámpara.

DID YOU GET IT? (¿COMPRENDISTE?) (Answers on page 217.)

Realmente, Eli y Juan no salen porque . . . (a) están enfermos. (b) tienen que dormirse a las 10. (c) desean una noche tranquila.

El español en tu vida

Spanish in your life

Practice what you've learned from Comics 48–55. (Answers on page 217.)

A. FRASES ÚTILES (*Useful Phrases*)

How would you say each of the following useful phrases in Spanish? **¿Cómo se dice?** (*How do you say it?*)

1. In my opinion . . . **¿Cómo se dice?**

2. Something to make us remember. **¿Cómo se dice?**

3. I was going to say to him (or to her) . . . **¿Cómo se dice?**

4. The same thing happened . . . **¿Cómo se dice?**

5. You look terrific! **¿Cómo se dice?**

B. ¿QUÉ VERBOS FALTAN AQUÍ? (*What verbs are missing here?*)

Look at the following selections from the comics. Write the verbs that are missing in each one.

1.

2.

3.

4.

5.

C. JUAN CUENTA SUS PENAS *(John talks about his troubles)*

In Comic 50, John comes home and tells Elly about all the awful things that happened at work that day. In Spanish he sometimes uses the preterite tense and sometimes the imperfect. Read through the explanation about when to use these tenses on pages 76–80, and, without looking back at the comic strip, underline the correct verb form in parentheses.

¡Ooohhh! ¡Me siento tan feliz de estar en casa! La señora Martínez no (1. vino/venía) a una cita de tres horas que (2. tuvo/tenía) esta mañana, así que (3. tratamos/tratábamos) de llenar el espacio con otros pacientes . . . Luego el sistema de la computadora de la recepción se (4. cayó/caía) por lo que (5. quedamos/quedábamos) fuera de acción por casi todo el día . . . Me (6. salté/saltaba) el almuerzo . . . Tenemos dos esterilizadores y uno (7. dejó/dejaba) de funcionar y después el sistema de succión (8. falló/fallaba). (9. Había/Hubo) tanta tensión entre el personal que (10. pensé/pensaba) que la oficina (11. fue/iba) a explotar . . . Doña Teresa (12. dejó/dejaba) a sus niños llorones en la sala de espera mientras le (13. hicimos/hacíamos) una limpieza bucal y uno de ellos (14. rompió/rompía) una lámpara . . . Mi silla dental se (15. atascó/atascaba) en la posición más baja y (16. tuve/tenía) que pasarme toda la tarde en esta posición . . .

Challenging Level

The Three Key Concepts

1. Implied command (for example: **quiero que, es importante que, nos gustaría que, te pido que**, etc.)

2. Expression of emotion (for example: **me alegro de que, tengo miedo de que, me sorprendo que**)

3. Expression of doubt or denial (**dudo que, es imposible que, no creo que**)

Remember that the subjunctive forms are used *after* these concepts, in the secondary idea, the one that is *subjoined* (*joined below*) to one of these concepts, not in the concept itself.

Look at the following examples taken from ***Por lo bueno o por lo malo:***

- Expression of emotion

  Indicative: **Es verdad que no *te quejas.*** *It's true that you don't complain.*

  Subjunctive: **Me sorprendo que no *te quejes* más.** *I'm surprised that you don't complain more.*

(Notice the first person present indicative of the *reflexive* verb **sorprenderse** in the primary clause of the subjunctive sentence above [**me sorprendo que** *I'm surprised*].)

The verb **quejarse** is an **-ar** verb and the regular present is **te quejas**. However, after the expression of emotion (**me sorprendo que**) the present subjunctive form **te quejes** is used. It's as though the emotion colors the following idea and alters the verb. Note that if there is no change of subject in the sentence, you can simply use the infinitive (e.g. **Me sorprendo de lo verlo.** *I am surprised to see it.*).

- Implied command

  Indicative: **Veo que tu y Papi *se cambian* de nuevo arriba.** *I see that you and Dad are moving back upstairs.*

  Subjunctive: **Quiero que tu y Papi *se cambien* de nuevo arriba.** *I want you and Dad to move back upstairs.*

The regular present of **cambiarse** is **se cambian**, but after the implied command (**Quiero que**), the present subjunctive **se cambien** is used. It is as though the force of the command spills over into the following idea and alters the verb.

- Doubt or unreality

Indicative: **Estoy segura de que me *gusta* esa expresión.** *I'm sure that I like that expression.*

Subjunctive: **No estoy segura de que me *guste* esa expresión.** *I'm not sure that I like that expression.*

The regular present of **gustar** is **gusta**, but after the expression of doubt (**no estoy segura de que**), the subjunctive **guste** is used. It's as though the doubt (or unreality) spreads a shadow over the following idea and changes the verb.

- Projection into the future

Indicative: **A veces *necesitas* un poco de amistad.** *Sometimes you need a little bit of friendship.*

Subjunctive: **Cuando *necesites* un poco de amistad, ¡me puedes llamar!** *Whenever you need a little bit of friendship, you can call me!*

The future is always uncertain and doubtful, so a projection into the indefinite future (**cuando necesites**) is followed by a subjunctive form. This is really part of the idea of doubt or unreality. This event could happen at any time, or it may not happen at all.

Back to Basics: How to Form the Subjunctives

How does the emotion, implied command, or doubt alter the form of the verb in the secondary idea? Basically, in the present tense, it interchanges the theme vowel: **-ar** verbs now use the **-e**, and **-er** or **-ir** verbs use the **-a**. Also, to form the present subjunctive, you always use the **yo** form of the indicative as your starting point, so an irregular verb like **tener** will begin with **teng-**.

Take the **yo** form, switch the theme vowel, and add the usual endings.

tener (to have)

(yo)	**tenga**	*I have*
(tú)	**tengas**	*you (familiar singular) have*
(él, ella, Ud.)	**tenga**	*he, she, it has; you (formal singular) have*
(nosotros[as])	**tengamos**	*we have*
(vosotros[as])	**tengáis**	*you (familiar plural in Spain) have*
(ellos, ellas, Uds.)	**tengan**	*they, you (general plural; formal plural in Spain) have*

And here are present subjunctives of regular verbs:

hablar (to speak, talk)

hable
hables
hable
hablemos
habléis
hablen

comer (to eat)

coma
comas
coma
comamos
comáis
coman

vivir (to live)

viva
vivas
viva
vivamos
viváis
vivan

pensar (to think) (stem-changing)

piense
pienses
piense
piensemos
pienséis
piensen

There are four irregular verbs in the present subjunctive that do not follow the rule for forming the subjunctive.

haber (aux. have)

haya
hayas
haya
hayamos
hayáis
hayan

ir (to go)

vaya
vayas
vaya
vayamos
vayáis
vayan

ser (to be)

sea
seas
sea
seamos
seáis
sean

saber (to know)

sepa
sepas
sepa
sepamos
sepáis
sepan

REALITY CHECK: How are you doing with all this? You might want to stop now and read some comics. Come back and read more someday, when you feel very bright and curious or for a ready reference.

How to Form the Imperfect Subjunctive

Sometimes you are talking about the past and need to use the subjunctive, so you use the imperfect subjunctive. For example, in Comic #56 there is a quote from Elly talking to her father: **Me sorprende que no *te quejes* más.** *I'm surprised that you don't complain more.*

(Notice the third person present indicative of the *non*-reflexive verb **sorprender** in the first clause of the subjunctive sentence above [**me sorprende que**]. In this case, **me** is an object pronoun [literally, *It is surprising to me that* . . .].) The verb **quejes** is in the subjunctive because it follows the expression of emotion, in this case, of surprise. If Elly wanted to talk about what she was feeling yesterday, she would say: **Me sorprendió que no te *quejaras* más.** *I was surprised that you didn't complain more.*

The verb **quejaras** is in the imperfect subjunctive (sometimes called the past subjunctive). If the verb in the main idea is in the preterite, imperfect, or conditional, then use the imperfect subjunctive when necessary in the secondary idea.

Good news! There are no irregular verbs in this tense. To form the imperfect subjunctive of all verbs, drop the **-ron** from the **ellos/ellas** form of the preterite and add these endings: **-ra, -ras,**

-ra, **-ramos**, **-rais**, **-ran**. (So if you learn the preterite well, it pays off for this tense.)

querer (to want, love): **ellos/ellas** form of preterite = **quisieron** – the **-ron** = **quisie-**

Now add the endings:

(yo)	**quisiera**
(tú)	**quisieras**
(él, ella, Ud.)	**quisiera**
(nosotros[as])	**quisiéramos**
(vosotros[as])	**quisierais**
(ellos, ellas, Uds.) . .	**quisieran**

Other examples:

hablar (to talk or speak)

hablara
hablaras
hablara
habláramos
hablarais
hablaran

comer (to eat)

comiera
comieras
comiera
comiéramos
comierais
comieran

vivir (to live)

viviera
vivieras
viviera
viviéramos
vivierais
vivieran

Alternate Forms for the Imperfect Subjunctive

The Spanish language puts a premium on elegance of sound, and offers you an alternate set of endings for the imperfect subjunctive. The **-se** endings are not as common as the **-ra** endings, but you should know about them to be able to recognize what they mean. In Comic #76, we have two examples when Elly asks April a question after reprimanding her for not cleaning her pet rabbit's cage: **¿Cómo te gustaría si *fueses* tú la que *tuvieses* que vivir en ese atroz, y asqueroso desorden?** *How would you like it if it were you who had to live in this atrocious and filthy mess?*

Here are examples of the **-se** forms for the imperfect subjunctive:

(yo)	**quisiese**	**hablase**
(tú)	**quisieses** . . .	**hablases**
(él, ella, Ud.) . . .	**quisiese**	**hablase**
(nosotros[as]) . . .	**quisiésemos** .	**hablásemos**
(vosotros[as]) . . .	**quisieseis** . . .	**hablaseis**
(ellos[as], Uds.) .	**quisiesen** . . .	**hablasen**

How to Form the Compound Tenses

Here is an example of how English and Spanish structure are sometimes very similar. Just as in English, Spanish has four compound tenses: present perfect, past perfect, future perfect, and conditional perfect. These are sometimes called the perfect tenses because they each refer to a particular point in time at which the action is *perfect*, in other words, complete or finished. The most common is the present perfect, which refers to an action that has been completed at the present time.

For example, Elly is furious because her daughter has not yet washed her dirty clothes and Elly thinks that at this present moment, she has had enough time to do this. **Ha tenido suficiente tiempo. ¿Cómo puede vivir de esa**

manera? *She has had enough time. How can she live like that?*

To form the compound tenses, in both the indicative and subjunctive, use the correct form of the auxiliary verb **haber** and the past participle (the **-ado** or **-ido**) form of the verb being used. That's why these tenses are called compound tenses, because they need two verbs, not one. Notice that the verb **haber** does not mean *to have* in the sense of possession as it does in English. (The verb **tener** is used for *to have* in the sense of possession.) **Haber** is used to mean *there is*, *there are* (as in **hay**), or simply as the auxiliary for the perfect tenses.

The Present Perfect

To form the present perfect, use the present of the verb **haber** plus the past participle.

hablar (to talk, to speak)

he hablado	*I have spoken*
has hablado	*you* (familiar) *have spoken*
ha hablado	*he, she, it has; you* (formal) *have spoken*
hemos hablado	*we have spoken*
habéis hablado	*you have spoken* (familiar plural, Spain)
han hablado	*they, you* (formal plural) *have spoken*

comer (to eat)

he comido
has comido
ha comido
hemos comido
habéis comido
han comido

vivir (to live)

he vivido
has vivido
ha vivido
hemos vivido
habéis vivido
han vivido

Notice that the regular past participle in English is *lived*, because it ends in *-ed*, but that the verbs *to speak* and *to eat* both have irregular past participles, *spoken* and *eaten*. Spanish also has a number of verbs with irregular past participles, e.g., **abrir/abierto**, **morir/muerto**, **decir/dicho**, **hacer/hecho**, **ver/visto**.

The Past Perfect

This tense refers to action that had been completed before a certain moment in the past. For example, Elizabeth is thinking about a moment in the past before which she had decided to study for a particular career, and then later changed her mind. She talks with her friend, using the past perfect tense: ***Había decidido tomar Arte General, pero en realidad me gusta la Biología.*** *I had decided to take liberal arts, but actually I like biology.*

To form the past perfect tense, use the imperfect of the verb **haber** and the past participle.

hablar (to talk, to speak)

había hablado	*I had talked*
habías hablado	*you* (familiar) *had talked*
había hablado	*he, she, it, you* (formal) *had talked*
habíamos hablado	*we had talked*
habíais hablado	*you had talked* (familiar plural, Spain)
habían hablado	*they, you* (formal plural) *had talked*

ver (to see)

habría visto
habías visto
había visto
habíamos visto
habíais visto
habían visto

The Future Perfect

This tense refers to a time in the future when the action *will have been* completed, or it is used to express the possibility that the action *may have been* completed at the present moment. This is the case in the following example when Elly asks April if she could possibly already have gotten bored with her new toy. **Cariño, no** *te habrás aburrido* **ya de tu nuevo juguete, ¿verdad?** *Darling, you can't possibly have already become bored with your new toy, right?*

To form the future perfect tense, use the future of **haber** and the past participle of the verb.

hablar (to talk, to speak)

habré hablado	*I will have talked*
habrás hablado	*you (familiar) will have talked*
habrá hablado	*he, she, it, you (formal) will have talked*
habremos hablado	*we will have talked*
habréis hablado	*you will have talked (familiar plural, Spain)*
habrán hablado	*they, you (formal plural) will have talked*

hacer (to do, to make)

habré hecho
habrás hecho
habrá hecho
habremos hecho
habréis hecho
habrán hecho

The Conditional Perfect

Use this tense to refer to an action that *would have been* completed at a particular moment in certain circumstances. Anthony uses it when he tells Elizabeth that if St. Valentine's Day had been created for lovers, it would have been put in July rather than in the cold month of February. **Porque si fuera para los amantes, lo** *habrían puesto* **en julio.** *Because if it were for lovers, it would have been put in July.*

To form the conditional perfect tense, use the conditional of **haber** and the past participle of the verb. (Notice that the verb **poner** has an irregular past participle, **puesto**.)

poner (to put)

habría puesto	*I would have put*
habrías puesto	*you would have put*
habría puesto	*he, she, it, you (formal) would have put*
habríamos puesto	*we would have put*
habríais puesto	*you would have put (familiar plural, Spain)*
habrían puesto	*they, you (formal plural) would have put*

hablar (to talk, to speak)

habría hablado
habrías hablado
habría hablado
habríamos hablado
habríais hablado
habrían hablado

How to Form the Present Perfect Subjunctive and the Past Perfect Subjunctive

There are times when you will want to use a perfect tense in a secondary idea after an implied command, an expression of emotion, or an expression of doubt or unreality. Two compound subjunctive tenses are available for this: the present perfect subjunctive to use for reference to the present or the future, and the past perfect subjunctive to use for reference to the past or a conditional action.

Elly uses the present perfect subjunctive to respond to her daughter Elizabeth's accusation that she is an obsessive-compulsive person. **¿De veras? Me alegro de que me lo *hayas hecho* ver.** *Really? I'm glad that you have made me see it.*

To form the present perfect subjunctive or the past perfect subjunctive, use the present subjunctive or the imperfect subjunctive of **haber** and the past participle of the verb.

The Present Perfect Subjunctive

hacer (to do, to make)

haya hecho	*I have made*
hayas hecho	*you* (familiar) *have made*
haya hecho	*he, she, it has made; you* (formal) *have made*
hayamos hecho	*we have made*
hayáis hecho	*you* (familiar plural, Spain) *have made*
hayan hecho	*they, you* (formal plural) *have made*

hablar (to talk, to speak)

haya hablado
hayas hablado
haya hablado
hayamos hablado
hayáis hablado
hayan hablado

The past perfect subjunctive

Notice that you can use **-ra** endings or the alternate **-se** endings for the past perfect subjunctive. There is no difference in meaning.

comer (to eat)

hubiera comido	*I had eaten*
hubieras comido	*you had eaten*
hubiera comido	*he, she, it, you* (formal) *had eaten*
hubiéramos comido	*we had eaten*
hubierais comido	*you* (familiar plural, Spain) *had eaten*
hubieran comido	*they, you* (formal plural) *had eaten*

decir (to say, to tell)

hubiese dicho
hubieses dicho
hubiese dicho
hubiésemos dicho
hubieseis dicho
hubiesen dicho

Now that you know something about the subjunctive, watch for it in the *For Better or For Worse* comics and in other written Spanish. Listen for it when you hear spoken Spanish or watch Spanish movies or TV. Above all, be brave and try using it yourself!

WORKING WITH WORDS AND PATTERNS

- **¿Te duele . . . la (espalda, cabeza, pierna)?** *Does your . . . (back, head, leg) hurt you?* ~ Literally, *To you does (it) hurt the back?* The verb **doler (ue)** is similar to the verb **gustar** and patterns with an indirect object pronoun (**me, te, le, nos, os, les**). Use this useful formula to ask someone about their aches and pains, filling in the appropriate body parts. (See **Las partes del cuerpo** in **El español en su vida**, page 164.) Remember to use the plural verb if necessary, as in **¿Te duelen . . . los pies (las manos, los hombros)?** *Do your . . . feet (hands, shoulders) hurt you?* To talk about your own aches and pains, use **me** instead of **te**. **Me duele la espalda.** *My back aches (hurts me).* **Me duelen los pies.** *My feet ache (hurt me).*

- **molestar . . . soportar** *to bother . . . to put up with (endure, tolerate)* ~ These verbs are false cognates because they look like the English verbs *to molest* and *to support*. Be sure to use them in the correct way. **Me molesta su actitud.** *His attitude bothers me.* **No soporto su arrogancia.** *I can't stand (put up with) her arrogance.* (The verb **soportar** never means *to support financially*. For that, use **mantener**.)

- *Highlight on the subjunctive:* **Me sorprende que no te quejes más.** *I'm surprised (i.e., It surprises me) that you don't complain more.* ~ The present subjunctive (**no te quejes**) occurs here after an expression of emotion and the connecting word **que** (*that*). (See pages 140–142.) Notice that **quejarse** is a reflexive verb and requires a reflexive pronoun.

- **Deprime a los demás.** *It depresses others.* ~ The verb **deprimir** means *to depress*, so you can say: **Me deprime la lluvia.** *Rain depresses me.* To talk about *getting depressed*, use the verb as a reflexive verb: **deprimirse. Yo no me deprimo fácilmente.** *I don't get depressed easily.* **A mi primo no le gusta su trabajo y se deprime todos los lunes.** *My cousin doesn't like his work and gets depressed every Monday.*

KEY WORDS AND PHRASES

¿Te duele de nuevo la espalda . . . ? Is your back aching again . . . ?

Oh, siempre me está molestando . . . Oh, it's always bothering me . . .

rodillas . . . manos . . . interiores . . . knees . . . hands . . . insides . . .

todo lo que tienes que soportar all that you have to put up with

No tiene sentido quejarse. It doesn't make sense to complain.

sentir pena por mí mismo to feel sorry for myself

¿Y él te levanta el ánimo? And he raises your spirits (improves your mood)?

mucho peor que yo much worse off than I (am)

56 ¿Qué te duele hoy, Abuelo?

What hurts you today, Grandpa?

WHAT YOU CAN LEARN   Talking about aches and pains, expressing surprise about someone's actions

PUTTING IT ALL TOGETHER (RESUMIÉNDOLO TODO). Fill in the blanks. (Answers on page 217.)

El abuelo se levanta y toma sus píldoras. Eli le pregunta, «¿(1) _____ _____ de nuevo la espalda, Papá?» Contesta de inmediato, «Oh, siempre me está molestando, querida, y también mis (2) _____ , mis manos, mis interiores . . . » Luego, Eli le dice, «Con todo lo que tienes que (3) _____, me sorprende de que no (4) _____ _____ más.» Su padre le explica que cuando (5) _____ _____ _____ pena por mí mismo, tomo el teléfono y llamo a mi amigo Pedro.»

DID YOU GET IT? (¿COMPRENDISTE?) Choose the best answer for this comprehension question. (Answer on page 217.)

¿Por qué el abuelo llama a su amigo Pedro? Porque Pedro . . . (a) está mucho mejor que él. (b) está mucho peor que él. (c) es un buen médico.

WORKING WITH WORDS AND PATTERNS

- **¡Qué dormilón(-a)!** *What a sleepyhead!* ~ Use **qué** in front of a descriptive word to express amazement at someone's extreme actions, in this case, (supposed) oversleeping. (Other examples: **¡Qué mentiroso(a)!** *What a liar!* **¡Qué trabajador(-a)!** *What a worker!*) Notice the **-on(-a)** ending, called an *augmentative*, used to emphasize large size or extreme qualities. **¡Qué hombrón!** *What a big man!* **¡Qué mujerona!** *What a big woman!* **¡Qué comilón(-a)!** *What a big eater!* (**Comilona** can also refer to a *big feast* or *eating orgy*.)

- *Highlight on the subjunctive:* **Cuando se despierte . . .** *When she wakes up . . .* ~ Here the subjunctive form (**se despierte** from the verb **despertarse**) is used because the speaker is projecting into the future which is always uncertain. This is different from saying *she will wake up* and using the future tense. Use the subjunctive in verbs after **cuando, antes de que, tan pronto como, hasta que,** or similar expressions when you are referring to future action. (See pages 140–142.)

- **cantarle a alguien las cuarenta . . .** *to give someone a piece of your mind . . .* **se las voy a cantar ahora mismo** *I'm going to give it to her right now* (the **las** refers to **las cuarenta**) ~ This is popular slang (from Spain and parts of Latin America) which literally means *I'm going to sing her (him, you, them) the 40* but it can be translated in various ways: *giving someone a piece of your mind*, *telling them off*, or *telling them a thing or two*. What does the 40 refer to? It could refer to getting the winning number of points in certain card games or it could be the 40 **razones** (*reasons*) that someone is out of line.

KEY WORDS AND PHRASES

Ya casi es mediodía.
It's already almost noon.

Cuando se despierte . . .
When she wakes up . . .

Le voy a cantar las cuarenta. I'm going to give her a piece of my mind (*slang*).

nada de eso none of that (never mind)

ahora mismo right now

Se fue a patinar. She went skating.

¡Qué dormilona!

What a sleepyhead!

WHAT YOU CAN LEARN   Threatening to give someone a piece of your mind, referring to future action with the subjunctive

PUTTING IT ALL TOGETHER (RESUMIÉNDOLO TODO). Fill in the blanks. (Answers on page 217.)

Eli está lavando ropa. Entra en el dormitorio de Isabel y cree que su hija está todavía en la cama. Piensa, «(1) _____ _____ _____ mediodía. ¿Cómo puede dormir tanto? ¡Cuando (2) _____ _____, le voy a (3) _____ _____ _____!» Luego, Abril, su hija menor, le pregunta, «¿(4) _____ _____ a Isabel, mamá? ¡Se fue a (5) _____ a las seis de la mañana!»

DID YOU GET IT? (¿COMPRENDISTE?) Choose the best answer for this comprehension question. (Answer on page 217.)

¿Qué lección aprende Eli? Aprende que . . . (a) no conoce tan bien a su hija. (b) conoce perfectamente bien a su hija. (c) su hija es una dormilona.

WORKING WITH WORDS AND PATTERNS

- *Highlight on the subjunctive:* **¡Quiero que guardes esta ropa . . .** *I want you to put away this clothing . . .* ~ Use the subjunctive after an expression of implied command (telling what you want someone to do), even though the infinitive is used in English. Literally, you are saying, *I want that you might put away this clothing . . .* If there is no change of subject, use the infinitive: **Quiero guardar esta ropa.** *I want to put away this clothing.* (See page 140.)

- *Highlight on the subjunctive:* **. . . para que no termine en el suelo!** *. . . so that it doesn't end up on the floor!* ~ Use the subjunctive after **para que**, **a fin de que**, or other expressions that imply purpose (since this is a kind of implied command) when there is a change of subject. (In this case, *you* are to put the clothing away so that *it* doesn't end up on the floor.)

- **¡No lo soy! . . . ¡Sí, lo eres!** *I am not! . . . Yes, you are!* ~ Notice that **lo** is used in Spanish to complete the phrase. It means: "No, I'm not *it* (that which you are calling me)" and "Yes, you are *it* (that which I am calling you)." This is similar to **No lo sé** (*I don't know it*), the Spanish way of saying *I don't know.*

- **en el lavaplatos** *in the dishwasher* ~ As a general rule, say the action first and the object second in Spanish when using a compound word for a gadget or appliance, just the opposite of the English word order. So, **lava** (*wash*) goes first and **platos** (*dishes*) second: it is the "wash-dishes" instead of the *dishwasher.* These words are usually masculine since **el aparato** (the *apparatus*) is understood: **el abrecartas** the *letter opener,* **el cortalápices** the *pencil sharpener.*

- *Highlight on the subjunctive:* **Me alegro de que me lo hayas hecho ver.** *I'm glad that you have made me see it.* ~ Use the subjunctive after an expression of emotion when there is a change of subject. (*I am glad that you have made me see it.*) Here the present perfect subjunctive (**hayas hecho**) is used because the second part of the sentence refers to an action that has been completed at the present moment. (See page 143.)

KEY WORDS AND PHRASES

¡Dobla! ¡Dobla! ¡Dobla! Fold! Fold! Fold!

Quiero que guardes esta ropa. I want you to put away this clothing.

no está nunca desordenada is never sloppy

cajones . . . armarios . . . pares de zapatos drawers . . . closets . . . pairs of shoes

Enderezas las alfombritas. You straighten the carpets.

Hasta doblas la ropa interior. You even fold the underwear.

un comportamiento obsesivo-compulsivo obsessive-compulsive behavior

de ahora en adelante trataré de . . . from now on I will try to . . .

¡Eres una fanática del orden!

You're a neatness freak!

WHAT YOU CAN LEARN   Telling someone what you want them to do, saying you're glad that someone has told you something, talking about keeping the house in order

PUTTING IT ALL TOGETHER (RESUMIÉNDOLO TODO). (Answers on page 217.)

Eli está pasando la aspiradora y limpiando. Ve a su hija y le dice, «Isabel, (1) _____ _____ _____ esta ropa ahora, para que no (2) _____ en el suelo.» Isabel le responde, «¡Pero, mamá! ¡Eres una fanática del orden! Pones los tarros y botellas en el (3) _____ antes de reciclarlos. ¡Si hasta doblas la ropa interior! ¡Eso es un comportamiento obsesivo-compulsivo!» Eli contesta, «¿De veras? (4) _____ _____ _____ me lo hayas hecho ver.» Más tarde, Abril la ve. Está sentada en la mesa, leyendo y tomando café y la cocina está totalmente (5) _____ . Abril le pregunta a su padre, «¿Qué le pasa a mamá?»

DID YOU GET IT? (¿COMPRENDISTE?) (Answer on page 217.)

¿Por qué está preocupada Abril? Porque su mamá . . . (a) está leyendo y tomando café. (b) no ha preparado la cena. (c) no parece normal.

WORKING WITH WORDS AND PATTERNS

- **Isabel piensa en su futuro.** *Elizabeth thinks about her future.* ~ Use **pensar *de*** when talking about someone's *opinion* of something, **¿Qué piensas *de* las películas mexicanas?** *What do you think about Mexican movies?* Use **pensar *en*** when referring to thinking *about* someone or something. **Juanita siempre piensa *en* su esposo.** *Jane is always thinking about her husband.*

- **los folletos que te dio el asesor** *the brochures the advisor gave you* ~ Notice the difference in Spanish versus English word order. In Spanish it can be subject/verb, but it is more flexible and can also be verb/subject. This is especially common in secondary clauses. **Hablaba con mi novia cuando entró su padre.** *I was talking with my girl-friend when her father walked in.*

- **He estado pensando . . . que has estado haciendo . . . investigación.** *I have been thinking . . . that you have been doing . . . research.* ~ Any tense can be turned into a progressive by adding the **-ando/-iendo** form (the present participle), which is equivalent to the *-ing* form in English. **Estoy pensando. Estaba pensando. Estaré pensando.** In this comic strip, the present perfect progressive is used twice to talk about what someone *has been thinking or doing.* (See page 6 for more on the present perfect tense.)

- **Había decidido tomar arte general . . .** *I had decided to take liberal arts . . .* ~ Use the past perfect tense (imperfect forms of **haber** with the past participle) to refer to an action you *had done* before a certain point in the past. (See pages 143–144.)

- *Highlight on the subjunctive:* **Cuanto más variada sea . . . , mejor.** *The more varied . . . is, the better.* ~ Use this formula (**cuanto más . . . sea . . . , mejor**) to talk about the link between something being a certain way in the future and your satisfaction. The subjunctive is used (**sea**) because the quality is projected into a possible (but never certain) future. (See page 140.) **Cuanto más grande sea tu auto, mejor.** *The bigger your car will be, the better.*

los folletos the brochures

el asesor de estudios the academic advisor

He estado pensando en leerlos. I have been thinking about reading them.

Había decidido tomar . . . I had decided to take . . .

Me gustaría trabajar . . . viajar. I would like to work . . . to travel.

a final (fin) de cuentas after all (when all is said and done)

59 Isabel piensa en su futuro

Elizabeth thinks about her future

WHAT YOU CAN LEARN Discussing plans for the future, talking about what you have been doing, saying what you would like to do

PUTTING IT ALL TOGETHER (RESUMIÉNDOLO TODO). (Answers on page 217.)

Una amiga de Isabel encuentra los (1) _____ que le dio el asesor de estudios. Isabel le explica, «(2) _____ _____ tomar arte general, pero en realidad me gusta la biología . . . quiero entrar a estudiar pedagogía. Pero también (3) _____ _____ _____ un tiempo . . . viajar. A final de cuentas quiero enseñar en una escuela superior, por lo que cuanto (4) _____ _____ _____ mi experiencia, mejor.» La amiga de Isabel se va, y su padre Juan entra. Le pregunta, «¡Isabel! Veo que (5) _____ _____ _____ un poco de investigación. ¿Cuáles son tus planes para el futuro?» Ella contesta, «No sé.»

DID YOU GET IT? (¿COMPRENDISTE?) (Answers on page 217.)

¿Por qué contesta Isabel, «No sé»? Porque en realidad . . . (a) no ha estado pensando en su futuro. (b) quiere trabajar y viajar y no le interesa la universidad. (c) puede hablar con su amiga de sus planes pero no con su padre.

WORKING WITH WORDS AND PATTERNS

- **Mira . . . Come tu comida . . . Recoje tus platos.** *Look . . . Eat your food . . . Pick up your plates.* ~ You tell a friend or child what to do with the familiar imperative forms, the ones used for people you address as **tú**.

- *Highlight on the subjunctive:* **No juegues . . . No esperes . . . No me discutas . . . No uses tanto champú.** *Don't play . . . Don't wait . . . Don't talk back to me (discuss with me) . . . Don't use so much shampoo.* ~ Tell a friend or child *not* to do something by using **no** + the present subjunctive **tú** form. (See pages 140–141.) Notice that in Spanish all commands in the negative (singular or plural, familiar or formal) use **no** + the relevant *subjunctive* form.

- *Highlight on the subjunctive:* **que yo limpie por ti . . . hasta que hayas recogido todos tus juguetes** *so that I will clean up for you . . . until you have picked up all of your toys* ~ In Spanish, to refer to action occurring at an indefinite point in the future, you must use the subjunctive when there is a change of subject. April tells her dolls, "Don't wait for me to clean up after you!" There is a change of subject here because *you* is understood to be the subject of *don't wait*, and *me* (or *I*) the subject of *clean up*. Similarly, April says, "(There will be) No more TV until you've picked up all your toys!" The subjunctive is required because the completion of the action is projected to an indefinite time in the future.

- **¡Tienes que bañarte hoy!** *You have to take a bath today!* ~ Instead of a direct command, you can tell someone to do something by using the common formula for obligation: **tener que** + infinitive, in the *you* form. **Tienes que pagar la cuenta ahora.** *You have to pay the bill now.*

- **¡Me estaba escuchando a mí misma!** *I was listening to myself!* ~ Notice that this is the imperfect progressive, made by adding the **-ando** or **-iendo** form to the imperfect. Use **mismo(a)** when you want to emphasize that you are referring to yourself. **¡Yo misma no comprendo mi invención!** *I myself don't understand my invention!*

KEY WORDS AND PHRASES

¡Mira como está de desordenado tu cuarto! Look how sloppy your room is!

¡Come tu comida, no juegues . . . ! Eat your food, don't play . . . !

¡Recoge tus platos! Pick up your plates!

¡Nada de TV hasta . . . ! No (more) TV until . . . !

¿Me estabas escuchando . . . ? Were you listening to me . . . ?

¡Me estaba escuchando a mí misma! I was listening to myself!

WHAT YOU CAN LEARN   Telling a friend or child what to do, telling a friend or child what not to do

PUTTING IT ALL TOGETHER (RESUMIÉNDOLO TODO). (Answers on page 217.)

Abril está jugando con su casita y regañándoles a sus muñecas. «¡Mira como está de desordenado tu cuarto! ¡(1) _____ tu comida, no juegues con ella! ¡Recoge tus platos! ¡No esperes (2) _____ _____ _____ por ti! ¡Nada de TV hasta que (3) _____ _____ todos tus juguetes! . . . ¡No me discutas! ¡Tienes que bañarte hoy! ¡(4) _____ _____ tanto champú!» Entra su madre Eli y Abril le pregunta, «¿Me estabas escuchando, Mami?» Eli contesta, «¡Me estaba escuchando (5) _____ _____ _____!»

DID YOU GET IT? (¿COMPRENDISTE?) (Answers on page 217.)

¿Por qué dice Eli que estaba escuchando a sí misma? Porque Abril . . . (a) tiene un cuarto muy desordenado. (b) estaba imitando las palabras de su mamá. (c) quería que sus muñecas aprendieran buenos hábitos.

WORKING WITH WORDS AND PATTERNS

- **¿Tienes algo planeado . . . ?** *Do you have something (anything) planned . . . ?* **¿ . . . ir a alguna parte . . . visitar a alguien?** *. . . to go somewhere (anywhere) . . . to visit someone (anyone)?* ~ When discussing possible plans, use **algo** (*something*), **alguna parte** (*somewhere*), or **alguien** (*someone*) to refer to *what* a person may want to do or *where* he or she may want to go or *whom* he or she may want to visit. Notice that in English we generally use the words *anything*, *anywhere*, or *anyone* in this context.

- *Highlight on the subjunctive:* **¿Hay algo que necesite ser arreglado?** *Is there something (anything) that needs to be fixed? . . .* **Nada que me venga a la cabeza.** *Nothing that comes to mind.* ~ Use the subjunctive in a descriptive clause following an indefinite or negative subject. In the first sentence, **algo** is vague and indefinite, because there may or may not be something needing fixing, so **necesite** is in the subjunctive. In the second sentence, **Nada** is negative because it means *nothing*, something that does not exist, so **venga** is in the subjunctive. (See page 140.)

- **Me encanta cuando me puedo . . .** *I'm thrilled (delighted) when I can . . .* ~ Literally, the common expression **Me encanta** means *It enchants me.* This expresses emotion, but since the clause following it does not start with **que**, it does not need a subjunctive. If the following clause starts with **que**, this expression requires a subjunctive. **Me encanta que *estés* aquí.** (subjunctive) *I'm thrilled (that) you are here.* **Me encanta cuando *estás* aquí.** (no subjunctive) *I'm thrilled when you are here.*

- **¡sin sentirme culpable!** *without feeling guilty!* ~ Spanish always uses an infinitive after a preposition, even though in English the gerund (*-ing*) is used. **Se fueron sin *hablar* con nosotros.** *They left without talking with us.* **En vez de *escribir* una carta, mandaron un email.** *Instead of writing a letter, they sent an e-mail.*

KEY WORDS AND PHRASES

¿Tienes algo planeado para hoy? Do you have anything planned for today?

¿Quieres ir a alguna parte . . . ? Do you want to go anywhere?

¿Hay algo que necesite ser arreglado? Is there anything that needs to be fixed?

¿Algo por hacer? Anything to be done?

pasar el día en mi taller to spend the day in my workshop

¡sin sentirme culpable! without feeling guilty!

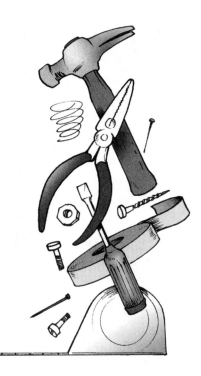

61 ¡A trabajar sin culpa!

To work without guilt!

WHAT YOU CAN LEARN   Asking about someone's plans for the day, talking about not feeling guilty

PUTTING IT ALL TOGETHER (RESUMIÉNDOLO TODO). (Answers on page 217.)

Juan se levanta, se viste y saluda a Eli con un beso. «¡Buenos días, querida! ¿Tienes (1) _____ _____ para hoy?» Eli responde que no. Juan continúa con sus preguntas, «¿Quieres ir (2) _____ _____ _____ . . . visitar a alguien? ¿Hay algo que (3) _____ ser arreglado? ¿Algo por hacer?» Eli contesta, «Nada que me (4) _____ _____ _____ _____.» Luego, Juan va a trabajar, pensando, «Me encanta cuando me puedo pasar el día en mi taller . . . ¡sin (5) _____ _____!»

DID YOU GET IT? (¿COMPRENDISTE?) (Answers on page 217.)

¿Por qué le pregunta Juan a Eli sobre sus planes para el día? Porque Juan . . . (a) quiere trabajar y no sentirse culpable. (b) necesita que ella lo ayude en su taller. (c) piensa pasar el día haciendo algo especial.

WORKING WITH WORDS AND PATTERNS

- **Tengo miedo.** *I'm scared (afraid).* ~ Literally, *I have fear*. Use **tener** for expressing fear, hunger, thirst, sleepiness, guilt, and other conditions that in English are expressed with the verb *to be*. **Tengo hambre.** *I am hungry.* **Tenemos sed.** *We are thirsty.* **Los niños tienen sueño.** *The kids are sleepy.* (See page 4.)

- **Echo de menos a Isabel.** *I miss Elizabeth.* ~ Use the common idiom **echar de menos** when talking about feeling lonely for some person, place or thing. Literally, it means *to throw for less* (someone or something). In Latin America, the verb **extrañar** is also used, with the same meaning. **Extrañamos (Echamos de menos) a nuestros antiguos vecinos que se mudaron el año pasado.** *We miss our former neighbors who moved away last year.*

- *Highlight on the subjunctive:* **No quiero dormir sola.** *I don't want to sleep alone.* **¡Quiero que tú y papi se cambien de nuevo arriba!** *I want you and Dad to move back upstairs!* ~ To express what you want to do (or not do), you can use **(no) querer** + an infinitive. **Quiero viajar por tren. No quiero viajar por avión.** *I want to travel by train. I don't want to travel by plane.* But when you tell others what you want *them* to do, you have a change of subject, and so you have to use a secondary clause and a subjunctive. **Quiero que ustedes viajen por tren.** *I want you to travel by train.*

- **la habitación de Isabel** *Elizabeth's room* ~ For the room, say **la habitación**, **el cuarto**, or **la pieza**. These are all synonyms. For a *conference room* or a *room for public use*, say **la sala**.

- **Y dijo que se sentiría bien . . .** *And she said that she would feel fine . . .* **Que eso la haría sentirse mayor** *That this would make her feel older* ~ These are classic examples of the use of the conditional to express the future of the past. In the present, the first sentence would be: *She says that she will feel fine.* But, if you put that sentence in the past, the *will* changes to *would*.

KEY WORDS AND PHRASES

Echo de menos a Isabel.
I miss Elizabeth.

¡Quiero que tú y papi se cambien . . . ! I want you and Dad to move . . . !

la habitación de Isabel
Elizabeth's room

Y dijo que se sentiría bien. And she said that she would feel fine.

Que eso la haría sentirse mayor. That this would make her feel older.

. . . siempre funcionan bien en teoría.
. . . always work well in theory.

62 Tengo miedo, Mamá

I'm scared, Mom

WHAT YOU CAN LEARN   Expressing fear, saying you miss someone, telling people what you want and don't want

PUTTING IT ALL TOGETHER (RESUMIÉNDOLO TODO). (Answers on page 217.)

Abril no puede dormir y baja la escalera. Despierta a su madre y le dice, «¿Mami . . . ? (1) _____ _____. No quiero dormir sola allá arriba. (2) _____ _____ _____ a Isabel.» Eli le responde, «Cielo mío, Isabel ahora está en la universidad.» Abril insiste, «¡Quiero que tú y Papi se (3) _____ de nuevo arriba! . . . » Eli se ablanda, «¿Por qué no te vuelves a tu cama y yo duermo en la (4) _____ _____ _____ esta noche?» Juan protesta, «Abril tiene al perro . . . ¡Y dijo (5) _____ _____ _____ _____!» Eli piensa, «Esas cosas siempre funcionan bien en teoría.»

DID YOU GET IT? (¿COMPRENDISTE?) (Answers on page 217.)

¿Qué piensa Eli con respecto a la disciplina de los hijos? Piensa que lo más importante es . . . (a) tomar decisiones y no cambiarlas. (b) hablar con los niños sobre todas las posibilidades. (c) ser flexible y responder a la situación actual.

WORKING WITH WORDS AND PATTERNS

- **¿Un resfrío y la gripe . . . ?** *A cold and the flu . . . ?* ~ To say *I have a cold*, you can say **Tengo un resfrío** or **Estoy resfriado(a).** To say *I have the flu*, say **Tengo gripe** (or in Mexico and some other places, **Tengo gripa**).

- **estornudos . . . tos . . . mal del estómago** *sneezes . . . cough . . . stomach upset* ~ As often happens, the nouns **el estornudo** and **la tos** have corresponding verbs: **estornudar** and **toser. Estornuda (Está estornudando) mucho.** *He is sneezing a lot.* **Tose (Está tosiendo) toda la noche.** *She is coughing all night long.* When someone sneezes, it is common to say, **¡Salud!** The expression **mal de** + part of the body can be used for many health problems. **Estoy mal de la espalda (del corazón, de los riñones).** *I have a bad back (a bad heart, bad kidneys).*

- *Highlight on the subjunctive:* **Un remedio . . . guarantizado para hacer que se sienta mejor . . .** *A medicine . . . guaranteed to make you feel better . . .* ~ Always use the subjunctive after **para hacer que** because this phrase expresses purpose and influence of one thing or person on another, as well as a projection into the future. Here the reflexive verb **sentirse** is in the subjunctive: **se sienta.**

- **un remedio** *medicine* ~ This cognate for the English word *remedy* is commonly used to talk about a medicine, but **el medicamento** is also used a lot. The word **medicina** exists, but in most places it is used only to refer to the field of study. **Ahora tengo que tomar mi remedio (medicamento).** *I have to take my medicine now.* **Alejandro estudia medicina en la universidad.** *Alexander is studying medicine at the university.*

- **¿Aló . . . ?** *Hello?* ~ How you say *Hello* on the telephone depends on what part of the Spanish-speaking world you are calling or answering in. The word **Aló** is universal and will be understood anywhere, but it is not the most common greeting in many places. Mexicans usually say **Bueno** (*Well, Good*) when calling or answering the phone; Spaniards, **Dígame** (*Tell me*); Cubans (whether in Cuba or Miami) **Oigo** (*I hear*). In the rest of Latin America, people usually say **Aló** or **Hola.**

KEY WORDS AND PHRASES

¿Un resfrío y la gripe la hacen sentirse miserable? Are a cold and flu making you feel miserable?

¿Padece de estornudos . . . ? Are you suffering from sneezing (sneezes) . . . ?

¿Tos? ¿Mal del estómago? A cough? Stomach upset?

un remedio ya probado y verdadero a tried and true medicine

para hacer que se sienta mejor to make you feel better

Resfriada y miserable

Down with a cold and miserable

WHAT YOU CAN LEARN   Talking about having a cold or flu, greeting on the telephone

PUTTING IT ALL TOGETHER (RESUMIÉNDOLO TODO). (Answers on page 217.)

Isabel está en su cuarto en la universidad, tosiendo y sonándose. Pone el radio y escucha, «¿Un (1) _____ _____ _____ _____ la hacen sentirse miserable? ¿Padece de estornudos? ¿Tos? ¿(2) _____ _____ _____? Un (3) _____ ya probado y verdadero, guarantizado para hacer (4) _____ _____ _____ _____ . . . » Isabel apaga el radio y toma el teléfono. Llama a su madre y dice, «¿(5) _____? ¿Mami?»

DID YOU GET IT? (¿COMPRENDISTE?) (Answers on page 217.)

¿Cuál es el remedio «ya probado y verdadero» para los problemas de Isabel? . . . (a) una conversación con su mamá (b) las pildoras que tiene en su baño (c) el medicamento que describen en el radio

El español en tu vida

Spanish in your life

Practice what you've learned from Comics 56–63. (Answers on pages 217–218)

A. ¿QUÉ SE DICE? (*What do you say?*)

1. Your father looks all bent over and in pain. **¿Qué se dice?**

2. You are very angry with someone and decide, when that person wakes up, you will tell her (or him) off. **¿Qué se dice?**

3. Someone insults you by labeling you in a certain way and you defend yourself by denying it. **¿Qué se dice?**

4. You want to reassure someone that nothing needs to be done and everything is fine. **¿Qué se dice?**

5. You are afraid. **¿Qué se dice?**

B. PALABRAS CLAVES (*Key words*)

What key words are missing in the following comics? Fill in each blank with the correct Spanish word.

1.

2.

3.

4.

5.

C. LAS PARTES DEL CUERPO (*Parts of the body*)

Label the following drawing with the missing parts of the body, which can be found in the comic strips (#56 and #63) and notes.

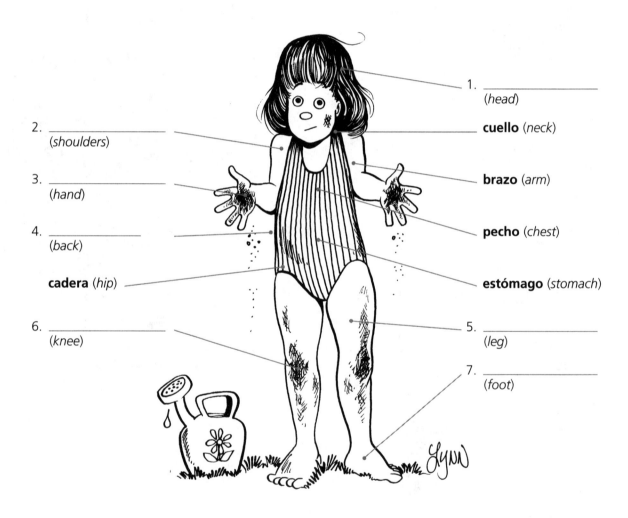

1. _____
   (*head*)

   cuello (*neck*)

   brazo (*arm*)

   pecho (*chest*)

   estómago (*stomach*)

2. _____
   (*shoulders*)

3. _____
   (*hand*)

4. _____
   (*back*)

   cadera (*hip*)

5. _____
   (*leg*)

6. _____
   (*knee*)

7. _____
   (*foot*)

D. ABRIL Y SU CASITA DE MUÑECAS

Make a list in Spanish of all the things in the picture that you can name.

WORKING WITH WORDS AND PATTERNS

- **¡Pruébatela!** *Try it on!* ~ Use the verb **probar** when talking about trying something on or trying something out for the first time. **Nunca he comido paella, pero quiero probarla.** *I've never eaten paella, but I want to try it.* For the familiar command, the form is **prueba**. Add the reflexive pronoun **te** to emphasize that you are trying it on yourself and **la** for *it* (since it refers to **una chaqueta**, which is feminine: **prueba + te + la = ¡Pruébatela!** *Try it on!*

- **Esa chaqueta se te ve de maravilla.** *That jacket looks like a million dollars on you.* ~ Here is a good formula for complimenting a friend when he or she looks great in some outfit. **Esa (Ese) . . . se te (le, les) ve de maravilla.** Literally, it means, *That _____ sees itself like a marvel on you.*

- *Highlight on the subjunctive:* **Deja que te compre algunas cosas.** *Let me buy a few things for you.* ~ When you say *Let me do something*, you are really telling someone to permit that you do something. There is an expression of implied command and a change of subject so you have to use the subjunctive.

- *Highlight on the subjunctive:* **Me siento feliz de que podamos comprar juntas.** *I feel happy that we can shop together.* ~ After an expression of emotion, use the subjunctive in a clause with a change of subject. (See page 139.)

- *Highlight on the past subjunctive:* **Hubo una época en que no querías que te vieran en público con tu madre.** *There was a time when you didn't want anyone to see you in public with your mother.* ~ After an expression of implied command ending in **que**, you need a subjunctive when there is a change of subject. Since the main part of the idea is in a past tense (the imperfect), the *past subjunctive* (not the present) must be used in the second part. (See page 145.)

- *Highlight on the past subjunctive:* **Eso era antes que empezara a comprar todo . . .** *That was before she began to buy everything . . .* ~ The phrase **antes (de) que** and certain others (**para que, con tal de que**) always take the subjunctive after them because of their meaning.

KEY WORDS AND PHRASES

De veras que las eché de menos. I really missed (both of) you.

¡Mira esa belleza! Look at that beauty (that gorgeous thing)!

¡Pruébatela! Try it on!

Esa chaqueta se te ve de maravilla. That jacket looks great on you.

Deja que te compre algunas cosas. Let me buy some things for you.

Hubo una época en que no querías que te vieran . . . There was a time when you didn't want anyone to see you . . .

¡Caramba . . . ! ¡Esto es divertido! Wow . . . ! This is fun!

WHAT YOU CAN LEARN   Complimenting a person on how he or she looks in an outfit, telling someone to let you do something, uses of the present and past subjunctive

PUTTING IT ALL TOGETHER (RESUMIÉNDOLO TODO). (Answers on page 218.)

Isabel está en casa, de visita de la universidad, y va de compras con su mamá y con su hermanita Abril. Ve en un escaparate una chaqueta que le gusta y Eli le dice, «¡(1) _____!» Luego, exclama, «¡Esa chaqueta (2) _____ _____ _____ _____ , Isabel! ¡Yo te la compro!» Cuando su hija protesta, insiste, «¡(3) _____ _____ _____ _____ algunas cosas para la universidad!» Después, Isabel dice, «¡Esto es (4) _____!» Eli dice, «Me siento feliz, querida. Hubo una época en que no querías (5) _____ _____ _____ en público con tu madre . . . » Luego, Abril observa, «Eso era antes que empezara a comprar todo con su propio dinero . . . »

DID YOU GET IT? (¿COMPRENDISTE?) (Answers on page 218.)

¿Qué ha comprendido Abril? . . . (a) la necesidad de la comunicación (b) la importancia del dinero (c) la dificultad de encontrar ropa

WORKING WITH WORDS AND PATTERNS

- **¡Qué chiquero!** *What a pigsty!* ~ Another common way of saying, *What a mess!* is **¡Qué lío!** (literally, *What a tie-up!*). There are also many regional variations on this theme. In the Southern Cone: **¡Qué despelote!** (*What an undoing of hair!*) In Costa Rica: **¡Qué zambrote!** (*What a Moorish festival!*) In Mexico: **¡Qué desmadre!** (*What an unmothering!*) In Peru: **¡Qué laberinto!** (*What a labyrinth!*) In Spain: **¡Qué follón!** (*What a ruckus!*)

- **¡Esto es ridículo!** *This is ridiculous!* ~ Use the neuter form **esto** for *this*, when referring to a whole situation. When referring to a specific object, use **éste** or **ésta**, depending on whether it is masculine or feminine. **Este es el mejor auto del mundo.** *This is the best car in the world.* **Esta fue la silla de mi abuelo.** *This was my grandfather's chair.* **¿Cómo? ¿Los niños se fueron sin pedir permiso? ¡Esto es el colmo!** *What? The children left without asking permission? That's the last straw!* (**Esto** refers to the whole situation.)

- **¡No lo puedo tolerar!** *I can't put up with it!* ~ Use this formula for many occasions by inserting a different infinitive at the end. You can also put the **lo** (*it*) at the very end by attaching it to the infinitive. **No lo puedo comprender. No puedo comprenderlo.** *I can't understand it.* **No lo puedo alcanzar. No puedo alcanzarlo.** *I can't reach it.*

- **¡No lo puedo creer!** *I can't believe it!* ~ You can express the sentiment with the Spanish rhyme: **Si no lo veo, no lo creo.** *If I weren't seeing it, I wouldn't be believing it.*

- **Se está tranquilizando con la edad.** *(She) is calming down with age.* ~ To describe a slow and gradual change, you can use the present progressive. (See page 6.) Notice that you can put the reflexive pronoun either at the very beginning of the verb as it is in the comic strip, or else you can attach it to the present participle and put it at the very end. **Se están adaptando a sus nuevas circunstancias. Están adaptándose a sus nuevas circunstancias.** *They are adjusting to their new circumstances.*

KEY WORDS AND PHRASES

¡Qué chiquero! What a pigsty!

¿Cómo puede vivir de esa manera? How can she live that way?

¡Esto es ridículo! This is ridiculous!

¡No lo puedo tolerar (creer)! I can't put up with (believe) it!

Se está tranquilizando con la edad. (She) is calming down with age.

todo mi lavado all my laundry

No dijo ni una palabra. She didn't even say one word.

65 Tanta ropa sucia

So much dirty clothing

WHAT YOU CAN LEARN   Griping about a mess, venting frustration, expressing disbelief

PUTTING IT ALL TOGETHER (RESUMIÉNDOLO TODO). (Answers on page 218.)

Eli entra en el cuarto de Isabel y piensa, «¡(1) _____ _____! Isabel tiene que volver a la universidad ya . . . ¡Y mira toda esa (2) _____ _____!» Piensa, «¿Cómo puede vivir de esa manera? ¡(3) _____ _____ _____! ¡No lo puedo tolerar!» Más tarde, entra en el cuarto de Isabel, pero esta vez lo encuentra . . . limpio y ordenado. Mientra tanto, Isabel y su amiga van en auto a la lavandería, e Isabel observa, «¡(4) _____ _____ _____ _____ . . . ! Pero mi mamá (5) _____ _____ _____ con la edad . . . ! Dejé todo mi lavado para el último día . . . ¡y no dijo ni una palabra!»

DID YOU GET IT? (¿COMPRENDISTE?) (Answers on page 218.)

¿Qué muestra la tira? . . . (a) Eli no comprende el punto de vista de su hija. (b) Isabel no comprende el punto de vista de su mamá. (c) Ninguna de las dos comprende el punto de vista de la otra.

WORKING WITH WORDS AND PATTERNS

- **Se está poniendo frío . . .** *It's getting cold . . .* /**que uno se está poniendo viejo . . .** *that one is growing old* ~ To talk about a change that is taking place gradually, use the present progressive. In these two examples the verb is **ponerse** (*to get, to become*), a reflexive verb that requires the use of **se**.

- **¡Se acerca el invierno!** *Winter is coming (approaching)!* ~ Notice that word order in Spanish is more flexible than in English and the subject can come before the verb or, as in this case, after the verb. You could say, **¡El invierno se acerca!** and that would be just as correct and would not change the meaning. The choice is dictated by personal taste or style.

- *Highlight on the subjunctive:* **No estoy muy segura de que me guste esa expresión.** *I'm not so sure that I like that expression.* ~ After a statement of doubt or unreality, the subjunctive is used if there is a change of subject in the second part. (See page 139.) Here the subject of the first part is **yo** (*I*), but in the second part, the subject of the verb **gustar** is **esa expresión** since literally you are saying, . . . *that expression is pleasing to me.* **No estoy seguro *de poder encontrar* el auto.** *I'm not sure that I'll be able to find the car.* (No change of subject, so an infinitive is used, not a subjunctive.) **No estoy seguro *de que llegue* Lorena.** *I'm not sure that Lorena will arrive.* (Change of subject from **yo** to Lorena, so a subjunctive is used.)

- **el golpe de darse cuenta que uno se está poniendo viejo** *the shock (blow) of realizing that one is getting old* ~ Don't be fooled by the deceptive cognate **realizar**. In Spanish, this means *to realize* only in the sense of *to realize a dream or ambition.* **Daniel realizó su sueño de construir su propia casa.** *Daniel realized his dream of building his own house.* To say *to realize* in the sense of *to understand something*, use the expression **darse cuenta (de)** (literally, *to give oneself an account of*). **Me di cuenta de mis limitaciones.** *I realized* (i.e., *understood*) *my limitations.*

KEY WORDS AND PHRASES

¡Se está poniendo frío! It's getting cold!

Puedo oler la escarcha . . . I can smell the frost . . .

Lo puedo sentir en mis huesos. I can feel it in my bones.

que se podría decir . . . that one could say . . .

No estoy muy segura de que me guste . . . I'm not so sure that I like . . .

uno es tonto y descontrolado one (a person) is dopey and out of control

. . . puede ser la mejor época de la vida . . . can be the best stage of life

66 En el invierno de la vida

In the wintertime of life

WHAT YOU CAN LEARN   Describing gradual changes, expressing doubt, talking about the stages of life

PUTTING IT ALL TOGETHER (RESUMIÉNDOLO TODO). (Answers on page 218.)

El abuelo Jaime está dando un paseo con su novia Iris cuando ella le dice, «¡(1) _____ _____ _____ _____, Jaime! ¡Se acerca el invierno!» Jaime dice, «Supongo que se podría decir que estamos en el invierno de nuestras vidas . . . .» Iris contesta, «(2) _____ _____ _____ de que (3) _____ _____ esa expresión.» Jaime continúa, «En la "primavera de la vida" (4) _____ _____ _____ _____ _____—en el "verano de la vida" uno está trabajando . . . Pero el invierno puede ser (5) _____ _____ _____ de la vida!»

DID YOU GET IT? (¿COMPRENDISTE?) (Answers on page 218.)

Según Jaime, ¿por qué puede ser el invierno la mejor época de la vida? . . . (a) Porque uno se da cuenta de que se está poniendo viejo. (b) Porque uno espera que sea largo, calientito y feliz. (c) Porque uno está teniendo bebés.

WORKING WITH WORDS AND PATTERNS

- *Highlight on the subjunctive:* **. . . te tengo que pedir que lleves tus cosas** *I have to ask you to take your things* ~ Literally, this means: *I have to ask that you take your things.* The subject of the first part is **yo** (*I*) and of the second part is **tú** (*you*), so the subjunctive must be used after the implied command given in the verb **pedir** which means *to ask for something, to request.* (See pages 139–140.)

- **¿Cuántas veces me lo has pedido ya?** *How many times have you asked it of me already?* ~ The small word **ya** often appears in conversation for emphasis. It can be translated to English in different ways: *already, now, really,* or even, *soon.* **Ya he visto esa película.** *I've already seen that movie.* **¡Ya voy!** *I'm coming right now!* **Ya lo creo.** *I really believe that.* **Ya veremos.** *We shall soon see (what happens).*

- **¡Si estos juguetes . . . no están en tu cuarto . . . , lo voy a tirar todo a la basura!** *If these toys . . . are not in your room . . . , I'm going to throw everything in the garbage!* ~ To make such a threat, use this formula: **Si** + clause with verb in the regular present tense, + clause in future tense (or with **ir a** + infinitive). You explain first the condition, and then the consequence. This is seen as a logical statement of connection in Spanish, and the subjunctive is not used.

- **¡Son mías!** *They're mine!* ~ The short possessives (**mi, tu, su, nuestro, vuestro**) are used *in front of* the person or thing referred to: **mis juguetes** *my toys,* **tu casa** *your house,* **sus perros** *his* (*her, their, your* [formal] *dogs*), **nuestra reunión** *our meeting.* In other positions, use the long possessives: **mío, tuyo, suyo, nuestro, vuestro.** (Notice that **nuestro** and **vuestro** do not change.) **Los niños tienen una maleta. Aquí está la mía, pero dónde está la suya?** *The children have a suitcase. Here is mine, but where is theirs?*

- **Pero la próxima vez . . .** *But next time . . .* ~ Use **vez** or **veces** for *time* or *times,* when referring to a specific moment or moments: **una vez** *once* (*one time*), **algunas veces** or **a veces** *sometimes* (*at times*), **aquella vez** *that time.*

KEY WORDS AND PHRASES

¿Cuántas veces te tengo que pedir . . . How many times do I have to ask you . . .

. . . que lleves tus cosas arriba? . . . to take your things upstairs?

al final del día at the end of the day

Lo voy a tirar todo a la basura. I'm going to throw it all in the garbage.

Lo siento. Hablaba en serio. I'm sorry. I was talking seriously. (I meant what I said.)

El camión las recogerá mañana . . . The truck will pick them up tomorrow . . .

¡Una buena amenaza . . . A good threat . . .

. . . es aquella que no hay que cumplir! . . . is one that doesn't have to be kept (fulfilled)!

Los juguetes de Abril

April's toys

WHAT YOU CAN LEARN   Asking someone to do something, making a threat, saying you're sorry

PUTTING IT ALL TOGETHER (RESUMIÉNDOLO TODO). (Answers on page 218.)

Eli descubre juguetes en la escalera y grita, «Abril, ¿cuántas veces te (1) _____ _____ _____ _____ _____ tus cosas arriba? ¡Si estos juguetes y libros y ropa (2) _____ _____ _____ _____ _____ al final del día, lo voy a tirar todo a la basura!» Un poco más tarde, Eli empieza a recoger los juguetes, cuando llega Abril y protesta, «¡No puedes tirarlas! ¡Son mías!» Eli responde, «(3) _____ _____. Hablaba en serio» Abril arma un escándalo y Eli dice, «Está bien. Puedes llevar tus cosas arriba, pero (4) _____ _____ _____ . . . » Luego, Eli se sienta y piensa, «¡Una buena (5) _____ es aquella que no hay que cumplir!»

DID YOU GET IT? (¿COMPRENDISTE?) (Answers on page 218.)

Al fin, ¿cómo pudo comunicarse Eli con su hija Abril? . . . (a) con la acción (b) con una pregunta (c) con una amenaza

WORKING WITH WORDS AND PATTERNS

- **nos damos cuenta de** *we realize* ~ Use the expression **darse cuenta de** to say *realize* in the sense of *to understand* or *comprehend something*. Since this does not imply command, emotion, doubt or unreality, the subjunctive is not used after it. Notice that the reflexive pronoun changes to match the subject.

- **el cocinar, la limpieza, la ropa recién doblada** *the cooking, the cleaning, the freshly folded clothes* ~ The first item in this short list of household chores is **el cocinar**, *the cooking*. Use **el** + the infinitive when you want to talk about a verb as if it were a noun. **El correr es mi ejercicio favorito.** *Running is my favorite exercise.*

- **Querida mamá . . . Con amor** *Dear Mom . . . With love* ~ These are typical ways of beginning and ending a friendly letter. Usually you will start with **Querido(a)** and the name, or **Queridos(as) amigos(as)**, but there are many common expressions you can use to close: **Con cariño** (*With affection*), **Un abrazo** (*A hug*), or **Besos y abrazos** (*Hugs and kisses*—but in reverse order). For business letters, begin with **Estimado(a) señor** or **Estimados(as) señores** and close with **Atentamente**.

- *Highlight on the subjunctive:* **Queremos que sepas que . . .** *We want you to know (that you know) that . . .* ~ This is a handy formula to show appreciation. After an expression of implied command (**queremos que**) the subjunctive must be used when there is a change of subject. That is why **sepas** (from the verb **saber**, *to know*) is in the subjunctive.

- **Lo dábamos por hecho.** *We took it for granted.* ~ This common idiom can also be **dar por sentado. La verdad es que la damos por sentada.** *The truth is that we take her for granted.*

- **Gracias por ser una mamá tan fantástica.** *Thanks for being such a fantastic Mom.* ~ Change this useful phrase to suit the circumstances when you wish to thank someone for their help or favors over a period of time. **Señor Méndez, gracias por ser un jefe tan comprensivo.** *Mr. Mendez, thank you for being such an understanding boss.*

- **esa tarjeta tan bella** *such a lovely card* ~ Here is the way to say *such a* (*lovely, good, difficult*, etc.). . . . After the person or thing you are talking about, put **tan** + the adjective: **unos regalos tan lindos** *such lovely gifts*.

KEY WORDS AND PHRASES

viviendo fuera de casa
living away from home

nos damos cuenta de todo we realize
everything

nos diste tus valores, tu juicio . . . you gave us your values, your judgment . . .

queremos que sepas . . .
we want you to know . . .

te apreciamos ahora más que nunca we appreciate you more than ever

esa tarjeta tan bella
such a beautiful card

De hecho, compartido entre los dos . . .
In fact, split between the two of us . . .

Happy Mother's Day!

WHAT YOU CAN LEARN Expressing appreciation, formulas for beginning and ending letters, thanking someone for their help

PUTTING IT ALL TOGETHER (RESUMIÉNDOLO TODO). (Answers on page 218.)

La familia se ha reunido para honrar a Eli. Isabel le dice, «(1) ¡_____ _____ _____ _____ _____, Mamá!» Eli lee la tarjeta: «Querida mamá, Ahora que estamos viviendo fuera de casa, (2) _____ _____ _____ de todo lo que siempre has hecho por nosotros. Y queremos que sepas (3) _____ _____ _____ ahora más que nunca. (4) _____ _____ _____ una mamá tan fantástica. Con amor, Miguel e Isabel.» Eli exclama, «Ohhhhh . . . ¡No puedo creer que . . . me dieron (5) _____ _____ _____ _____!»

DID YOU GET IT? (¿COMPRENDISTE?) (Answers on page 218.)

Después de que Eli lee la tarjeta, ¿cómo cambia Miguel la atmósfera emocional? Miguel explica como compraron la tarjeta y da una explicación muy . . . (a) complicada. (b) sentimental. (c) práctica.

WORKING WITH WORDS AND PATTERNS

- **esta boda** *this wedding* ~ You can also say: **el casamiento** or **el matrimonio** for *wedding*. The word **matrimonio** has another meaning too: *married couple*. **¿Viene el matrimonio García?** *Are the Garcías coming?*

- *Highlight on the subjunctive:* **Quiero que esta boda sea perfecta . . .** *I want this wedding to be perfect . . .* ~ Use the subjunctive in an idea that comes after an expression of implied command **(Quiero que)** when there is a change of subject **(yo/esta boda)**. (See pages 139–140.) You can adapt this pattern for other occasions. **Quiero que esta fiesta sea maravillosa.** *I want this party to be marvelous.*

- *Highlight on the subjunctive:* **Así que entendamos bien las cosas.** *So let's understand things well. (Let's get things straight.)* ~ To give a *Let's . . .* command to a person or a group, use the **nosotros** form of the present subjunctive. **¡Caminemos un poco!** *Let's walk a little!*

- **a la derecha . . . a la izquierda . . .** *to the right . . . to the left . . .* ~ Use these phrases to tell someone to go right or left. To tell them to go straight ahead, say: **¡Derecho!** *Straight ahead!*

- **¿Novio? Tú y el padrino entran ahora . . .** *Groom? You and the best man come in now . . .* **¿Novia? Toma el brazo de tu padre.** *Bride? Take your father's arm.* ~ Deanna's mother gives instructions to the bridal party and sometimes she uses the regular present tense to tell people what they are doing or will be doing, as when she speaks to the groom (**tú y el padrino entran**). At other times she uses the command forms, as in the second example when she speaks to the bride (**toma**). You can give instructions either way, or mix them. **Niños, van primero a la farmacia y luego regresan a casa. Compren todas las cosas de la lista.** *Children, you go first to the drugstore and then you return home* (regular present tense). *Buy everything on the list* (**ustedes** command form).

- **el padrino** *the best man . . .* **la madrina** *the maid (matron) of honor* ~ Besides being roles in a wedding, these words also mean *godfather* and *godmother*, the adults appointed for a child at baptism to be his or her special guardians for life. The words **novio** and **novia** also have another meaning: *boyfriend* and *girlfriend*.

KEY WORDS AND PHRASES

¡Su atención, por favor! (May I have) your attention, please!

Quiero que esta boda sea . . . I want this wedding to be . . .

la iglesia . . . dos ensayos the church . . . two rehearsals

¡Los ujieres! Tomen a las damas solteras del brazo. Ushers! Take the single ladies by the arm.

¿Novio? Tú y el padrino entran ahora. Groom? You and the best man come in now.

La madrina y las damas de compañía . . . The maid of honor and bridesmaids . . .

siguen en orden de su estatura. follow in order of their height.

¿Novia? Toma el brazo de tu padre. Bride? Take your father's arm.

69 — Preparativos para la boda

Wedding preparations

WHAT YOU CAN LEARN — Saying what you want something to be like, giving a series of instructions, talking about a wedding

PUTTING IT ALL TOGETHER (RESUMIÉNDOLO TODO). (Answers on page 218.)

Es el ensayo para la boda en la iglesia. La madre de Deana da instrucciones, «¡Su atención, por favor! Quiero que (1) _____ _____ _____ _____ . . . Así que (2) _____ _____ las cosas . . . La familia y amistades del novio van (3) _____ _____ _____, los de la novia, a la izquierda . . . ¿Novio? Tú y el padrino (4) _____ ahora . . . La madrina y las damas de compañía siguen y por favor (5) _____ al compás de la música . . . ¿Novia? . . . ¡Sonríe! ¡Y no te olvides, querida! ¡Este es tú día!»

DID YOU GET IT? (¿COMPRENDISTE?) (Answer on page 218.)

¿Por qué parece cómico cuando la madre de Deana le dice a la novia, «¡Este es tu día!»? Parece cómico porque . . . (a) la boda realmente tiene lugar al día siguiente. (b) la persona que manda es la madre de Deana. (c) nadie ha comprendido las instrucciones.

WORKING WITH WORDS AND PATTERNS

- **Nos hemos reunido aquí . . .** *We have gathered here together . . .*
  ~ Use the verb **reunirse** whenever you want to say *to get together* or
  to meet. Remember that it is a reflexive verb and so must have the
  correct reflexive pronoun to agree with the subject of the sentence.
  The pronoun goes in front of the whole verb, or else it can be
  attached to an infinitive or present participle at the end. **¿Cuando
  nos reunimos tú y yo?** *When are you and I getting together?*
  Reflexive pronoun attached to infinitive: **El jefe quiere reunirse con
  sus empleados todas las semanas.** *The boss wants to meet with
  his employees every week.* Reflexive pronoun attached to present participle: **Los socios del club están reuniéndose ahora mismo.** *The
  members of the club are meeting together right now.*

- **para presenciar** *to witness (attend, be present at)* ~ The verb **presenciar** means *to attend* or *witness*, but it does not mean *to witness* in
  the official or legal sense. Official or legal witnesses are **testigos**.

- **Te tomo a ti.** *I take you.* ~ The phrase **a ti** is redundant here, since
  te *(you)* is already stated. It is used for emphasis, the equivalent of
  saying in English, *I take you*, with the last word said in a louder and
  more forceful way. Use the redundant phrase to emphasize what you
  are saying. **¡A mí me encantan estas flores!** *I like these flowers!*
  (even if some other people don't).

- **Ya puedes besar a la novia.** *You may now kiss the bride.* ~ Don't
  forget to put the personal **a** in front of the object of an action when
  it is a person rather than a thing. That is why the priest says: **besar *a*
  la novia.**

- **uno de los días más felices de mi vida** *one of the happiest days
  of my life* ~ The word **más** means either *more* or *most* and the difference is shown through context. Usually, to show that **más** means
  most, put the definite article right in front of it. **Hoy es un día más
  feliz que ayer.** *This is a happier day than yesterday.* **Hoy es *el día
  más feliz* de toda la semana.** *Today is the happiest day of the
  whole week.*

KEY WORDS AND PHRASES

**Nos hemos reunido
aquí . . .** We have
gathered here together . . .

**para presenciar y
celebrar** to witness and
celebrate

**en el sagrado vínculo
del matrimonio** in the
sacred bond (link)

Te tomo a ti. I take you.

**Ya puedes besar a la
novia.** You may now kiss
the bride.

**uno de los días más
felices de mi vida**
one of the happiest days
of my life

70 La boda de Miguel y Deana

Michael and Deanna's wedding

WHAT YOU CAN LEARN   What is said at a wedding ceremony, how to say this is one of the happiest days of your life

PUTTING IT ALL TOGETHER (RESUMIÉNDOLO TODO). (Answers on page 218.)

Miguel y Deana se casan. El sacerdote anuncia, «Queridos familiares y amigos . . . (1) _____ _____ _____ aquí hoy . . . para (2) _____ y celebrar la unión de Deana Sobinski y Miguel Patterson . . .» Eli empieza a llorar mientras Miguel dice, «Yo, Miguel, te (3) _____ _____ _____, Deana . . . » Luego, el sacerdote le indica, «Ya puedes (4) _____ _____ _____ _____.» Eli mira a Juan y le dice, «Oh, Juan . . . Este tiene que ser uno de (5) _____ _____ _____ _____ de mi vida . . . »

DID YOU GET IT? (¿COMPRENDISTE?) (Answer on page 218.)

¿Por qué parece confundido Juan cuando Eli uno de los días más felices de su vida? Parece confundido porque . . . (a) Eli está llorando. (b) Eli no es una persona emotiva. (c) Eli nunca habla durante las ceremonias.

WORKING WITH WORDS AND PATTERNS

- **¡Sí, te llamo más tarde!** *Yes, I'll call you later.* ~ You can use the present tense instead of the future when talking about something you will be doing very soon. **Bueno, salimos en diez minutos.** *All right, we will be leaving in ten minutes.*

- **¡Aló! ¿Qué tal?** *Hello! How are you?* ~ You can use this way of answering the telephone and you will be understood. But there are other ways that are more common in different parts of the Spanish-speaking world, including the following: **¡Bueno!, ¡Dígame!, ¡Hola!,** and **¡Oigo!**

- **Oh, nada, aquí sentado** *Oh, nothing, sitting here* ~ Michael pretends to be answering the question, *What are you doing?* Notice that in English we would say, *Oh, nothing, sitting here . . .* But in Spanish the past participle **sentado** (*seated*) is used, not the present participle **sentando** (*sitting*). This is because the Spanish mind sees this action as completed, a condition or state that a person is in.

- **en un restaurante carísimo** *in a very, very expensive restaurant* ~ Add **-ísimo(a)** or **ísimos(as)** to adjectives to express forcefully that the person, place or thing possesses the quality to a great degree. This is called the absolute superlative of an adjective. **¿Son bellas las flores? Hombre, ¡son bellísimas!** *Are the flowers lovely? Man, they are very very lovely!* **¿Es inteligente tu profesor? Pues, sí. Es inteligentísimo.** *Is your teacher intelligent? Well, yes. He is very, very intelligent.* Notice that even though the adjective ends in **-e** (**inteligente, elegante**), the ending must be **-ísimo** or **-ísima.**

- **intentando tener una cena romántica con mi esposa** *trying to have a romantic dinner with my wife* ~ Use **intentar** or **tratar de** when you want to say that you are trying to do something. **Siempre intento (trato de) contestar mis emails en seguida.** *I always try to answer my e-mails right away.*

¡Sí, te llamo más tarde! Yes, I'll call you later!

De acuerdo . . . O.K. (Agreed) . . .

¡Aló! ¿Qué tal? Hello! How are you?

sentado en un restaurante carísimo seated in a very, very expensive restaurant

intentando tener una cena romántica trying to have a romantic dinner

Por supuesto, está aquí mismo. Of course, he's right here.

A cell phone rings!

WHAT YOU CAN LEARN   Phrases to use on the phone

PUTTING IT ALL TOGETHER (RESUMIÉNDOLO TODO). (Answers on page 218.)

Miguel y Deana están cenando cuando suena un celular. Un hombre de otra mesa contesta y conversa. Finalmente, se despide, «¡Si, (1) _____ _____ _____ _____! De acuerdo, Luis.» Miguel toma un panecillo y empieza a hablarle como si fuera un teléfono, «¡(2) _____! ¿Qué tal? ¿Yo? Oh, nada, (3) _____ _____ en un restaurante (4) _____ intentando tener una cena romántica . . . ¿Qué? Por supuesto, está aquí mismo.» Entonces Miguel le ofrece el panecillo al señor con el celular, diciéndole, « . . . (5) _____ _____ _____.» Toda la gente se pone a reír.

DID YOU GET IT? (¿COMPRENDISTE?) (Answers on page 218.)

Juzgando de sus acciones, ¿qué opina Miguel del uso de los celulares en los restaurantes? . . . (a) Es normal. (b) Es elegante. (c) Es irritante y descortés.

El español en tu vida

Spanish in your life

Practice what you've learned from Comics 64–71. Answers on page 218.

A. FRASES ÚTILES (*Useful phrases*)

How would you say each of the following useful phrases in Spanish? **¿Cómo se dice?**

1. That jacket looks great on you! **¿Cómo se dice?**

2. This is fun! **¿Cómo se dice?**

3. I can't stand it! **¿Cómo se dice?**

4. I'm sorry. I meant it. (I spoke seriously.) **¿Cómo se dice?**

5. Let's get things straight. (Let's understand things well.) **¿Cómo se dice?**

B. PALABRAS CLAVES (*Key words*)

What key words are missing in the following comics? Fill in each blank
with the correct Spanish word.

1.

2.

3.

4.

5.

C. EN LA IGLESIA (*In the church*)

Make a list in Spanish of all the items in the
picture that you can name.

_____

_____

_____

_____

WORKING WITH WORDS AND PATTERNS

- *Highlight on the subjunctive:* **¡Quizás en el próximo siglo tendremos robots . . . !** *Maybe in the next century we will have robots . . .!/* **Quizás podamos ir al espacio . . .** *Maybe we can go into space . . .* ~ It's easy to speculate in Spanish since there are three ways to say *maybe* (or *perhaps*): **quizás, tal vez,** or **acaso.** If you want to suggest more doubt about whether or not the action will happen, use the subjunctive; less doubt, use the indicative. So, it seems that April thinks that we probably *will have* robots in the next century (since she uses the indicative of tener: **tendremos**), but that *we may* or *may not* go to space (since she uses the subjunctive of **poder: podamos**).

- **Van a haber muchos cambios . . .** *There are going to be many changes . . .* ~ This is one way of giving the future tense of **hay** (*there is, there are*). **Hay** comes from the verb **haber** and this is the **ir a +** infinitive form.

- *Highlight on the subjunctive:* **Espero que existan teles tridimensionales y coches que vuelen.** *I hope that there will be three-dimensional TVs and cars that fly.* **Espero que podamos salvar las ballenas . . .** *I hope that we can save the whales . . .* ~ Use the subjunctive after **Espero que** since it expresses emotion and also an implied command for the future.

- **y cambiar el tiempo cuando queramos** *and change the weather whenever we want to* ~ Use the subjunctive after **cuando** when it refers to a future or possible moment in the future. Here it refers to a *possible* moment, *whenever* wanted or desired. Notice that the word **tiempo** can be either *time* or *weather* and the meaning must be drawn from context. As you saw before, it meant *time* in the phrase **viajar en el tiempo,** but here it means *weather,* as we see when we read the sentence that follows.

- *Highlight on the subjunctive:* **¡Para que todas las fiestas sean con sol!** *So that all the holidays will be sunny (with sunshine)!* ~ Always use subjunctive after **para que** (*so that*) since it expresses implied command. The term for holidays is **días de fiestas** or **días feriados,** but it can also be understood simply from **fiestas.**

KEY WORDS AND PHRASES

¡Quizás en el próximo siglo tendremos . . . Perhaps in the next century we will have . . .

¿Para qué? ¡Si ya tienes uno! For what? If you already have one!

Van a haber muchos cambios. There are going to be many changes.

Espero que existan teles tridimensionales. I hope there will be 3D TVs.

Espero que podamos salvar las ballenas. I hope we will be able to save the whales.

y cambiar el tiempo cuando queramos and change the weather whenever we want to

para que todas las fiestas sean con sol so that all holidays will be sunny

¿Qué esperas tú que cambie . . . ? What do you hope will change . . . ?

What changes will there be?

WHAT YOU CAN LEARN Discussing future possibilities, saying what you wish will happen

PUTTING IT ALL TOGETHER (RESUMIÉNDOLO TODO). (Answers on page 218.)

El abuelo y Abril charlan. Dice la niña, «¿Sabes, abuelo? ¡Quizás en el próximo siglo (1) _____ robots para hacer el té!» Abril continúa, «(2) _____ _____ _____ muchos cambios . . . (3) _____ _____ teles tridimensionales reales y coches que vuelen. (4) _____ _____ _____ al espacio ¡o hasta viajar en el tiempo! Espero que podamos salvar las ballenas . . . » Luego pregunta, «¿Qué (5) _____ _____ _____ en el próximo siglo, abuelo?» Y éste le contesta, «La gente.»

DID YOU GET IT? (¿COMPRENDISTE?) (Answers on page 218.)

¿Qué diferencias hay entre la visión de Abril y la de su abuelo con respecto al futuro? . . . (a) Abril es pesimista y su abuelo es optimista. (b) Abril piensa en la tecnología y su abuelo piensa en la psicología. (c) No hay diferencia.

WORKING WITH WORDS AND PATTERNS

- **¡Gracias por llevarme a cenar!** *Thanks for taking me out to dinner!* ~ When someone has just done a favor for you, thank them with this phrase: **Gracias por** + infinitive.

- **Con gusto.** *With pleasure.* ~ There are different ways of saying *You're welcome.* You can also say: **de nada** (literally, *for nothing*), **no hay de qué** (literally, *there is nothing of which* [*to thank me*]), or **¿para qué?** (literally, *for what?*).

- **¿tú crees que el Día de San Valentín lo crearon . . .** *do you believe that Valentine's Day was created . . .* ~ You can use the impersonal *they* construction (third-person plural) in Spanish as an equivalent for the passive voice, that is, you can say *they did something* instead of *something was done*. Here, the literal translation would be: *do you believe that Valentine's Day it they created . . . ?*

- **para los amantes o por el bien de los centros comerciales** *for lovers or for the good of the shopping centers* ~ A whole book could be written on the differences between **por** and **para**. Since in English there is only one word—*for*—it takes time for English speakers to learn the difference. One way of looking at it is to think of **para** with an arrow going forward and **por** with an arrow coming from behind. **Mañana salimos para Madrid.** *Tomorrow we leave for Madrid.* **Esta carta es para usted.** *This letter is for you.* **El soldado murió por la patria.** *The soldier died for the fatherland.* (Whenever *for* means *for the sake of*, use **por**.) **Ella fue a la tienda por pan.** *She went to the store for bread.* (That is, her motive or reason for going was bread.)

- *Highlight on the past subjunctive:* **Porque si fuera para los amantes, lo habrían puesto en julio.** *Because if it were for lovers, it would have been put in July.* ~ Use a past subjunctive (either the imperfect or the pluperfect) in a contrary-to-fact *if*-clause. This is the kind of clause that presents what *would* happen *if something else were true.* Since it is unreal, the subjunctive must be used. In the second part of the sentence, the conclusion, use the conditional or conditional perfect. (See pages 140 and 80–81.)

KEY WORDS AND PHRASES

¡Gracias por llevarme a cenar! Thanks for taking me out to dinner!

Con gusto. With pleasure. (You're very welcome.)

¿Tú crees que el Día . . . lo crearon . . . ? Do you think that the day . . . was created . . . ?

o por el bien de los centros comerciales or for the good of the shopping centers

porque si fuera para los amantes . . . because if it were for lovers . . .

lo habrían puesto en julio. they would have put it in July.

El Día de San Valentín

Valentine's Day

Thanking someone for doing you a favor, talking about what could be and what might have been.

PUTTING IT ALL TOGETHER (RESUMIÉNDOLO TODO). (Answers on page 218.)

Es el Día de San Valentín. Isabel y su novio Antonio acaban de cenar en un restaurante y salen al frío. Isabel dice, «¡(1) _____ _____ _____ a cenar!» Antonio responde, «¡(2) _____ _____, Isabel!» Al llegar a la casa de Isabel, se besan. Isabel pregunta, «Antonio, ¿tú crees que el Día de San Valentín (3) _____ _____ para los amantes o por el bien de los centros comerciales?» Sin vacilar, Antonio le contesta, «¡Por el bien de los centros comerciales! . . . Porque (4) _____ _____ para los amantes, (5) _____ _____ _____ en julio.»

DID YOU GET IT? (¿COMPRENDISTE?) (Answers on page 218.)

Ese dia, ¿qué obstáculo hay para el amor de Isabel y Antonio? . . . (a) el clima del invierno (b) la falta de dinero (c) una diferencia de opinión

WORKING WITH WORDS AND PATTERNS

- *Highlight on the past subjunctive:* **Te quisiera hacer un regalo** *I would very much like to give you a gift.* ~ Notice that in Spanish you say **hacer un regalo** (*to make a gift*) instead of *to give*, or else you use the verb **regalar** (*to give a gift*) and say, **Quisiera regalarte algo** *I would like to give you something.* Use **quisiera**, the imperfect subjunctive form of **querer**, to express what you would like to do in an extremely refined and courteous way. (See pages 141–142 for imperfect subjunctive forms.) This means the same thing as **me gustaría** or **quiero** except that it is more polite and refined.

- **lo que realmente me gustaría** *what I'd really like* ~ Use **lo que** for *what* when it is not used to ask a question and means *that which.*

- **Yo estaba pensando en un anillo de la amistad.** *I was thinking about a friendship ring.* ~ Use **pensar en** for *to think about* in the sense of having an image of something in your mind and **pensar de** for *to think about* in the sense of having an opinion of something. **¿Piensas mucho en tu novio, Ana?** *Are you thinking a lot about your boyfriend, Anna?*

- **es tan poco romántico** *(it) is so unromantic* ~ Use **poco** (*not very*) when you want to say the opposite of **muy** (*very*) to describe a quality. In English we often do this by putting *un-* in front of the adjective. **Esos libros son poco interesantes.** *These books are uninteresting.*

- *Highlight on the subjunctive:* **Cuando necesites un poco de amistad . . .** *Whenever you need a little bit of friendship . . .* ~ If **cuando** refers to some indefinite moment (or moments) in the future (which may or may not happen), the present subjunctive should be used. (See page 140.) When it refers to a real present or habitual time (which actually happens), the regular (indicative) present is used. **Escucho música cuando trabajo en la computadora.** *I listen to music when(ever) I work on the computer.* (Real, customary time, indicative.) **Amigos míos, ¡vengan a visitarnos cuando quieran!** *My friends, come visit us whenever you want to!* (Indefinite time in the possible future, subjunctive.)

KEY WORDS AND PHRASES

Te quisiera hacer un regalo. I would very much like to give you a present.

¡Qué dulce eres! How sweet you are!

¿Sabes lo que realmente me gustaría? Do you know what I would really like?

Yo estaba pensando en un anillo de la amistad. I was thinking about a friendship ring.

cuando necesites un poco de amistad whenever you need a little bit of friendship

74 Buscando el regalo perfecto

Looking for the perfect gift

WHAT YOU CAN LEARN

Expressing what you wish to do in a very courteous way, telling someone directly what you would really like, talking about an action that will happen "whenever"

PUTTING IT ALL TOGETHER (RESUMIÉNDOLO TODO). (Answers on page 218.)

El abuelo Jaime toma café con su novia Iris en un centro comercial, y luego le dice, «Iris, (1) _____ _____ _____ un regalo para el Día de San Valentín.» Iris contesta, «Ay, Jaime . . . ¡Qué dulce eres! ¿Sabes (2) _____ _____ realmente me gustaría? ¡Un teléfono celular!» Jaime está sorprendido y protesta, «Yo (3) _____ _____ _____ un anillo de la amistad . . . Un teléfono celular es (4) _____ _____ _____ . . . » Iris explica, «No, no lo es . . . (5) _____ _____ un poco de amistad . . . ¡me puedes llamar!»

DID YOU GET IT? (¿COMPRENDISTE?) (Answers on page 218.)

¿Quién es más romántico y quién es más práctico? . . . (a) El es más romántico y ella es más práctica. (b) Ella es más romántica y él es más práctico. (c) Los dos son parecidos: muy prácticos.

WORKING WITH WORDS AND PATTERNS

- **Entonces, con nuestros muchachos en control . . .** *Then, with our boys in control . . .* ~ There are several different way to say *boys* in Spanish. For very young boys, pre-teens, say **niños**; for adolescents or young men in their 20s, **muchachos**, **jóvenes**, or **chicos**.

- **No hay nada más que cosas sobre la guerra.** *There's nothing else but things about war.* ~ When talking about something in general, e.g., money, love, war, business, use the definite article in Spanish (even though you don't use it in English). **El dinero es la raíz de todos los males.** *Money is the root of all evil(s).* But when you are talking about *some* money, love, war, etc., then do not use the definite article. **¡Vamos! Tengo dinero.** *Let's go! I have money.*

- **en prácticamente todas las estaciones de la tele** *on practically all the TV stations* ~ Just as you can say *TV stations* or *channels* in English, you can use various words for this in Spanish: **estaciones**, **cadenas**, or **canales de la tele**.

- *Highlight on the past perfect subjunctive:* **Tuvo que hacerlo o el otro soldado le hubiera disparado a él.** *He had to do it or the other soldier would have fired at him.* ~ Here the second verb **hubiera disparado** is in the pluperfect (also called past perfect) subjunctive. (See pages 143–144.) This is appropriate because the verb expresses what *could have happened.* Notice that in Spanish the reference to *him* is repeated with **le** and then, **a él**, for emphasis.

- *Highlight on the subjunctive:* **¡Vaya! ¡El abuelo nunca me dijo nada de eso!** *Wow! (Good heavens!) Grandpa never told me anything about that!* ~ Use the third-person singular present subjunctive of **ir** to express surprise (either *pleasant* or *unpleasant*). **¡Vaya! ¡Qué regalo más bonito!** *Wow! (Oh, my goodness!) What a beautiful present!* **¡Vaya! ¡Qué desastre!** *Good grief! What a disaster!* Notice that it is correct in Spanish to use the double (or even triple) negative, e.g., . . . **nunca me dijo nada** . . . .

- **es una cosa . . . que debemos recordar** *it is something (that) we should remember* ~ The best way to express moral, psychological, or social obligation is usually with the verb **deber** *to ought to*, which often translates as *should.* **Debes visitar a tu primo que está enfermo.** *You should visit your cousin who is sick.*

KEY WORDS AND PHRASES

Entonces, con nuestros muchachos en control . . . Then, with our boys in control . . .

No hay nada más que . . . There's nothing else than (except) . . .

Tu abuelo peleó en la última guerra mundial. Your grandfather fought in the last world war.

¿Disparó a alguien? Did he shoot anyone?

o el otro soldado le hubiera disparado or the other soldier would have shot him

Porque la guerra se libró por nuestra libertad. Because the war was fought for our freedom.

Es una cosa tan importante que debemos recordar. It's such an important thing that we should remember.

mientras otros tratan tanto de olvidarlo while others try so hard to forget it

Hablando de la guerra

Talking about war

WHAT YOU CAN LEARN   Talking about what might have been or could have been, expressing surprise, saying what we should do

PUTTING IT ALL TOGETHER (RESUMIÉNDOLO TODO). (Answers on page 218.)

Abril escucha la voz de la tele: «Entonces, con (1) _____ _____ en control . . ., avanzamos . . . . » Entra Juan y Abril se le queja, «Papi, no hay nada más que cosas (2) _____ _____ _____ en prácticamente todas las estaciones . . . » Juan dice que su abuelo peleó en la última guerra mundial. Abril le pregunta, «¿Disparó a alguien?» Le contesta que sí y agrega, «Tuvo que hacerlo o el otro soldado (3) _____ _____ _____ _____ _____.» Sorprendida, la niña exclama, «¡ (4) _____! El abuelo nunca me dijo nada de eso.» Juan dice, «Es una cosa tan importante que (5) _____ _____. Mientras otros tratan tanto de olvidarlo.»

DID YOU GET IT? (¿COMPRENDISTE?) (Answers on page 218.)

¿Sobre quién o quiénes aprende Abril algo nuevo? . . . (a) sobre unos muchachos (b) sobre otro soldado (c) sobre su abuelo

WORKING WITH WORDS AND PATTERNS

- **Ven aquí.** *Come here.* ~ For certain very common verbs, there are short irregular forms for the informal commands. So, when you are telling a friend or family member what to do, use these: **ven**, **ten**, **pon**, **haz**, **di**, **ve**, and **sal** for the usual suspects (**venir**, **tener**, **poner**, **hacer**, **decir**, **ver**, and **salir**).

- **No le has limpiado la habitación.** *You haven't cleaned his living quarters (room).* ~ As is often the case in Spanish, it is better to use the definite article (**el**, **la**) than the possessive (**mi**, **su**) when ownership is obvious. So, Elly says literally: *You have not cleaned to him the room* . . . The use of **le** (*to him*) makes the ownership clear in this case.

- **Le hacen falta cama nueva y agua limpia . . .** *He needs a new bed and clean water . . .* ~ Here is one of those times when Spanish word order is completely the reverse of English word order. So (to English speakers) it seems backwards! Literally, *To him it makes a lack (of) a new bed . . .* The useful idiom **Le hace falta** = *He (She, It) needs* . . . is similar in a way to the verb **gustar**; the subject in the Spanish sentence is the object in the English one. Be sure to change the verb to match the subject if it is plural, as in the example given here.

- *Highlight on the past subjunctive:* **¿Cómo te gustaría si fueses tú la que tuvieses que vivir en ese atroz, y asqueroso desorden?** *How would you like it if it were you who had to live in this atrocious and filthy mess?* ~ In Spanish, instead of the past subjunctive forms having just one set of endings (**-ra**), they have two (**-ra**, **-se**). (See page 142.) Here Elly uses the **-se** ending as she asks her daughter to put herself in the place of the unfortunate rabbit and so uses a contrary-to-fact clause: *if it were you—but it is not—the one who had to* . . . The **-ra** endings could also be used and there would be no difference to the meaning.

- **Hay veces que hago unas preguntas verdaderamente estúpidas.** *There are times that I ask really stupid questions.* ~ In general, use the verb **preguntar** to say *to ask questions.* **Necesito preguntar.** *I have to ask (some questions).* But if you want to use the noun **pregunta**, then use it with **hacer.** **Necesito hacerle una pregunta.** *I have to ask him (her) a question.*

KEY WORDS AND PHRASES

¡Cava cava! Dig dig! (sound of bunny digging)

Ven aquí. Come here.

No le has limpiado la habitación en siglos. You haven't cleaned his quarters (cage) in centuries.

Le hacen falta cama nueva y agua limpia . . . He needs a new bed and clean water . . .

si fueses tú la que tuvieses que vivir . . . if it were *you* who had to live . . .

en ese atroz y asqueroso desorden in this atrocious and filthy mess (disorder)

WHAT YOU CAN LEARN Talking about needs, asking people to put themselves in someone else's place, describing a filthy mess

PUTTING IT ALL TOGETHER (RESUMIÉNDOLO TODO). (Answers on page 218.)

Eli oye el señor B., el conejo de Abril que está cavando en su jaula. Llama a su hija, «Abril, (1) _____ _____ _____ _____ la jaula de tu conejo. No le has limpiado la habitación en siglos. (2) _____ _____ _____ cama nueva y agua limpia.» Eli empieza a subir la escalera y le grita a Abril, «¿Cómo te gustaría (3) _____ _____ *tú* la que tuvieses que vivir en ese (4) _____ _____ _____ _____?» Entra en la habitación de Abril y ve que está totalmente sucia y desordenada. Eli piensa, «Hay veces que (5) _____ unas preguntas verdaderamente estúpidas.»

DID YOU GET IT? (¿COMPRENDISTE?) (Answers on page 218.)

¿Qué comprende Eli cuando entra en la habitación de Abril? . . . (a) Que le hace falta una nueva cama. (b) Que hay un problema más grande que la jaula sucia. (c) Que el Sr. B. está cavando porque su habitación está asquerosa.

WORKING WITH WORDS AND PATTERNS

- **Ese disfraz es de lo más mono.** *That costume is the cutest thing.* ~ The noun **mono** means *monkey* but as an adjective, it means *cute, dainty,* or *pretty.* **Vamos al zoológico a ver los monos.** *Let's go to the zoo to see the monkeys.* **Tus nuevos zapatos son muy monos.** *Your new shoes are very cute.*

- **Nos va a llevar al barrio de Maplewood.** *He's going to take (drive) us to the Maplewood neighborhood.* ~ This is the usual way to say that someone will take you someplace in a car. The word *lift* that is so often used in English does not have a Spanish equivalent, so generally to say, *Can you give me a lift to the party?*, you say, **¿Puedes *llevarme* a la fiesta?** *Can you take me to the party?* However, in Mexico, the slang phrase **dar un aventón** is close to the English expression, *to give (someone) a lift* or *ride.* (Literally, **aventón** means *push* or *shove.*)

- *Highlight on the subjunctive:* **Seguro que los vecinos de Maplewood no quieren que los niños de otros vecindarios vayan allá.** *For sure the Maplewood residents (neighbors) don't want children from other neighborhoods going there.* ~ Use the subjunctive after an expression of implied command (**no quieren**) when there is a change of subject. (See pages 139–140.) The subject of the first part is **los vecinos de Maplewood** (*the Maplewood residents*) and the subject of the second part is **los niños de otros vecindarios** (*children of other neighborhoods*). English handles this with an infinitive or gerund: *the residents . . . don't want the children to go there* (or *going there*).

- **trato o truco** *trick or treat* ~ Halloween is a traditional holiday of Canada and the United States. It occurs around the same time as the **Día de los muertos** (*Day of the Dead*), which is honored in most parts of the Spanish-speaking world and celebrated with great pageantry in Mexico and Central America. However, due to the influence of the English-speaking countries, some children in Spain and Latin America celebrate Halloween, and the expression **trato o truco** is used.

- **¡Qué disfraces más estupendos llevan!** *What super (stupendous) costumes you are wearing!* ~ This common type of compliment, with the word **qué** (*what*) followed by a noun, must have the word **más** after it in Spanish, although *more* or *most* is not used in English.

KEY WORDS AND PHRASES

Ese disfraz es de lo más mono. That costume is the cutest thing.

¿Crees que me darán más dulces . . . ? Do you think they'll give me more candies . . . ?

si voy de adorable o si voy de horrible if I go (looking) adorable or . . . horrible

Nos va a llevar al barrio de Maplewood. He's going to take us to the . . . neighborhood.

No quieren que los niños . . . vayan allá. They don't want the children . . . to go there.

¡Qué disfraces más estupendos llevan! What super costumes you are all wearing!

¿Y a quién tenemos aquí? And whom do we have here?

¡Qué disfraz más mono!

What a cute costume!

WHAT YOU CAN LEARN   Complimenting someone on what he or she is wearing, talking about what some people want others to do

PUTTING IT ALL TOGETHER (RESUMIÉNDOLO TODO). (Answers on page 218.)

Es la noche de Halloween. Abril está disfrazada como mariquita y Eli exclama, «¡Corazón, ese disfraz es de lo más (1) _____ !» Abril dice, «El papá de Becky (2) _____ _____ _____ _____ esta noche, Mamá. Vamos a ir al barrio de Maplewood.» Eli le advierte, «Seguro que los vecinos de Maplewood (3) _____ _____ _____ los niños de otros vecindarios (4) _____ allá.» Abril se va y suena el timbre. Eli ve a tres niños en disfraces, y los saluda, «¡Hola, chicos, (5) _____ _____ _____ _____ llevan! ¿Y a quién tenemos aquí?» Uno de los niños contesta, «No nos conoce. ¡Somos de Maplewood!»

DID YOU GET IT? (¿COMPRENDISTE?) (Answers on page 218.)

¿Qué lección aprende Eli? (a) Que su barrio es generoso. (b) Que los disfraces horribles son los mejores. (c) Que las costumbres cambian.

CHALLENGING LEVEL   **195**

WORKING WITH WORDS AND PATTERNS

- **Lo guías con este botón y con el otro controlas la velocidad.** *You guide it with this button and with the other you control the speed.* ~ In giving instructions, you can explain things in the present tense (using either the **tú** or **usted** forms as appropriate), the way John does here. Later on John switches to giving direct commands.

- **No, así no. ¡Dirígelo así!** *No, not like that. Steer it like this!* ~ The magic word for saying *like this*, *like that*, or *in this way* is **así**. When showing someone how to do something, you can simply say: **Así, por favor.** Or you can say, as John does later, **¡Así es como se hace!** *Here's how you do it!* The second phrase is the informal command form of the verb **dirigir** (*to direct* or *steer*).

- *Highlight on the subjunctive:* **Deja que te enseñe.** *Let me show you.* ~ Here once again John uses an informal command (from the verb **dejar** *to leave* or *let*) but it is followed by a subjunctive, **enseñe** from the verb **enseñar** (*to show* or *teach*) because a clause depending on a command (direct or implied) is in the subjunctive. Literally, this means: *Allow that I show to you . . .*

- *Highlight on the subjunctive:* **Retrocedamos y giremos . . .** *Let's go backwards and turn . . .* ~ Use the **nosotros** form of the present subjunctive to give a command involving yourself and others. (See pages 139–140.) This is translated as *Let's* + verb in English.

- **Cariño, no te habrás aburrido de tu nuevo juguete, ¿verdad?** *Sweetie, you haven't gotten bored already with your new toy, have you?* ~ You can often use reflexive verbs to talk about getting or becoming a certain way. The verb **aburrirse** means *to get* or *become bored*. Elly uses the future perfect tense, which refers to *what will have happened* at a certain time in the future or, in this case, *what possibly could have happened by now*. (See page 140.)

- *Highlight on the subjunctive:* **¡Primero tengo que esperar a que papá se aburra!** *First I have to wait for Dad to get bored!* ~ Use the subjunctive after the verb **esperar** when there is a change of subject and there is a projection into a future time (since the future is always vague and uncertain).

KEY WORDS AND PHRASES

¡Te he comprado un coche teledirigido!
I bought you a remote controlled car!

No, así no. ¡Dirígelo así!
No, not like that. Steer it like this!

Deja que te enseñe. Let me show you how.

¡Hacia la izquierda! ¡Hacia la derecha!
To the left! To the right!

¡Este pequeño sí que vuela! This little guy really flies!

No te habrás aburrido de . . . ya. You haven't already gotten bored with . . .

(78) El nuevo juguete

The new toy

WHAT YOU CAN LEARN   Giving detailed instructions, talking about boredom

PUTTING IT ALL TOGETHER (RESUMIÉNDOLO TODO). (Answers on page 218.)

Juan llega a casa y anuncia, «¡Mira, Abril! ¡Te he comprado un coche teledirigido! Ves cómo funciona. (1) _____ _____ con este botón.» Abril toma el remoto, pero Juan le grita, «¡No, así no! . . . Deja (2) _____ _____ _____.» Juan vuelve a tomar el remoto y dice, «Retrocedamos y (3) _____ . . . bien, ¡hacia la izquierda! ¡Hacia la (4) _____! . . . ¿Ves?» Abril entra en la casa. Eli la saluda con una pregunta, «Cariño, no te habrás aburrido de tu nuevo juguete ya, ¿verdad?» Abril responde, «¡Primero tengo que esperar a (5) _____ _____ _____ _____!»

DID YOU GET IT? (¿COMPRENDISTE?) (Answers on page 218.)

¿Qué problema tiene Abril con su coche teledirigido? . . . (a) No le interesa para nada. (b) A su papá le gusta demasiado. (c) No sabe controlarlo.

WORKING WITH WORDS AND PATTERNS

- **Trae un sentimiento tan bello.** *It carries such a lovely sentimental value (literally, sentiment).* ~ To say, *such a . . . thing* (or *person*), use **una cosa o persona tan . . . Lee un libro tan interesante.** *She is reading such an interesting book.*

- **Siento herirle los sentimientos a Juan.** *I'm sorry that I will hurt John's feelings.* ~ Since there is no change of subject, the subjunctive is *not* required after the expression of emotion (**sentir**). When referring to a part of the body or a feeling or an object that obviously belongs to the person talked about, use the indirect object instead of a possessive. Literally, this is *I'm sorry to hurt to John the feelings.*

- *Highlight on the subjunctive:* **Tendré cuidado cuando se lo diga.** *I will be careful when I tell it to him.* ~ Use the subjunctive (in this case, **diga**) after **cuando** when there is an action projected into the future, since to the Spanish mind the future is vague and uncertain. For habitual or past action after **cuando**, do *not* use the subjunctive. **Siempre visito a mis tíos cuando voy a Guanajuato.** *I always visit my uncle and aunt when I go to Guanajuato.*

- *Highlight on the past subjunctive:* **Quizás no lo debiera haber hecho . . .** *Maybe I shouldn't have done it . . .* ~ Use the past subjunctive of the verb **deber** to suggest doubt and to soften the meaning of *should*. The sentence would still mean the same thing if you used the regular present tense: **Quizás no lo debo haber hecho.** (See page 140.)

- *Highlight on the subjunctive:* **Y por favor dime si quieres que la ponga de vuelta . . .** *And please tell me if you want me to put it back . . .* ~ You have to use a subjunctive after an expression of implied command (**quieres que**) when there is a change of subject (See pages 139–140.)

KEY WORDS AND PHRASES

La mamá de Juan hizo esta almohada. John's mother made this pillow.

Trae un sentimiento tan bello. It holds such a lovely sentimental value.

Siento herirle los sentimientos a Juan. I'm sorry that I'll hurt John's feelings.

La voy a guardar. I'm going to put it away.

Tendré cuidado cuando se lo diga. I will be careful when I tell him about it.

Quizás no lo debiera haber hecho. Maybe I shouldn't have done it.

Dime si quieres que la ponga de vuelta. Tell me if you want me to put it back.

¿QUÉ ALMOHADA MÁS CÓMODA!

79 Una almohada muy especial

A very special pillow

WHAT YOU CAN LEARN   Talking about feelings, explaining your actions with sensitivity

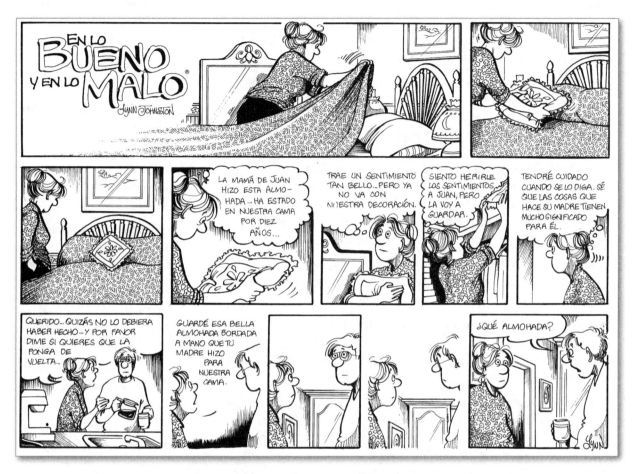

PUTTING IT ALL TOGETHER (RESUMIÉNDOLO TODO). (Answers on page 218.)

Eli está haciendo la cama en su alcoba cuando se fija en una pequeña almohada, y piensa, «(1) _____ _____ _____ _____ hizo esta almohada . . . Pero ya no va con nuestra decoración. Siento (2) _____ los sentimientos a Juan, pero lo voy a guardar. Tendré cuidado cuando (3) _____ _____ _____.» Más tarde, Eli habla con Juan en la cocina y le dice, «Querido . . . Quizás no lo (4) _____ haber hecho . . . y por favor dime si quieres que (5) _____ _____ _____ _____ . . . Guardé esa bella almohada que tu madre hizo para nuestra cama.» Luego, Juan pregunta, «¿Qué almohada?»

DID YOU GET IT? (¿COMPRENDISTE?) (Answers on page 218.)

¿Qué proverbio es el más apropiado para esta tira? . . . (a) Cada cabeza es un mundo. (b) Cuando hay amor, hay dolor. (c) Más vale tarde que nunca.

WORKING WITH WORDS AND PATTERNS

- **un lío amoroso** *a love affair* ~ Literally, a **lío** is a *bundle* or *package*, and by extension, a *mess*, *fix*, or *jam*, so a **lío amoroso** would be a *love mess*. Another common way of talking about a *love affair* is **una aventura amorosa**, literally, *a love adventure*.

- **Ultimamente se le ha visto con la estrella del Pop Vanesa Velour.** *Recently he has been seen with the Pop (music) star Vanessa Velour.* ~ In English *he has been seen* is in the passive voice since the subject *he* is receiving the action instead of doing it. In Spanish a **se** construction is often used for this, as here: **se le ha visto** (*one has seen him*). If the subject is a person, the impersonal **se** construction is used with **le** or **les** for men and **la** or **las** for women (or **le**, **les** if used as an indirect object). If the subject is a thing, a normal reflexive construction is used. **La casa se vendió ayer.** *The house was sold yesterday.* (Literally, *the house sold itself yesterday*.)

- **¿Alguna vez has pensado en . . . ?** *Have you ever thought about . . . ?* ~ Use **alguna vez** for *ever* when talking about an open and inclusive period of time, either past or future.

- **No me gustaría hacer algo así a mi familia.** *I wouldn't want to do anything like that (of that kind) to my family.* ~ Use **algo así** (literally, *something like that*) for *that sort of thing*, *anything of that kind*, *a thing like that*.

- **Además, tendría que perder unos 15 kilos . . . tostarme la piel . . . endurecer estos michelines . . .** *Besides, I would have to lose around 15 kilos . . . get a tan . . . harden up these love handles* ~ Use the conditional (**tendría que**) when talking about what you *would have to do* in certain circumstances or to achieve a particular goal.

- **¡Por lo que me siento feliz tal y como están las cosas!** *Because of all that I feel happy just the way things are!* ~ Literally, **por lo que** means *for all of which*. The **lo** refers back to all that went before. The second part means literally *such and how things are*, but it's convenient to remember that **tal y como** means *just the way*.

KEY WORDS AND PHRASES

la estrella de «Asquerosamente rico» star of (the program) "Filthy Rich"

Se le ha visto con . . . He has been seen with . . .

un parlamentario de su esposa a spokesperson for his wife

hacer algo así a mi familia to do something like that to my family

(tendría que) tostarme la piel un poco (I would have to) get a bit of a tan

endurecer estos michelines (I would have to) firm up these love handles (literally, these tires)

luego habría todo ese andar escondido then there'd be all that running around, hiding

tal y como están las cosas just the way things are

80 Imaginando un lío amoroso

Imagining a love affair

WHAT YOU CAN LEARN   Asking if someone has ever thought about something, listing what you would have to do to attain a goal, saying you are happy with the way things are

PUTTING IT ALL TOGETHER (RESUMIÉNDOLO TODO). (Answers on page 218.)

Eli y Juan miran la tele. El locutor dice, «Chet Whiffle, la estrella de "Asquerosamente rico," ¡se está separando de su esposa . . . ! Ultimamente (1) _____ _____ _____ _____ con la estrella del Pop Vanesa Velour.» Eli pregunta, «Juan . . . ¿(2) _____ _____ has pensado en tener un lío amoroso?» Juan responde, «¡No! No me gustaría . . . Además, (3) _____ que perder unos 15 kilos . . . hacer ejercicio . . . (4) _____ _____ _____ un poco . . . endurecer estos michelines . . . me siento feliz (5) _____ _____ _____ están las cosas!» Juan está sorprendido cuando Eli le da un almohadazo.

DID YOU GET IT? (¿COMPRENDISTE?) (Answers on page 218.)

¿Por qué se enoja Eli con Juan? . . . (a) Porque él nunca ha pensado en tener un lío amoroso. (b) Porque es obvio que él ha pensado en tener un lío amoroso. (c) Porque él ha tenido unos líos amorosos en el pasado.

El español en tu vida

Spanish in your life

Practice what you've learned from Comics 72–80. (Answers on page 218.)

A. ¿QUÉ SE DICE? (*What do you say?*)

Imagine yourself in the following situations. Use the cues from the comics and fill in the blanks with the missing Spanish words.

1. What do you say to thank someone for taking you out to dinner? **¿Qué se dice?**

2. How do you explain that someone had to perform an unpleasant action? **¿Qué se dice?**

3. How do you tell someone to come here and take a look (at something). **¿Qué se dice?**

4. How do you say, "Maybe I shouldn't have done it . . . ? **¿Qué se dice?**

B. ¿CUÁL ES LA PREGUNTA? (*What's the question?*)

Look at the following selections from the comics and insert the most likely question.

1.

2.

3.

4.

5.

C. EN EL CENTRO COMERCIAL (*At the mall*)

Make a list of all the things in the picture you can name in Spanish.

_____

_____

_____

_____

_____

D. EN LA DESPENSA DE LOS PATTERSON (*In the Pattersons' pantry*)

Examine the drawing below. Label all the objects you can with their Spanish names.
(The words for them have all been used in the comics up to this point.)

1. _____   9. _____

2. _____   10. _____

3. _____   11. _____

4. _____   12. _____

5. _____   13. _____

6. _____   14. _____

7. _____   15. _____

8. _____   16. _____

Original English Text of the *For Better or For Worse* Comic Strips

The text of the original comic strips in English is included below for your information. Inevitably some changes occurred when the comics were adapted into Spanish. Consequently, the English will not always present an exact translation of the Spanish that appears in the strips reproduced in this book.

Key

E: Elly; **J:** John; **M:** Michael; **Ez:** Elizabeth; **A:** April; **G:** Grandpa; etc.: other incidental characters will be indicated by a name or description and then given an abbreviation, e.g., Friend, and then **F**; *italic*: signs, sounds; | break between frames of the comic strips.

#1. **E:** Ahhh. | *Sale* | *Take Out*; **E:** Thank you, honey!; | **E:** Every now and then I need a me day!

#2. *Relax & rejuvenate with luxurious "Heavenly Bliss" bath beads . . . a soothing blend of natural herbs & aromatic oils . . .* | **E:** Aaahhhhhhh. | **A:** Mom? Mom! | **A:** Momeeeeeeeeeeeeeee | **E:** April! I'm coming! What's wrong?! | **A:** Nothing . . . We just wanted to know where you were.

#3. **J:** Hi there, April! What's the matter—are you tired?; **A:** Yeah . . . | **A:** I've been going around in circles all day!

#4. **A:** I'm nine years old now, Mom! I'm actually nine!; **E:** Yes! | **E:** And you know what the best thing about being nine is?; **A:** What? | **E:** You're old enough to help clean up the mess!!

#5. *Back to School*; *Sale* | *Bread Cereals Pancake Syrup Mix Baking Supplies* | **E:** I don't know what to do, John . . . She's been like this all afternoon! | **J:** Seems to me that somebody needs a nap!! | **E:** Z.

#6. **A:** Mom . . . I've got something to tell you. | **E:** What is it, April? | **A:** Mom . . . I hafta go to the bathroom. | **E:** We'll be home soon, honey.; **A:** I can't wait. | **E:** But there's no place to stop.; **A:** Please? | **E:** Ok, as soon as I see a gas station I'll pull over. | **A:** Owoooooohhh!; **E:** OK! There's a place. I'll pull over now! | *Confectionary* | **E:** Excuse me, can we use your washroom? It's an emergency! **Clerk:** Of course!

#7. **Ez:** Hey, Mom, can I have the car? **E:** Sure | **Ez:** I'm taking your red coat, is that OK? **E:** Uh huh. | **Ez:** Where are the keys?!; **E:** In the pocket!

#8. *Kabooommmmmm* | **A:** Mom, there's a big thunderstorm outside—an' I can't find Edgar anywhere! | **A:** He's scared of thunder, an' I wanna know where he is! | **E:** Well, when Farley was with us, he used to go and hide under the porch. | *Kabooom!*

#9. **A:** Oh, wow! A porcupine! | **A:** Dad! Grampa, look! There's a porcupine up in that tree! | **J:** Where? I don't see him.; **G:** Neither do I.; **A:** He's right there!! | **J:** It must be an old nest, April.; **G:** Or a bunch of dried leaves. | **A:** But it's a porcupine! Honest!! | **G:** Wait a minute! I see him!; **A:** Do you?!! | **G:** See? He's at the very top of that tall birch over there!; **J:** Sorry—I don't see anything. | **J:** Well! I guess you were right, honey!; **A:** Daddy . . . | **A:** How come grown-ups believe other grown-ups . . . but they don't believe me?

#10. *Rringgg!!!* | *Bus Stop*; **Boy (B):** I'm first in li-ine, I'm first in li'ine—nah, nah, nah-naaa nah! | **B2:** I'm next! **B3:** Then me! **B4:** I'm next. | **B:** You're last, April! April's last in li-ine! Ha-ha! | **B:** Here comes the bus! I'm first an' yer last. I'm first an' yer last! | *Screech!*

#11. *Boom Boom Boompa* | *Boom Boom Boompata* | *Boompa Booom . . . Boomm Boom . . .* | **Ez:** What do you think, Candace? Did everyone have a good time?; **C:** In my experience, Liz . . . | **C:** The measure of a good party is the length of time one takes to recover from it.

#12. *Honk! Honk!* | *Honk!* | **E:** Off to the beach?; **Ez:** Yeah! We've got food an' everything, Mom. | **E:** Sounds like fun!—Can I come? | **Ez:** Sure! Why not!; **Boy:** That'd be great, Mrs. P.! | **E:** No, I'm just kidding. I've got too much to do here.; **B:** Too bad. | **Ez:** Whew! That was close!; **Boy2:** Yeah! | **E:** Every now and then, I like to shake them up a little!

#13. **E:** *Snifffff Aaahhhh* | **E:** I feel really good today! | **E:** I know why . . . I feel thin! | **E:** My stomach feels a little flatter. | **E:** Yes! I've lost a few pounds! | **E:** I've been trying to diet and it hasn't been easy . . . but, I have lost weight! | **E:** I feel so good today . . . I'm going to do something I really enjoy!! | *The Joy of Baking*; *Flour*

#14. *Art Gallery* | *Zwedenthrog. The art and the artist.* | **Old Man (OM):** Impressive, isn't it. | **OM:** He was in his "amoeba" period when he did these.; **E:** Yes, it's all very, um, fluid. | **OM:** Do you like Zwedenthrog?; **E:** Some of it is interesting.; **OM:** Come here often?; **E:** I run in on my lunch hour sometimes. | **OM:** Really? Care to share a table in the cafeteria?; **E:** No thanks, I'm meeting someone. | *Gallery* | **Friend:** You should be flattered, El—to a guy in his 80s we're still a couple of "sweet young things"!

#15. *Bus Stop* | **E:** April! I'm glad you're home. Would you take this to Carol across the street, please? | **A:** But, Mom! It's raining!

#16. *Kaboom!* | **Deanna (D):** You have an umbrella! | **D:** But, it's so small! | **M:** I know. That's why I bought it. | **M:** The smaller the umbrella . . . the closer the girl!!

#17. **E:** You're right, John. When it comes to disciplining animals . . . | **E:** You have to catch them in the act! | *Bake Sale. Don't touch!*

#18. **E:** Yes! It was worth it! It was all worth it! Yess! | **M:** I dunno, Sis . . . The older she gets . . . the weirder she gets!

#19. *Scratch Scratch Scratch* | **J:** Hey, there, Ed. How's it going? | **J:** Good boy. How's my good boy? | **J:** Come here, Eddy! Come on! Come here! | *Whap Whappita Whap* | **J:** Thaaat's a gooood boy! | *Squirm Kick Struggle* | **J:** Amazing, isn't it . . . | **J:** Dogs always seem to know when they're going to have a bath!

#20. *Clean, Polish, Wipe, Dust* | **J:** She needs a good scraping an' the starter's busted. I'm going to get a new part. | **E:** Wait! The propane tank's empty! | **J:** Hey, Kids! It took all day, but we're ready to barbecue! | **Ez:** Gee, Dad . . . I'm sorry, but I'm meeting some friends for pizza! | **A:** An' I'm going to Becky's for supper an' a sleepover, remember? | *Double Burg. Bacon Burg. Chicken Burg. Fries. Big Bigger Huge*

#21. *Art Supplies; Wrapping Paper* | **J:** How about cleaning up, now.; **Ez:** Ok, Dad —we're just waiting for the news to come on. | **J:** Well, I'm glad to see that my kids are finally interested in what's going on in the world! | **TV:** Hello, this is Peter Mansbridge, with the CBS Evening News.

#22. *Toss* | *Snapp!! Chomp. Chew. Gulp!* | *Snapp!* | *Chomp. Drool. Munch* | *Pant, Pant, Drool, Whine! Drool, Slurp, Slobber, Whimper.* | **E:** What are you doing, Dad? | **E:** I fed the dogs a few minutes ago!

#23. **TV:** *Boompa-Thud, Boompa Thud, Ka-Boompa Thud!* | **TV:** An' we're comin' up to the big one—here on Rock Hits Ninety Nine! | **TV:** Ok dudes an' dudettes! Get ready to shake it with Bulk Crude an' The Flammable Liquids!! | **TV:** Ooaahhh nedjer nedjer hot luv bayy-bee | **E:** April, how can you concentrate with all this noise?; **A:** I'm OK. | **E:** I'm going to turn it down a little.; **A:** No! I like it! | **E:** Honey, you can't do homework and listen to this! It's impossible! | **A:** Mom, I'm not doing homework! Honest! | **A:** . . . I'm studying!

#24. *Z* | *Bop!* | *Whap!* | *Chomp!* | *Whappita Whappita Whappita* | *Whump* | *Boink!* | **Ez:** You know, Dawn . . . Sometimes I really miss my brother. | **Dawn:** Yeah, me too.

#25. *Rrriinggg!* | *Rringg!!* | *Rringgg!* | *Rringg!!* | **M:** Hi, Grandpa—it's Michael! Happy Father's Day! | **M:** So, could I speak to Dad, please.; **G:** Sure thing! | **G:** Talk to John . . . | **G:** Mmm. . . Fresh brewed Java! | **E:** Strange . . . | **E:** Would anyone know why the phone is off the hook?

#26. **A:** Aaaghh!! | **A:** I don't wanna do this project. Don't wanna do it!! | I hafta look up all this stuff! It's just too much! | **A:** I hate this! Why do I hafta do this? | **A:** Stoopid, dumb, crummy, stoopid. | **A:** It's no fair! I won't do any more! . . . I quit!! | **A:** Snivel . . . Sniff. |

Cut, cut, snip, paste, clip. Color, write, clip, cut, paste. | **A:** There, it's done. I did it. | **A:** . . . I just had to get in the mood!

#27. **Anthony:** Man, we've been here so long, the windows have fogged over! | **Ez:** It won't wipe off! It's frozen.; *Chip, chip, chip! Scrape. Scratch.* | **Ez:** . . . At least you knew where I was!

#28. **Gordon (G):** Isn't this a beautifully decorated window, guys?; **M:** It's amazing, Gord! | **Deanna (D):** Michael, what are you doing? | **M:** I'm looking at it from the right height! | **M:** This is how I remember looking at Christmas windows when I was small. Everything seemed so real to me! | **M:** How I'd love to be able to see from the perspective of a child again! | **Little boy (LB):** Daddy? . . . | **LB:** Lift me up!

#29. *Beep, Beep, Boop, Fladdap!* | *Beep Bip Boop* | *Bip Bip Bip* | **A:** Money. Money. Money. Money. La, La, La, La. | **J:** It isn't free, April. This represents a lot of hard work!; **A:** I know. | **A:** We musta been in line for an hour!!

#30. **A:** How long are you going to stay with us, Grampa? | **G:** Put it this way . . . As long as I'm needed. | **Ez:** What are you doing, April. | **A:** Looking for something to break.

#31. **A:** Are you gonna wear that in the parade today, Grampa?; **G:** With pride. | **E:** Here comes your Grandpa, April. | **E:** These are the men and women of our city who fought for us in the Second World War.; **A:** Mom? . . . | **A:** . . .Why are there so few of them?

#32. **G:** That's strange . . . I know I poured myself a cup of coffee! | **G:** Oh, yes! I left it in the rec room while I was watching the news!! | **G:** Does anyone know why I'm down here?

#33. **M:** Deanna, your hands are freezing! Why weren't you wearing gloves?!! | **D:** I wanted to show off my engagement ring!!

#34. **Radio:** Once again, the local weather watch calls for freezing rain for the next 24 hours. | **A:** Mom, remember that plastic raincoat Grandma Carrie sent you?; **E:** Uh huh. | **A:** Could I please borrow it?; **E:** Of course, dear. | **E:** It's a little big. **A:** It's O.K. I'll manage. | **E:** Wow! That's amazing. Freezing rain and April is wearing a raincoat! | **E:** Finally, there's some common sense in that little head of hers!

#35. **E:** Hi, Honey–Did you have a nice day at the beach?; **Ez:** The best. | **Ez:** We played volleyball and swam for most of the day. | **Ez:** Then we all rowed over to Cove Island and had a picnic. | **Ez:** Later, we hiked up to the bluffs, and took pictures, then raced back to the park for baseball and a marshmallow roast! | **Ez:** It was an amazing day, Mom. I am totally exhausted! Too bad you weren't there! | **E:** Oh, I've had wonderful days like that, Elizabeth! | **E:** You know you're getting older when you'd rather remember a great time than relive it!!

#36. **E:** Honey, have you seen my gardening gloves?; **J:** I think I hung them up in the garage. | **A:** Know what I saw on TV, Mom? | **A:** This guy hung some gloves on

ORIGINAL ENGLISH TEXT OF THE *FOR BETTER OR FOR WORSE* COMIC STRIPS a nail like that an' a spider went inside one of the fingers. | **A:** Then, when he put his gloves on—it bit him, like this! | **A:** His finger swelled up so much, he had to go to the hospital! | **J:** Did your Mom find her gardening gloves, April?; **A:** Uh huh. | **A:** An' she's jumping up an' down on them!

#37. **E:** Elizabeth, why are you showing April how to do things like this?; **Ez:** I dunno. | **Ez:** Dad showed Michael, Michael showed me, an' I showed April!; **E:** Oh! | **E:** Other people hand their games, their legends, and their language down from generation to generation . . . | **J:** What's the matter, El?; **E:** . . . I'm worried about our culture!!

#38. **E:** John, what are you doing?; **J:** Getting rid of these plastic containers. | **E:** But . . .; **J:** Look! There's no room in this cupboard! | **J:** It's time we got rid of all the junk we've been collecting, El.; **E:** I guess you're right. | **E:** Are you really going to toss out these bottles?; **J:** Maybe not. They'd be good for nails. | **E:** What about these? They have tight-fitting lids.; **J:** Save 'em. | **E:** This is a good packing box!; **J:** Yeah, and this big tin can may come in handy. | **E:** I could use this for wrapping gifts or something.; **J:** Sniff? | **A:** I thought you were gonna recycle all these things, Daddy.; **J:** We did . . . | **J:** They were recycled from one part of the house to another.

#39. *Luxury Chocolate* | *Pingg!* | **J:** Elly . . . Did you just throw a whole box of chocolates into the trash?; **E:** Yes. | **E:** They've been in the cupboard for ages and none of us needs the calories or the fat. | **J:** But that was a whole unopened box!; **E:** Think of it as an act of willpower over want-power! | **J:** I guess you're right, we absolutely do not need the chocolates. | *Poingg!* | **J:** Save me the ones with the cherries.

#40. *Hobbies. Books. Lilliput's;* **Coworker (C):** Oooh, my feet are killing me!! | **E:** Mine, too! | **C:** It's 6 o'clock, El.; **E:** Great. Time to close up the shop and go home! | **C:** Sorry, we're closing, now. **Woman (W):** Can't we come in?; **W2:** Please? | **W:** You have so many wonderful things in here!!!; **C:** But . . . | **C:** Umm. Is there something I can help you with? | **W:** No, thanks. We're just looking.

#41. *Whak!* | **Ez:** I hate this stuff! | **Ez:** Oh, man! Check out the homework I hafta do . . . Like, this totally bums me! | **Ez:** It's such a great day, and I'm stuck in here doing this!! | **Ez:** It's not fair! | **Ez:** *Grumble, Snort! Write, Snuff, Grumble* | **Ez:** Know what? I can't wait 'til I'm out of school completely! | **Ez:** . . . Then I won't have to do stuff I hate on the weekend!

#42. **E:** Great. I've just bathed and brushed both dogs, and they're outside, rolling in the dirt. | **E:** I washed and folded April's clothes and she's left them in a heap. | **E:** I've just cooked a nice dinner and nobody will be here to eat it. | **E:** I cleaned out the garage and now there's more junk in it than there was before. | **E:** And it looks like I've gained back the 6 pounds I lost. | **E:** I wonder . . . who coined the phrase "The futility of man"?

#43. *Emilio's For Him* | *Men's Wear* | **Sales Assistant (SA):** May I help you?; **E:** Yes, my husband needs some summer clothes. | **SA:** Shorts? Socks? Shirts? | **E:** Yes, these are his size. | **SA:** What do you think?; **E:** The shirt is good . . . the shorts are baggy. | **E:** We'll take this, the beige pants, the striped shirt, the cream vest and a spring jacket . . . something with breast pockets. | **SA:** Thank you, madam. . . Sign here.; *Brrrttt Whtttt Bppp* | **E:** Well, I'm so delighted with the clothes we just bought—aren't you, John? | **J:** I don't know . . . Was I there?

#44. **J:** *Toss. Turn. Toss.* | **E:** Can't sleep?; **J:** Nope. | **E:** Neither can I. | **J:** I saw something strange today, Elly. Two toads in the back lane were fighting! | **J:** It wasn't an ordinary little "spat." They were really going at one another! | **E:** It was probably over a female.; **J:** I didn't see one. | **E:** Oh, she'd be around somewhere.; **J:** I didn't think toads fought! | **E:** All males fight over females. | **E:** John? Would you fight over me? | **J:** I guess I took too long to answer.

#45. *Brush. Brush. Brush.* | *Thump. Thump. Thump.* | **Ez:** Mom, can I have some money for lunch? | **E:** Why don't you just make yourself something Liz?; **Ez:** Like what? | **E:** . . . a sandwich?; **Ez:** Where's the bread?; **E:** In the cupboard. | **Ez:** Do we have any cheese?; **E:** It's in the fridge. | **Ez:** What else could I have?; **E:** Celery sticks? | **Ez:** Celery sticks?! That means I have to wash an' cut them up!! | **Ez:** How about an apple, then?; **Ez:** I don't like that kind. | **Ez:** A granola bar?: **Ez:** They've got raisins in them.; **E:** A pudding cup?; **Ez:** There's no vanilla. | **Ez:** Don't we have anything that's fast and easy and something I like?! | **E:** Here.; **Ez:** What is it? | **E:** . . . Some money for lunch.

#46. **Radio (R):** That's our fitness report. Now let's talk about diet! | **R:** Despite ample information people are still not consuming enough vegetables! New evidence shows that . . . | **R:** And remember your health-watch regimen? Drink at least 6 to 8 glasses of water a day! *Glug glug glug* | *Water* | *Glupp, gulp, grgl, gulp glugg* | **Moira:** Good night, Elly!; **E:** 'Night, Moira. | *Rmmmm* | *Washroom* | *Police* | *Highway Next Exit* | **E:** . . . That's the first time in my life I've ever been stopped for drinking and driving!

#47. **E:** The dinner I'm going to starts at 6, John, so I've prepared everything for you here. | **E:** There's a nice casserole in the fridge. Just put it in the microwave and then into the oven at 350° 'til it bubbles . . . | **E:** Put frozen peas into a covered Pyrex dish and microwave on high for 3 minutes, stir and heat again . . . | **E:** I bought buns, there's a fresh garden salad and for dessert, there's . . .; **Ez:** We'll be fine, Mom—honest! | *Burgorama Dogorama Spudzorama!!*

#48. **E:** Mmmmm. | **E:** For me, John . . . this time of year is pure heaven! | **E:** The smell, the colors, the markets, the cool, fresh winds. | **E:** Of all the seasons—I think I like this best. | **J:** We've seen a lot of autumns together, haven't we, El.; **E:** More than 20! | **J:** I guess you could say we're in the "autumn of our lives"! | **E:** That's a nice analogy, John—comparing a long-lasting relationship to this time of year.; **J:** Yeah . . . | **J:** For one thing, there's fewer bugs.

#49. **A:** Why are people selling poppies today, Mom?; **E:** They're a symbol, April. Something to make us remember. | **E:** A man called John McCrae wrote a beautiful poem about poppies that grew in Flanders fields. | **E:** Also in the fields were crosses, marking the graves of soldiers who died fighting the war. | **A:** Why do I hafta wear a poppy?! | **A:** I'm not really sure what a war is!; **E:** I know. | *Lest we forget*; **E:** And that, I think, is the best reason of all!

#50. **J:** Ohhh I am so glad to be home!! *Peel peel peel peel* | **J:** Mrs. Nedwitt didn't show up for a three hour appointment this morning, so we juggled patients, trying to fill the space . . . | **J:** Then our computer at the front desk went down, so we were out of commission for most of the day. I missed lunch . . .| **J:** We have two sterilizers and one stopped working. Then, the suction system backed up. There was enough tension among the staff I thought the place would explode! | **J:** Melviss Danel left her whiny kids in the reception area while we did her cleaning and one of them broke a lamp . . . | **J:** My dental chair locked into the "down" position, so I spent all afternoon working in a position like this!! | **J:** How was your day?; **E:** Fine! | **E:** I was going to tell him it was terrible!!

#51. *Z* | *Snappp!* **Ez:** Uh? | **Ez:** Last night I had a bath and got into a comfortable bed with clean sheets . . . but I tossed and turned until midnight! | **Ez:** Same thing the night before . . . | **Ez:** And the night before that. *Z* | *Snappp!!!* **Ez:** Uh? | **Ez:** Why is it so hard to sleep at night . . . | **Ez:** And so easy to sleep when you're studying! *Z*

#52. **E:** That was a nice party.; **J:** Yes, I talked to the Vincents, the Piches, the Neils, Kestys, Porters, Grahams and the Kamachis. | **E:** Did you talk to the Scotts?; **J:** Uh huh, also the Landriaults, Fuzys, Hernandez', Bains, O'Gradys, McParlands, Arthurs, Brennes, Palecznys and the Latours! | **E:** Great!; **J:** Yeah . . . | **J:** I just wish I could remember one single conversation.

#53. *Wake-Up Willie, Alarm Clock, Santa's Village*; **A:** Look, Dad! See that? I want it for Christmas!! | **A:** I want a "Wake-Up Willy" an' a rocket sleigh! | **A:** An' a real camera an' . . . an' . . . | **J:** April, Christmas is a time for giving! There is a joy in giving to others that far outweighs any other pleasure.; **A:** I know. | **A:** But somebody has to receive or there'd be nobody to give stuff to!; **J:** So? | *Clock Shack* **A:** . . . I was just trying to help out.

#54. **A:** Elizabeth, you're going out with Anthony?; **Ez:** Uh huh, what's wrong with that? | **A:** Oh, nothing! . . . It's just New Year's Eve an' you guys are supposed to be "involved" with other people. | **Ez:** Well, the other people aren't here, April—and besides . . . | **Ez:** Anthony and I have known each other since we were kids. We're going out for "old time's sake." *Ding*

Donggg!! | **Anthony (An):** Hey, you!; **Ez:** Hey yourself!; **An:** You look amazing.; **Ez:** So do you. | **A:** Did you see that? Those guys are like almost engaged to other people, an' they're dating again! | **A:** Man, this could wreck their other relationships!; **E:** Well, it's their business, April. We keep our opinions entirely to ourselves.

#55. **J:** Hah! When I was 16, I went to my first all night party. Don't know how I kept my folks from finding out! | **E:** I think I was 18. At 4 A.M., we all went down to English Bay and ran in the sand barefoot! | **E:** Remember our first New Year's Eve together, John? It was on the Toronto Island ferry!; **J:** We were both students . . . and I was crazy about you. | **J:** The next year the party was at the frat house. What a brawl!; **E:** I'm surprised you remember it!! | **J:** We were married by the following year.; **E:** Uh-huh. We went to "The Crow's Nest" and danced 'til the sun came up! | **J:** Remember when we had our own party?; **E:** 16 people came, and all we could afford was chips and beer! | **J:** Then there was the time we took Michael with us.; **E:** He was so tiny. We put him in a basket and he slept through the whole thing. | **J:** Man, we've seen some wild and crazy New Years' Eves!; **E:** And survived the mornings after. | **J:** But now, after almost 25 years together, we've discovered that those all-night celebrations aren't nearly as meaningful as a quiet evening alone!; **E:** Right! | **J:** 'Cause neither of us can stay awake past 10!!! *Snorggg*

#56. **E:** Is your back bothering you again, Dad? | **G:** Oh, it's always bothering me, dear—and, so are my knees, my hands, my innards . . . | **E:** With all you put up with, I'm surprised you don't complain more.; **G:** No point in complaining. | **G:** It doesn't make me feel better . . . and it depresses everyone else. | **G:** So, when I've had enough and start feeling sorry for myself, I just pick up the phone and call my friend Frank. | **E:** And he cheers you up?; **G:** Sure does. | **G:** He's worse off than I am!!

#57. *Creeek* | **E:** It's almost noon. How can she sleep for so long?!! | **E:** When she wakes up, I'm going to tell her just exactly what I think! | **E:** No, by heavens, I am going to tell her now! | **A:** Are you looking for Elizabeth, Mom? | **A:** She went skating at 6 o'clock this morning!

#58. *Sssssss* | *Fold Fold Fold Fold* | **E:** Elizabeth, I want you to put away these clothes now, so they don't end up on the floor.; **Ez:** Cheeze, Mom! | **Ez:** You are such a neat freak!; **E:** I am not a neat freak! | **Ez:** You are! For example: the kitchen is never cluttered, every drawer is organized, every closet is clean. | **Ez:** You line up pairs of shoes, you straighten floor mats, you put cans and bottles in the dishwasher before you recycle them. You even fold the underwear! | **Ez:** This is obsessive-compulsive behavior!; **E:** Really? . . . I'm glad you pointed it out. | **E:** From now on, I'll try not to inflict this disorder on my family. | **A:** . . . What's wrong with Mom?

#59. Friend (F): Are these the brochures the guidance counselor gave you, Liz?; **Ez:** Yah! | **Ez:** I've been thinking about reading them. | **F:** So, which universities are you gonna apply to?; **Ez:** I've narrowed it down to three. | **Ez:** I was going to take general arts, but I really like biology, so I'll check out sciences first. | **Ez:** I want to get into teacher's college eventually . . . | **Ez:** But I'd also like to work for a while, take a year off and travel. | **Ez:** Ultimately, I want to teach high school, so the more varied my experiences, the better. | **J:** Elizabeth! I see you've been doing some research! . . . What are your plans for the future?; *University of Toronto. University of Western Ontario* | **Ez:** I dunno.

#60. A: Tsk! | **A:** Look at your messy room! | **A:** Eat your dinner, don't play with it!! | **A:** Pick up your dishes! Don't expect me to clean up after you! | **A:** No TV 'til you pick up all your toys! | **A:** I said now, not later! | **A:** Don't argue with me. You do have to have a bath tonight! | **A:** Don't use so much shampoo! | **A:** Were you listening to me, Mom?; **E:** No, April. | **E:** I was listening to me!

#61. J: Morning, Honey! Got anything planned for today?; **E:** Mmm . . . I don't think so, John. | **J:** Want to go anywhere? Visit anyone?; **E:** Nope. | **J:** Does anything need to be fixed? Any chores to be done?; **E:** None I can think of. | **J:** April doesn't need to be driven anywhere? We don't need groceries?; **E:** No, everything's fine! | **J:** Just thought I'd ask. | **J:** I love it when I can spend the day in my workshop guilt free!!

#62. A: Mom?; **E:** Uhhh? | **A:** I'm scared. I don't wanna sleep upstairs by myself. I miss Elizabeth! | **E:** Honey, Elizabeth is at the university now. | **A:** I want you an' Daddy to move upstairs again. I don't wanna be alone! | **E:** Why don't you go back to bed, and I'll come and sleep in Elizabeth's room tonight. **A:** Sniff . . . OK. | **J:** Elly, we talked about this! April has the dog in her room, she has her radio, her toys. She said she'd be fine! | **J:** She even said she wanted to be alone—that it would make her feel all grown up!; **E:** I know. | **E:** These things always work well in theory.

#63. *Cough Snivel Cough Cough A-Hack! Cough Cough | Koff Wheeze Snuffl Cough Koff. . . Whonk!! | Cough Koff Cough Hack! Cough Cough | Snivel | Whonk! | Clack!; Sniff Sniff Sniff* | **Radio (R):** Cold and flu got you feeling miserable? Sneezing? Coughing? Upset stomach? | **R:** One tried and true remedy, guaranteed to make you feel better. *Click* | **Ez:** Hello, Mom?

#64. E: It's so nice to have you home for a few days.; **Ez:** Yeah. | **Ez:** I've really missed you guys! | *Candy Shack* **Ez:** Whoa! Check out the cool jacket!; **E:** Try it on!; *Back to School* | **E:** The jacket looks great, Elizabeth. I'll buy it for you.; **Ez:** No Mom! I can . . . | **E:** Hey, let me get you some new things for school, OK?; **Ez:** OK!; *Cashier* | **Ez:** Gee, thanks Mom! This is fun! | **E:** I'm so glad we can shop together now, honey! | **E:** There was a time when you didn't want to be seen in public with your mother! | **A:** That was before she started buying everything with her own money!

#65. E: What a pigsty! | **E:** Elizabeth has to go back to college, now—and look at all these dirty clothes! | **E:** Well, she's an adult now. It's her stuff and it's not my problem. | **E:** *Fume!* | **E:** She's had lots of time. How can she live like that?! | **E:** This is ridiculous! I can't stand it! Where is that girl?!! | **Ez:** I can't believe I'm saying this, Dawn—but my mother is getting cool in her old age . . . | **Ez:** I left all my laundry 'til the last day—and she never said a word!; *Lou's Laundromat, 24 Hrs*

#66. Iris (I): It's getting colder, Jim. I can smell the frost in the air! | **I:** Winter's coming, I can feel it in my bones!; **G:** I can feel it everywhere! | **G:** I guess you could say we're in the winter of our lives! | **I** I'm not sure I like that expression!; **G:** I do! | **G:** In the "spring of your life," you're silly and out of control. In the "summer," you're having babies, paying mortgages and struggling with careers . . . | **G:** In the "autumn of your life," you have children to put through university . . . and the shock of discovering you're not getting any younger . . . | **G:** But winter can be the best time of all!; **I:** Why?! | **G:** We can just look forward to a long, warm, happy one!

#67. E: April, how many times do I have to ask you to take your things upstairs?!!; **A:** I dunno. | **A:** How many times did you ask me already? | **E:** April, if these toys and books and clothes are not taken up to your room by the end of the day, I'm throwing them all into the trash! | **A:** Mom? What are you doing?!; **E:** Throwing out your stuff. | **A:** You can't do that! It's mine!!!; **E:** Sorry, I meant what I said. | **E:** It'll be picked up first thing in the morning.; **A:** Aaaagh! | **E:** All right, you can take your things upstairs, but next time . . . | **E:** A really good threat is one you don't have to carry out!

#68. E: *Sniffff.* | **Ez:** Happy Mother's Day, Mom! | **Card (C):** Dear Mom, Now that we're living away from home we realize how much you've always done for us. | **C:** The cooking, the cleaning, the freshly folded clothes . . . We took it all for granted. | **C:** You took us places and taught us things. You gave us your values, your judgment and your time. You cared for us in sickness and in health. | **C:** And we want you to know that we appreciate you now, more than ever before.; **E:** *Snivel* | **C:** Thank you for being such a great Mom! Love—Michael and Elizabeth!; **E:** Ohhhh, that is sooo sweet!!! | **E:** I can't believe you two got together and gave me that beautiful card! | **M:** Actually, split 2 ways, it only cost us an even 2 bucks each!

#69. Deanna's Mother (DM): OK everyone, your attention please! | **DM:** I want this wedding to be perfect, so let's get things right. | **DM:** We only have the church for an hour, which gives us time for two rehearsals. | **DM:** Ushers, take the single ladies by the arm. Friends and family of the groom to the right, bride left! | **DM:** Music begins with "Air on a G String" by Bach. | **DM:** Groom? You and the best man come from the vestibule now. | **DM:** Ring bearer and flower girl enter now! Matron and maids of honor follow in order of height please and step in time to the music slowly! | **DM:** Bride? Take your father's arm, wait for the trumpet voluntary in "D" and now!!! | **DM:** Chin up! Smile! . . . and don't forget my darling | **DM:** This is your day!!

#70. **Priest (P):** Dear families and friends, we are gathered here today | **P:** To witness and to celebrate the union of Deanna Sobinski and Michael Patterson in holy matrimony; **E:** *Snifff* | **M:** I Michael, take thee, Deanna. | **D:** I Deanna, take thee, Michael.; **E:** *Sniffll* | **M:** With this ring, I thee wed. | **P:** You may now kiss the bride! | **E:** Oh, John | **E:** This has to be one of the happiest days of my life! *Sniff*

#71. *Beebedaeeebadeebadeebadeeba* | **Man:** *Yack yack yack yap yap* | **Man:** *Yap yack yap* | **Man:** Well, I'll call you later, Bob! OK! Ciao! | *Dingalingalingaling-alinggg!* | **M:** . . . Hey! What's up? Me? Oh, nothing, just sitting in an expensive restaurant trying to have a romantic evening with my wife. | **M:** What?!! Sure, no problem—he's right here!!! | **M:** It's for you.

#72. **A:** Know what, Grampa? Maybe in the new millennium we'll have robots that will make tea! | **E:** Why? You've already got one! | **A:** There's gonna be lots of changes in the next 1,000 years huh, Grampa.; **G:** I guess there will be. | **A:** I hope we have real 3-D TV shows an' cars that fly! | **A:** Maybe we'll be able to go to outer space—or even time travel!; **G:** There will be some amazing technology. | **A:** I hope we'll be able to save the whales an' change the weather whenever we want—so every holiday would be on a sunny day! | **A:** What do you hope will change in the new millennium, Grampa? | **G:** People.; *Refugees wait in freezing weather. Guerrilla forces open fire. Violence started by racist remarks.*

#73. *The Wine & Diner* | **Ez:** Thanks for taking me out to dinner!; **Anthony (An):** No problem, Liz! | **Ez:** Anthony . . . do you think Valentine's Day was made for lovers or for the sake of crass commercialism? | **An:** Crass commercialism.; **Ez:** Why? | **An:** 'Cause if it was for lovers . . . they'd have made it in July!

#74. *Food. Fine Jewelry.* | **G:** Iris, I'd like to give you a gift for Valentine's Day; **I:** Really? | **I:** Oh Jim, how sweet! Do you know what I'd really love to have? | **I:** A cell phone!; **G:** A cell phone? | **G:** I was thinking about a friendship ring! A cell phone is so unromantic.; **I:** No it isn't! | **I:** When you need a little friendship, you can ring!

#75. **TV:** Then, with our boys in control of this strategic area, we pushed forward . . . | *Ratta-Tattat Tatta Pop Poppp Bwang! Rattata Ttatat Atattatat* | **A:** Daddy, on just about every TV station, there's stuff about the war.; **J:** I know. | **J:** Your grandpa fought in the last World War, April.; **A:** Did he shoot anybody? | **J:** Yes, he did.; **A:** Really?!; **J:** He had to, or the other soldier would have shot him. | **A:** Wow! Grandpa never told me about that! | **J:** I know, he doesn't like to talk about it . . . he says it's just too painful.; **A:** Then,

why do they show the war on TV? | **J:** Because it was fought for our freedom and allows us to live the way we do today. | **J:** Strange, isn't it . . . that something so important for us to remember . . . | **J:** Is something that others try so hard to forget.

#76. *Scratch Dig Dig Dig!* | *Scratch Dig Dig Dig* | **E:** April, come here and look at your rabbit's cage! | **E:** Poor Mr. B, you haven't cleaned his room for ages! | **E:** He needs fresh bedding and clean water and get rid of any food he hasn't eaten. | **E:** Honestly! How would you like it if you had to live in an awful, disgusting mess?!! | **E:** Now and then . . . I ask some really stupid questions.

#77. **E:** Honey, that's the cutest costume! You look absolutely adorable.; **A:** Really? | **A:** I've been trying to decide . . . | **A:** Would I get more stuff if I looked adorable or disgusting? | **A:** Becky's Dad is taking us out tonight, Mom. We're gonna go to Maplewood.; **E:** What? | **E:** Why don't you stay here on Sharon Park Drive?; **A:** The candy's better on Maplewood. | **E:** Honey, this is a very generous neighborhood. | **E:** Besides, I'm sure the people on Maplewood don't want kids coming from the other side of town! | *Ding dongg!* **Kids (K):** Trick or treat! | **E:** Hi there. What great costumes! Who do we have here?; **K:** You don't know us! | **K:** We're from Maplewood!

#78. *Toys & Treasures* | **J:** Look April—I bought you a remote control car! | **J:** See how it works? You steer with this thumb and the other controls the speed. | **J:** No, not like that, steer it this way! | **J:** Wait, you're not doing it right! Let me show you! | **J:** Let's back it up and turn . . . OK, left! Right! This baby can really fly! | **J:** See? This is how it's done! | **E:** You're not bored with your new toy already, are you honey?; **A:** No . . . | **A:** I hafta wait until Dad gets bored with it first!

#79. **E:** John's mother made this pillow. It's been on our bed for years . . . | **E:** It has such sweet sentiment—but it doesn't match the décor any more. | **E:** I hate to hurt John's feelings but I'm putting it away. | **E:** I'll be sensitive about the way I tell him. I know that his Mom's handicrafts mean a lot. | **E:** Honey? This may have been the wrong thing to do—and please tell me if you'd like me to put it back . . . | **E:** I've put away the lovely little hand-embroidered pillow your mother made for our bed. | **J:** What pillow?

#80. *Click!* | **TV:** Chet Whiffle, star of "Disgustingly Wealthy," is splitting with his wife of 30 years! | **TV:** He's been seen recently with young pop star Vanessa Velour!! When asked to comment, spokespersons for his wife said . . . | **E:** John, have you thought about having an affair?; **J:** Nope! | **J:** I wouldn't want to do something like that to my family! | **J:** Besides, I'd have to take off at least 30 pounds, I'd need to exercise, get a tan, tighten up some of this flab! | **J:** Then, there'd be all the sneaking around and excuses . . . | **J:** So I'm happy just the way things are!

English Text of the *Putting It All Together* (Moderate and Challenging)

In the *Moderate* and *Challenging* sections, your task of filling in the blanks in the *Putting It All Together* summary is made somewhat more difficult since we have presented this activity without English translations. If you find you require help in understanding the Spanish activities, you can find the complete translations below.

#31. It's Remembrance Day (Veterans' Day), and Grandpa puts on his hat and jacket. April asks him, "Are you going to wear that in the parade, Grandpa?" He answers her, "With great pride." April waits with her family, and her mother says to her, "Here comes your grandfather. These are the men and women of our country who fought for us." Then April asks her, "Mom, why are there so few?"

#32. Grandpa is in the kitchen and he suddenly says to himself, "How strange! I know that I served myself a cup of coffee!" Later he remembers: "Oh, yes! I left it in the living room (family room) while I was watching the news." He goes downstairs, picks up a magazine, and then realizes that he's forgotten why he is there.

#33. Michael is now engaged and talks with his fiancée, Deanna, on the telephone. She walks in the snow, takes a bus, and arrives at Michael's house. He takes her hands and sees that they are icy cold. He asks her, "Where are your gloves?" Deanna replies, "I wanted to show off my engagement ring!"

#34. April listens to the weather report on the radio. They say that there is going to be freezing rain for the next 24 hours. April talks with her mom about a raincoat that grandmother sent them. She asks her, "Could you lend it to me?" Elly gives it to her and April goes outside. Elly is amazed and thinks, "Wow! This is definitely something remarkable!"

#35. Elizabeth comes back home after spending the day at the beach. Her mom asks her, "Did you have a good time?" Elizabeth answers, "Terrific!" and she tells about the activities she participated in with her friends: "We played volleyball and we swam . . . we went off to Picnic Island . . . we hiked to the rocks and we took photos, and from there we ran back to the park . . . It was a fantastic day, Mommy. I'm totally exhausted! What a shame that you couldn't come!" Then, Elly assures her that she has had fantastic days too.

#36. Elly is looking for her gardening gloves. John says to her, "I think I hung them up in the garage." Elly goes to the garage and April begins to tell her what she saw on T.V. April relates: "A guy hung up his gloves on a nail and a spider slipped into one of the fingers. And then when he put his gloves on, it bit him LIKE THIS! His finger swelled up so much that he had to go to the hospital." Later, in the yard, John asks April, "Did your mother find her gloves?" and April says yes, "She's jumping on top of them!"

#37. Elizabeth takes out some socks from a drawer and teaches her little sister April how to fold them and put them on the doorknobs as a joke. (Then if someone wants to come in, he or she is going to have problems.) Elly sees them and asks Elizabeth, "Why are you teaching April things like this?" "I don't know," she answers. "Dad taught Michael, Michael taught me, and I taught April." Elly thinks to herself that other people pass on, from one generation to the next, their games, their legends, and their language. John asks her what the matter is and she replies, "I'm worried about our culture."

#38. John is carrying a bunch of plastic containers when Elly asks him, "John, what are you doing?" John explains and then comments, "It's about time that we get rid of all the garbage . . ." Elly asks him, "Are you really going to throw away all of these bottles?" John answers that he isn't because they are good for storing nails. Afterwards, they decide to keep many other things. April remarks to her father, "I thought you were going to recycle all these things, Dad." John replies, "We did. We recycled them from one place in the house to another."

#39. Elly throws an entire unopened box of chocolates in the garbage can, and John sees her. He asks her, "Elly, have you just thrown all the candies into the garbage?" She explains: "They'd been in the cupboard for quite some time and really we don't need the calories or the fat. Consider it an act of willpower . . ." John decides that Elly is right, but later he sees her eating the chocolates and says to her, "Save me the ones filled with cherries."

#40. Elly's co-worker complains: "Oh, my! My feet are killing me!" She looks at her watch and announces, "It's six o'clock." Elly says, "It's time to close the shop." Two women knock at the door. "May we come in?" they ask, "Please?" The co-worker replies, "I'm sorry, we are closing . . . " But the women come in anyway and say, "You have such beautiful things." They look at everything and stay quite a while but don't buy anything. Finally, they say, "We were only looking . . . "

#41. Elizabeth is very angry. She comes into the kitchen and screams, "I hate this thing!" She doesn't want to do her schoolwork. She complains, "Like, it totally irritates me! It's a fantastic day and I'm stuck here inside . . . It's not fair!" Elly listens to her without saying anything, while she cleans and scrubs. Elizabeth says, "You know? I can hardly wait to finish my studies. That way . . . I won't have to do things I hate!" The dog winks.

#42. Elly looks at the dogs outside, rolling around in the dirt. She thinks, "Great! I've just bathed and brushed the two dogs . . . I washed and folded April's clothes and she left them scattered all over. I cleaned out the garage and now there is more junk than before. And it seems that I gained back the three kilos that I lost. I wonder who could possibly have invented the phrase 'The futility of man' . . ."

#43. Elly and John enter a men's clothing store. The sales clerk greets them, "May I help you?" Elly answers, "Yes, my husband needs summer clothes." She chooses some pieces of clothing in his size and John tries them on. Elly looks at him and says, "The shirt is fine . . . The shorts are big on him." Later, they take a few things, pay for them and leave the store. Elly says that she is delighted with the purchases and asks John, "What do you think?" John replies, "I don't know. Was I there?"

#44. Elly and John have insomnia and are tossing and turning in bed. John tells Elly about something strange that he saw, "Two toads were fighting with each other in the yard. And it wasn't a simple little squabble . . ." Elly remarks, "It was probably for a female." John responds that he didn't see any. Elly asks him, "John, would you fight for me?" A few minutes go by, and Elly smacks him in the face with a pillow. John thinks, "I suppose I took a long time to answer."

#45. Elizabeth is about to leave for school when she calls to Elly, "Mom, can you give me money for lunch?" Elly says to her, "Why don't you make something for yourself . . . ? A sandwich?" Elizabeth asks, "Where is the bread? Do we have any cheese?" Then Elly suggests a few other things: celery, an apple, a granola bar, a pudding cup, but Elizabeth doesn't like them. Finally, Elly gives up and gives Elizabeth money to buy lunch.

#46. Elly is listening to the radio at the bookstore. The voice on the radio announces, "That was our report on physical well-being. Now, let's talk about diets. In spite of the ample information that exists on the topic, the public does not consume enough vegetables . . . to safeguard their health. Drink 6 or 8 glasses of water each day." Elly drinks a lot of water. Then, she gets into her car to return home. She feels the need to go to the bathroom and begins to speed. A policeman stops her and gives her a ticket. She thinks, "This is the first time in my life that I've been stopped for drinking and driving."

#47. Elly gets ready to go out. Then, she gives instructions to her family, "The dinner I'm going to is at six o'clock, John, and that's why I have left everything prepared for all of you. There's a tasty soup . . . You only have to put it in the microwave and later in the oven . . . Put the frozen vegetables in a covered plate and . . . you stir them and you heat them again. I bought buns, and there is fresh salad, and for dessert there is . . ." Elizabeth interrupts her, "It's OK, Mom

. . . Really!" Elly leaves. Everyone looks at each other. Then they all go out to eat fast food.

#48. It's autumn and Elly and John are walking through the forest. Elly comments, "In my opinion, John, this time of the year is heavenly. The aroma, the colors, the markets, the freshness of the wind. Of all the seasons, I believe that this is the one I like best!" John says, "I imagine we could say that we are in the autumn of our lives." Elly answers that it's a good analogy and John goes on, "Yes, to begin with, there are fewer bugs!"

#49. It's Remembrance Day (Veterans' Day) in Canada when people buy poppies in honor of the veterans who fought in past wars. April asks her mom why they are selling poppies, and Elly explains to her that it is a symbol, something to make us remember. Then she tells her the story of John McCrae, the Canadian who wrote the beautiful poem about the poppies that were growing in Flanders Field. April asks her, "Why do I have to wear this poppy? I'm not even very sure about what a war is." Elly replies, "I know. And that . . . is the best reason of all."

#50. John arrives home all tired out and exclaims, "Oh, I'm so happy to be home! Mrs. Martinez didn't show up for a three-hour appointment . . . , so we tried to fill the space with other patients . . . Then the computer system crashed . . . I skipped lunch . . . We have two sterilizers and one stopped working . . . There was so much tension among the personnel that I thought the office was going to explode . . . dear Mrs. Teresa left her crying children (in the waiting room) . . . and one of them broke a lamp . . ." Then, he asks his wife, "And how was your day?" Elly answers, "Stupendous."

#51. Elizabeth is in the library, trying to study. She thinks, "Last night I took a bath and went to bed in a comfortable bed with clean sheets . . . But I couldn't stop tossing and turning until midnight. The same thing happened the night before. And the night before that." At that moment Elizabeth almost falls asleep, but she wakes up abruptly. Then, she wonders, "Why is it so hard to sleep at night? And so easy to fall asleep when you're studying?"

#52. John and Elly go to an elegant Christmas party. They eat, drink, and talk with people. Afterwards, Elly says, "That certainly was a lovely party!" John answers, "That's right . . . I spoke with the Gonzalezes, the Reyes, and the Arces . . . " and then he mentions several other couples. Elly is impressed with this list and comments, "Fantastic!" Then John confesses, "I only wish that I could remember the conversations, even if it were just one . . . "

#53. John and Elly are shopping with April in a big store. April touches her father's arm and tells him, "Look, Daddy! Do you see that? I want it for Christmas!" Then, she shows him other things that she wants to receive. John explains to April that now is a time for giving . . . that there is a special joy in giving to others that is greater than any other pleasure. April listens to him and then says, "But someone has to receive or there will be nobody to give to . . . Well . . . I was just trying to help . . . "

#54. Elizabeth is getting dressed and her little sister, April, asks her, "Listen, Elizabeth, are you going out with Anthony?" "Yes," replies Elizabeth, "Is there anything wrong with that?" April says, "Oh, no . . . only that it's New Year's Eve and supposedly you both are 'involved' with other people . . ." Elizabeth explains, "Anthony and I have known each other since we were children . . ." The doorbell rings. Anthony comes in, looks at Elizabeth, and tells her, "Hey you! You look fantastic!" The two of them leave. April exclaims, "Good heavens! This could wreck their other relationships!" Elly says to her, "Well, that's none of our business." But her parents jump for joy.

#55. Elly and John are in bed, chatting. John remembers, "When I was 16, I went to my first party that lasted the whole night!" . . . Then, Elly asks her husband, "Do you remember our first New Year's together, John?" John answers, "We were both students . . . I was crazy about you . . ." The two of them keep on remembering. John says, "The next year we got married . . ." Finally, John states, "But now, after almost 25 years together, we've discovered that those all-night celebrations aren't nearly as significant as a peaceful night together." Then John hears a snore and turns off the light.

#56. Grandpa gets up and takes his pills. Elly asks him, "Is your back still aching, Dad?" He answers right away, "Oh, it's always bothering me, dear, and also my knees, hands, insides . . ." Then Elly says, "With all you have to put up with, I'm surprised that you don't complain more." Her father explains to her that when he begins to feel sorry for himself, he phones his friend Pedro so he'll lift up his spirits.

#57. Elly is doing the laundry. She goes into Elizabeth' s bedroom and believes that her daughter is still in bed. She thinks, "It's already almost noon. How can she sleep so much? When she wakes up, I'm going to give her a piece of my mind!" Then April, her younger daughter, asks her, "Are you looking for Elizabeth, Mom? She went out skating at six A.M.!"

#58. Elly is running the vacuum cleaner and doing the wash. She sees her daughter and says to her, "Elizabeth, I want you to put away this clothing now so that it doesn't wind up on the floor." Elizabeth replies to her, "But, Mom! You are a neatness freak! You put the jars and bottles in the dishwasher before recycling them. You even fold the underwear! That is obsessive-compulsive behavior!" Elly answers, "Really? I'm glad that you have made me see it." Later, April sees her. She is seated at the table, reading and drinking coffee and the kitchen is a complete mess. April asks her father, "What's the matter with Mom?"

#59. A friend of Elizabeth's finds the brochures the academic advisor gave her. Elizabeth explains "I had decided to take liberal arts, but really I like biology. I want to go into studying pedagogy. But I also would like to work a while . . . to travel. Finally, I want to teach in a high school, so the more varied my experience is, the better." Elizabeth's friend leaves, and her father John comes in. He asks her, "Elizabeth! I see that you have been doing a little bit of research. What are your plans for the future?" She answers him, "I dunno."

#60. April is playing with her dollhouse and scolding her dolls. "Look how messy your room is! Eat your food, don't play with it! Pick up your plates! Don't wait for me to wash them for you! No more TV until you have picked up all your toys! . . . Don't talk back to me! You have to take a bath today! Don't use so much shampoo!" Her mother Elly comes in and April asks her, "Were you listening to me, Mom?" Elly answers, "I was listening to myself!"

#61. John gets up, gets dressed, and greets Elly with a kiss. "Good morning, dear! Do you have anything planned for today?" Elly replies that she doesn't. John continues with his questions, "Do you want to go anywhere . . . visit anyone? Is there anything that needs fixing? Anything to be done?" Elly answers, "Nothing that comes to mind." Then, John gets to work, thinking, "I'm thrilled when I can spend the day in my workshop . . . without feeling guilty!"

#62. April can't sleep and comes downstairs. She wakes up her mother and says, "Mom . . . ? I'm scared. I don't want to sleep alone upstairs. I miss Elizabeth." Elly answers, "Dear heart, Elizabeth is at the university." April insists, "I want you and Dad to move back upstairs!" Elly gives in, "Why don't you go back to your bed and I'll sleep in Elizabeth's room tonight?" John protests, "April has the dog . . . And she said that she would be fine!" Elly thinks, "These things always work great in theory."

#63. Elizabeth is in her room at the university, coughing and blowing her nose. She turns on the radio and listens, "Does a cold and the flu have you feeling miserable? Are you suffering from sneezing? Cough? Stomach upset? A tried and true medicine, guaranteed to make you feel better . . ." Elizabeth turns off the radio and picks up the telephone. She calls her mother and says, "Hello? Mom?"

#64. Elizabeth is home from college, and she goes shopping with her mom and her little sister, April. She sees a jacket that she likes in a shop window and Elly says, "Try it on!" Later, she declares, "That jacket looks like a million dollars on you, Elizabeth! I'll buy it for you!" When her daughter protests, she insists, "Let me buy you some things for college!" Afterwards, Elizabeth says, "This is fun!" Elly says, "I'm happy, dear. There was a time when you didn't want to be seen in public with your mother." Then April observes, "That was before she started buying everything with her own money . . ."

#65. Elly goes into Elizabeth's room and thinks, "What a pigsty! Elizabeth has to return to college now . . .

And look at all that dirty clothing!" She thinks, "How can she live like that? This is ridiculous! I can't stand it!" Later, she goes into Elizabeth's room, but this time she finds it . . . clean and orderly. Meanwhile, Elizabeth and her friend are driving to the laundromat, and Elizabeth comments, "I can't believe it . . .! My mom is calming down with age . . .! I left all my laundry until the last day and she didn't even say one word about it!"

#66. Grandpa Jim is taking a walk with his girlfriend Iris when she says to him, "It's getting cold, Jim! Winter is coming!" Jim says, "I suppose you could say that we are in the winter of our lives . . ." Iris answers, "I'm not very sure that I like that expression." Jim continues on, "In the 'spring of life' we're stupid and wild—in the 'summer of life,' we're working . . . But the winter can be the best stage of life."

#67. Elly finds toys on the stairs and shouts, "April, how many times do I have to ask you to take your things upstairs? If these toys and books and clothing aren't in your room by the end of the day, I'm going to throw it all in the garbage!" A little bit later, Elly begins to pick up the toys when April comes and protests, "You can't throw them away! They are mine!" Elly responds, "I'm sorry. I was serious. [I meant what I said.]" April raises a fuss and Elly says, "OK. You can take your things upstairs, but next time . . ." Then, Elly sits down and thinks, "A good threat is one that doesn't have to be carried out!"

#68. The Patterson family has gotten together to honor Elly. Elizabeth says, "Happy Mother's Day, Mom!" Elly reads the card: "Dear Mom, Now that we are living away from home, we realize all that you have done for us. And we want you to know that we appreciate you now more than ever. Thanks for being such a fantastic Mom. With love, Michael and Elizabeth." Elly exclaims, "Ohhhhhh . . . I can't believe that you gave me such a lovely card!"

#69. It's the wedding rehearsal in the church. Deanna's mother gives instructions. "Attention, please! I want this wedding to be perfect . . . So let's get things straight [understand things well]. The family and friends of the groom go to the right and those of the bride, to the left . . . Groom? You and the best man enter now . . . The maid of honor and the bridesmaids follow, and please walk to the beat of the music . . . Bride? . . . Smile! And don't forget, dear! This is your day!"

#70. Michael and Deanna are getting married. The priest announces, "Dear relatives and friends . . . we have gathered here together today . . . to witness and celebrate the union of Deanna Sobinski and Michael Patterson . . ." Elly begins to cry while Michael says, "I, Michael, take you, Deanna . . ." Then the priest tells him, "You may now kiss the bride." Elly looks at John and says to him, "Oh, John, this has to be one of the happiest days of my life . . ."

#71. Michael and Deanna are dining when a cell phone rings. A man at another table answers and converses. Finally, he says goodbye, "Yes, I'll call you later! OK, Luis." Michael takes a roll and begins to talk into it as if it were a telephone, "Hello! How are you? Me? Oh, nothing, sitting here in a very, very expensive restaurant, trying to have a romantic dinner with my wife . . . What? Of course, he's right here." Then Michael offers the roll to the man with the cell phone, saying, "It's for you." All the people begin to laugh.

#72. Grandpa and April chat. The little girl says, "Know what, Grandpa? Maybe in the next century we'll have robots to make [us] tea!" April continues, "There are going to be many changes . . . I hope that there will be real 3D TVs and flying cars. Maybe we can go to space and even travel through time! I hope we'll be able to save the whales . . ." Then she asks, "What do you hope will change in the next century, Grandpa?" And he replies, "People."

#73. It's Valentine's Day. Elizabeth and her steady boyfriend Anthony have just finished eating supper in a restaurant and they go out into the cold. Elizabeth says, "Thanks for taking me out to supper!" Anthony replies, "With pleasure, Elizabeth!" When they arrive at Elizabeth's house, they kiss. Elizabeth asks, "Anthony, do you think that Valentine's Day was created for lovers or for the benefit of shopping malls?" Without hesitating, Anthony answers her, "For the benefit of shopping malls! Because if it were for lovers, they would have put it in July!"

#74. Grandpa Jim is having coffee with his lady friend Iris in a mall, and he says, "Iris, I would very much like to give you a gift for Valentine's Day." Iris answers, "Oh, Jim . . . How sweet you are! Do you know what I would really like? A cell phone!" Jim is surprised and protests, "I was thinking about a friendship ring . . . A cell phone is so unromantic . . ." Iris explains, "No, no it isn't . . . Whenever you need a little bit of friendship, you can call me!"

#75. April listens to the voice of the TV: "Then with our boys in control . . ., we advanced." John enters and April complains to him, "Daddy, there is nothing except things about war on practically all the stations." John says that her grandpa fought in the last world war. April asks him, "Did he shoot anyone?" He answers her that yes, he did, and adds, "He had to do it, or the other soldier would have shot him." Surprised, the little girl exclaims, "Wow, Grandpa never told me anything about that." John says, "It's such an important thing we should remember. While others try so hard to forget it."

#76. Elly hears Mr. B., April's rabbit, who is digging in his cage. She calls her daughter, "April, come here and look at your rabbit's cage. You haven't cleaned his living quarters in centuries. He needs a new bed and clean water." Elly starts up the stairs and shouts to

April, "How would you like it if you were the one who had to live in this atrocious and filthy mess?" She goes into April's room and sees that it is totally dirty and messy. Elly thinks, "There are times when I ask questions that are truly stupid."

#77. It's the night of Halloween. April is dressed up like a ladybug and Elly exclaims, "Darling, that costume is just the cutest thing!" April says, "Becky's dad is going to give us a lift tonight, Mom. We're going to Maplewood." Elly warns her, "For sure the Maplewood residents don't want children from other neighborhoods going there." April leaves and the doorbell rings. Elly goes to the door, sees two children in costumes, and greets them, "Hi, kids, what super costumes you have on! And whom do we have here?" One of the children answers, "You don't know us. We're from Maplewood!"

#78. John arrives home and announces, "Look, April! I've bought you a remote-controlled car! You see how it works! You guide it with this button." April takes the remote, but John shouts at her, "No, not like that! . . . Let me show you." John takes the remote again and says, "Let's go backwards and turn . . . good, to the left! To the right! . . . Do you see?" April goes into the house. Elly greets her with a question, "Sweetie, you haven't already gotten bored with your new toy, have you?" April answers, "First I have to wait for Dad to get bored!"

#79. Elly is making the bed in her bedroom when she notices a small pillow, and she thinks, "John's mother made this pillow. But now it doesn't go with our decor. I feel bad that I'll hurt John's feelings, but I'm going to put it away. I'll be careful when I tell him about it." Later on, Elly is talking with John in the kitchen and she says to him, "Dear . . . Maybe I shouldn't have done it . . . and please tell me if you want me to put it back . . . I put away that lovely pillow that your mother made for our bed." Then John asks, "What pillow?"

#80. Elly and John watch TV. The commentator says, "Chet Whiffle, the star of 'Filthy Rich,' is getting a separation from his wife . . . ! Recently he has been seen with pop star Vanessa Velour." Elly asks John, "John, have you ever thought about having a love affair?" John replies, "No! I wouldn't want to . . . Besides, I would have to lose about 15 kilos, do some exercise, get a bit of a tan, harden up these 'love handles' . . . I'm happy just the way things are!" John is surprised when Elly gives him a smack with the pillow.

Answer Key

Beginning

Before you read (page 4): 1. baño, 2. botella, 3. café, 4. desastre, 5. esfuerzo, 6. gran, 7. impresionante, 8. chaqueta, 9. necesitar, 10. placer, 11. porche, 12. proyecto, 13. cantidad, 14. recuperarse, 15. estación, 16. estomago, 17. extraño, 18. estudiando

#1   **Putting It All Together:** 1. llevar, 2. gracias, 3. vez, 4. necesito, 5. para

#2   **Working with Words and Patterns:** sales de baño, hierbas, lujoso, mezcla, tranquilizantes. **Putting It All Together:** 1. lujoso, 2. voy, 3. pasa, 4. Nada, 5. queríamos

#3   **Putting It All Together:** 1. Hola, 2. pasa, 3. cansada, 4. día, 5. vueltas

#4   **Putting It All Together:** 1. cumpleaños, 2. tengo, 3. Tienes, 4. edad, 5. ayudarme

#5   **Putting It All Together:** 1. ha, 2. toda, 3. sé, 4. Parece, 5. necesita

#6   **Putting It All Together:** 1. ir, 2. casi, 3. esperar, 4. confitería, 5. Podemos

#7   **Putting It All Together:** 1. bolsillo, 2. Puedo, 3. usar, 4. Está, 5. llaves

#8   **Putting It All Together:** 1. hay, 2. tormenta, 3. parte, 4. solía, 5. debajo

#9   **Putting It All Together:** 1. fantástico, 2. veo, 3. tampoco, 4. siento, 5. razón

#10 **Putting It All Together:** 1. parada, 2. primero, 3. fila, 4. última, 5. primera

El español en tu vida (Comics 1–10): **A.** 1. comida para llevar, 2. auto / perro, 3. basura, 4. truenos, 5. árbol / puercoespín, 6. parada de buses **B.** 1. Gracias, querido, 2. voy / pasa, 3. tengo / años, 4. Parece / necesita / siesta, 5. Perdón / Podemos / baño / emergencia

#11. **Putting It All Together:** 1. hacen, 2. crees, 3. pasaron, 4. acuerdo, 5. recuperarse

#12. **Putting It All Together:** 1. divertido, 2. acompañar, 3. Claro, 4. demasiado, 5. gusta

#13. **Putting It All Together:** 1. siento, 2. delgada, 3. perdido, 4. peso, 5. me

#14. **Putting It All Together:** 1. galería, 2. Impresionante, 3. menudo, 4. almuerzo, 5. compartir

#15. **Putting It All Together:** 1. alegro, 2. en, 3. Le, 4. lado, 5. lloviendo

#16. **Putting It All Together:** 1. paraguas, 2. pequeño, 3. sé, 4. lo, 5. cerca

#17. **Putting It All Together:** 1. pilla, 2. razón, 3. trata, 4. que, 5. masa

#18. **Putting It All Together:** 1. llevan, 2. pena, 3. hermanita, 4. cuánto, 5. se

#19. **Putting It All Together:** 1. chico, 2. perrito, 3. Ven, 4. crees, 5. les

#20. **Putting It All Together:** 1. quitando, 2. falta, 3. pieza, 4. están, 5. quedado

#21. **Putting It All Together:** 1. de, 2. parece, 3. esperando, 4. alegra, 5. lo que

El español en tu vida (Comics 11–21): **A.** 1. vez / desconcertarlos, 2. bien / gusta, 3. paraguas / chica, 4. Hay / manos, 5. hermanita / vieja, 6. saber / baño **B.** 1D, 2B, 3E, 4A, 5C

#22. **Putting It All Together:** 1. tomar, 2. almuerzo, 3. haciendo, 4. comer, 5. hace

#23. **Putting It All Together:** 1. escucha, 2. bulla, 3. Lo, 4. tareas, 5. estudiando

#24. **Putting It All Together:** 1. Sabes, 2. veces, 3. echo, 4. menos, 5. yo

#25. **Putting It All Together:** 1. Feliz, 2. Podría, 3. supuesto, 4. recién, 5. por

#26. **Putting It All Together:** 1. demasiado, 2. odio, 3. torpe, 4. justo, 5. estar

#27. **Putting It All Together:** 1. besándose, 2. Llevan, 3. tiempo, 4. puede, 5. sabías

#28. **Putting It All Together:** 1. escaparates, 2. parece, 3. recuerdo, 4. pequeño, 5. nuevo

#29. **Putting It All Together:** 1. cola, 2. Plata, plata, plata, 3. Esto, 4. esfuerzo, 5. como

#30. **Putting It All Together:** 1. quedar, 2. manera, 3. Mientras, 4. buscando, 5. romper

El español en tu vida (Comics 22–30): **A.** 1. ¿Qué estás haciendo? / hace sólo unos minutos, 2. Es imposible / De veras, 3. realmente echo de menos / yo también, 4. ¡No es justo! / ¡Me rindo!, 5. Llevamos aquí tanto tiempo / ¡No se puede limpiar!, 6. Lo sé / en la cola **B.** 1. Podría, 2. escaparates, 3. Algo **C.** 1. una botella (bottle), 2. una cámara (camera) 3. un árbol (tree), 4. las ventanas (windows), 5. un puercoespín (porcupine), 6. un reloj (clock), 7. una mesa (table), 8. una chaqueta (jacket), 9. la comida para llevar (take-out food), 10. las llaves (keys), 11. un perro (dog), 12. una basura (wastebasket / garbage [can]), 13. un paraguas (umbrella), 14. el teléfono (telephone), 15. un pastel (pastry/cake)

Moderate

#31. **Putting It All Together:** 1. usar, 2. desfile, 3. orgullo, 4. por, 5. pocos; **Did You Get It?:** a.

#32. **Putting It All Together:** 1. extraño, 2. serví, 3. La, 4. sala de estar, 5. veía; **Did You Get It?:** b.

#33. **Putting It All Together:** 1. nieve, 2. congeladas, 3. están, 4. guantes, 5. anillo; **Did You Get It?:** c.

#34. **Putting It All Together:** 1. tiempo, 2. lluvias heladas, 3. impermeable, 4. podrías prestar, 5. Vaya; **Did You Get It?:** a.

#35. **Putting It All Together:** 1. pasaste, 2. fuimos, 3. tomamos, 4. Fue, 5. agotada; **Did You Get It?:** a.

#36. **Putting It All Together:** 1. lo que, 2. araña, 3. se puso los, 4. Se le hinchó, 5. Encontró tu madre; **Did You Get It?:** c.

#37. **Putting It All Together:** 1. le enseña, 2. le estás enseñando 3. me enseñó a mi, 4. leyendas, 5. preocupada por; **Did You Get It?:** b.

#38. Putting It All Together: 1. recipientes, 2. estás haciendo, 3. hora de deshacernos, 4. botar, 5. ibas a reciclar; **Did You Get It?:** c.

El español en tu vida (Comics 31–38): **A.** 1. ¡Qué extraño!, 2. ¿Dondé están tus guantes?, 3. ¡Estoy totalmente agotada!, 4. ¿Sabes lo que vi en la tele? 5. No lo sé. **B.** 1. ¿Vas a usar eso en el desfile?, 2. ¿Me lo podrías prestar?, 3. ¿Lo pasaste bien en la playa?, 4. ¿Qué pasa? 5. ¿Qué estás haciendo?

#39. Putting It All Together: 1. Acabas de tirar, 2. alacena, 3. hace tiempo, 4. no necesitamos, 5. Guárdame; **Did You Get It?:** c.

#40. Putting It All Together: 1. me están matando, 2. Son las, 3. Hora de cerrar, 4. Podríamos entrar, 5. hermosas; **Did You Get It?:** b.

#41. Putting It All Together: 1. Odio, 2. me carga, 3. atascada, 4. veo la hora de, 5. tendré; **Did You Get It?:** c.

#42. Putting It All Together: 1. afuera, 2. Acabo de, 3. doblé la ropa, 4. desechos, 5. Me pregunto; **Did You Get It?:** b.

#43. Putting It All Together: 1. ¿Puedo ayudarles?, 2. de verano, 3. talla, 4. le quedan, 5. te parece; **Did You Get It?:** a.

#44. Putting It All Together: 1. vuelta, 2. probablemente, 3. hembra, 4. pelearías, 5. me tardé; **Did You Get It?:** b.

#45. Putting It All Together: 1. Me puedes dar, 2. tú misma, 3. algo de queso, 4. barra, 5. le gustan; **Did You Get It?:** b.

#46. Putting It All Together: 1. bienestar físico, 2. hablemos sobre, 3. salud, 4. vasos de agua, 5. la primera vez; **Did You Get It?:** c.

#47. Putting It All Together: 1. a las seis, 2. sopa sabrosa, 3. Pon, 4. panecillos, 5. postre; **Did You Get It?:** a.

El español en tu vida (Comics 39–47): **A.** 1. sólo estábamos mirando, 2. ¡Odio esta cosa!, 3. Acabo de cocinar, 4. ¿Puedo ayudarles?, 5. No me gustan de esa clase. **B.** 1.b, 2.a, 3.b, 4.c, 5.b; **C.** 1. unas barras de granola (granola bars), 2. unas pasas (raisins), 3. pan (bread), 4. una caja de dulces (box of candies), 5. café (coffee), 6. unos platos (plates), 7. el refrigerador (refrigerator), 8. una parilla (grill), 9. carne (meat), 10. sopa (soup), 11. unas botellas de agua (bottles of water), 12. unas manzanas (apples), 13. queso (cheese), 14. apio (celery), 15. unos panecillos (buns), 16. unas cerezas (cherries)

#48. Putting It All Together: 1. Para mí, 2. frescura del viento, 3. la que más me gusta, 4. Me imagino, 5. sabandijas; **Did You Get It?:** a.

#49. Putting It All Together: 1. para hacernos recordar, 2. crecían, 3. Por qué tengo que, 4. Ni siquiera, 5. Ya lo sé; **Did You Get It?:** c.

#50. Putting It All Together: 1. tan feliz de estar, 2. cita, 3. dejó de funcionar, 4. iba a explotar, 5. estuvo; **Did You Get It?:** b.

#51. Putting It All Together: 1. me acosté, 2. sábanas, 3. Lo mismo pasó, 4. dormir, 5. dormirse; **Did You Get It?:** b.

#52. Putting It All Together: 1. Ésa sí que fue, 2. los Pérez, 3. los Zurita, 4. me gustaría poder acordarme, 5. una sola; **Did You Get It?:** c.

#53. Putting It All Together: 1. Mira, 2. Navidades, 3. época para regalar, 4. cualquier otro placer, 5. estaba tratando de; **Did You Get It?:** a.

#54. Putting It All Together: 1. Víspera, 2. nos conocemos desde, 3. Te ves fantástica, 4. relaciones, 5. eso es asunto; **Did You Get It?:** a.

#55. Putting It All Together: 1. tenía, 2. Te acuerdas de, 3. éramos, 4. nos casamos, 5. hemos descubierto; **Did You Get It?:** b.

El español en tu vida (Comics 48–55): **A.** 1. Para mí, 2. Algo para hacernos recordar, 3. Le iba a decir, 4. Lo mismo pasó, 5. ¡Te ves fantástica! **B.** 1. creo / gusta, 2. escribió / crecían, 3. fue / hablé, 4. tratando / ayudar, 5. Fuimos / bailamos; **C.** 1. vino, 2. tenía, 3. tratamos, 4. cayó, 5. quedamos, 6. salté, 7. dejó, 8. falló, 9. Había, 10, pensé, 11. iba, 12. dejó, 13. hacíamos, 14. rompió, 15. atascó, 16. tuve

Challenging

#56. Putting It All Together: 1. Te duele, 2. rodillas, 3. soportar, 4. te quejes, 5. empieza a sentir; **Did You Get It?:** b.

#57. Putting It All Together: 1. Ya casi es, 2. se despierte, 3. cantar las cuarenta, 4. Estás buscando, 5. patinar; **Did You Get It?:** a.

#58. Putting It All Together: 1. Quiero que guardes, 2. termine, 3. lavaplatos, 4. Me alegro que, 5. desordenada; **Did You Get It?:** c.

#59. Putting It All Together: 1. folletos, 2. Había decidido, 3. me gustaría trabajar, 4. más variada sea, 5. has estado haciendo; **Did You Get It?:** c.

#60. Putting It All Together: 1. Come, 2. que yo limpie, 3. hayas recogido, 4. No uses, 5. a mí misma; **Did You Get It?:** b.

#61. Putting It All Together: 1. algo planeado, 2. a alguna parte, 3. necesite, 4. venga a la cabeza, 5. sentirme culpable; **Did You Get It?:** a.

#62. Putting It All Together: 1. Tengo miedo, 2. Echo de menos, 3. cambien, 4. habitación de Isabel, 5. que se sentiría bien; **Did You Get It?:** c.

#63. Putting It All Together: 1. resfrío y la gripa, 2. Mal del estómago, 3. remedio, 4. que se sienta mejor, 5. Aló; **Did You Get It?:** a.

El español en tu vida (Comics 56–63): **A.** 1. ¿Te duele de nuevo . . . ? 2. ¡Le voy a cantar las cuarenta!, 3. No lo soy., 4. ¡Todo está bien!, 5. Tengo miedo.; **B.** 1. soportar / quejes, 2. investigación / planes, 3. hayas / juguetes, 4. taller / culpable; 5. gripe / Mal; **C.** 1. cabeza, 2. hombros, 3. mano, 4. espalda, 5. pierna, 6. rodilla, 7. pie; **D.** balcón (balcony), banco (bench), baño (bath), carrito (buggy, stroller), casa (house), comedor (dining room), cuadro (picture), cuarto de baño (bathroom), dormitorio (bedroom), escalera (stairs), escritorio (desk), espejo (mirror), gato (cat), hija (daughter), hijo (son), hombre (man), inodoro (toilet), lámpara (lamp), madre (mother), mesa (table), mujer (woman, wife), muñeca (doll), niña (girl), niño (boy), padre (father), pelota (ball), perro (dog), planta (plant), plato (plate), porche (porch), sala de estar (living room, family room), silla (chair), sofá (sofa), techo (roof), teléfono (telephone), ventana (window)

#64. Putting It All Together: 1. Pruébatela, 2. se te ve de maravilla, 3. Deja que te compre, 4. divertido, 5. que te vieran; **Did You Get It?:** b.

#65. Putting It All Together: 1. ¡Que chiquero!, 2. ropa sucia, 3. ¡Esto es ridículo!, 4. No lo puedo creer, 5. se está tranquilizando; **Did You Get It?:** c.

#66. Putting It All Together: 1. Se está poniendo frío, 2. No estoy muy segura, 3. me guste, 4. uno es tonto y descontrolado, 5. la mejor época; **Did You Get It?:** b.

#67. Putting It All Together: 1. tengo que pedir que lleves, 2. no están en tu cuarto, 3. Lo siento, 4. la próxima vez, 5. amenaza; **Did You Get It?:** a.

#68. Putting It All Together: 1. Feliz Día de la Madre, 2. nos damos cuenta, 3. que te apreciamos, 4. Gracias por ser, 5. esa tarjeta tan bella; **Did You Get It?:** c.

#69. Putting It All Together: 1. esta boda sea perfecta, 2. entendamos bien, 3. a la derecha, 4. entran, 5. caminen; **Did You Get It?:** b.

#70. Putting It All Together: 1. Nos hemos reunido, 2. presenciar, 3. tomo a ti, 4. besar a la novia, 5. los días más felices; **Did You Get It?:** a.

#71. Putting It All Together: 1. te llamo más tarde, 2. Aló, 3. aquí sentado, 4. carísimo, 5. Es para usted; **Did You Get It?:** c.

El español en tu vida (Comics 64–71): **A.** 1. ¡Esa chaqueta se te ve de maravilla!, 2. ¡Esto es divertido!, 3. ¡No lo puedo tolerar!, 4. Lo siento. Hablaba en serio., 5. Entendamos bien las cosas.; **B.** 1. lavado / palabra, 2. segura / guste, 3. sepas / apreciamos, 4. presenciar / matrimonio; 5. supuesto / mismo. **C.** la iglesia, el novio, la novia, el padrino, el sacerdote, las damas de compañía, la niña de las flores, el niño que trae los anillos, las familias y los amigos de la novia y del novio . . . .

#72. Putting It All Together: 1. tendremos, 2. Van a haber, 3. Espero que existan, 4. Quizás podamos ir, 5. esperas tú que cambie; **Did You Get It?:** b.

#73. Putting It All Together: 1. Gracias por llevarme, 2. Con gusto, 3. lo crearon, 4. si fuera, 5. lo habrían puesto; **Did You Get It?:** a.

#74. Putting It All Together: 1. te quisiera hacer, 2. lo que, 3. estaba pensando en, 4. tan poco romántico, 5. Cuando necesites; **Did You Get It?:** a.

#75. Putting It All Together: 1. nuestros muchachos, 2. sobre la guerra, 3. le hubiera disparado a él, 4. Vaya, 5. debemos recordar; **Did You Get It?:** c.

#76. Putting It All Together: 1. ven aquí y mira, 2. Le hacen falta, 3. si fueses, 4. atroz y asqueroso desorden; 5. hago; **Did You Get It?:** b.

#77. Putting It All Together: 1. mono, 2. nos va a llevar, 3. no quieren que, 4. vayan, 5. qué disfraces más estupendos; **Did You Get It?:** c.

#78. Putting It All Together: 1. Lo guías, 2. que te enseñe, 3. giremos, 4. derecha, 5. que Papá se aburra; **Did You Get It?:** b.

#79. Putting It All Together: 1. La mamá de Juan, 2. herirle, 3. se lo diga, 4. debiera, 5. la ponga de vuelta; **Did You Get It?:** a.

#80. Putting It All Together: 1. se le ha visto, 2. Alguna vez, 3. tendría, 4. tostarme la piel, 5. tal y como; **Did You Get It?:** b.

El español en tu vida (Comics 72–80): **A.** 1. ¡Gracias por llevarme a cenar!, 2. Tuvo que hacerlo., 3. Ven aquí y mira., 4. Quizás no lo debiera haber hecho.; **B.** 1. ¿Qué esperas tú que cambie? 2. ¿Sabes lo que realmente me gustaría?, 3. ¿Y a quién tenemos aquí?, 4. no te habrás aburrido de tu nuevo juguete, 5. has pensado en tener un lío amoroso?; **C.** abrigo (coat), abuelo (grandfather), bocadillos (sandwiches), botella (bottle), café (café), caja (box), camisa (shirt), chaqueta (jacket), comida (food), hombre (man), lentes (glasses), mesa (table), mujer (woman, wife), niño (boy), padre (father), pantalones (pants), pañuelo (handkerchief), papas fritas (fries), pelo (hair), plato (plate), restaurante (restaurant), silla (chair), taza (cup), vaso ([drinking] glass), zapatos (shoes)

¡CÁLLATE! ESTOY ESTUDIANDO.

About the Authors

Lynn Johnston is the creator of the comic strip *For Better or For Worse*, which is distributed by United Feature Syndicate. It appears in more than two-thousand newspapers worldwide, in twenty countries, and eight languages, reaching 220 million readers every day. In the twenty-four years since it was developed, there have been thirty books of cartoons published.

Brenda Wegmann is an experienced teacher and author of ESL and Spanish language textbooks and instructional guides; she also teaches at the University of Alberta Faculty of Extension.